A Crossing of Paths

The True Untold Story of the
Hillside Strangler Case

Ron Crisp

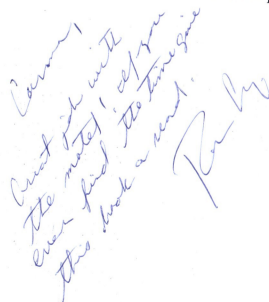

Printed in the United States

First printing 2011

ISBN-13: 978-1477407783

Old Flame Finders Publishing
12701-57 Sunset Harbor Rd.
Weirsdale, Florida 32195

www.oldflamepi@aol.com

Acknowledgements

I want to thank my editor, Jeanie MacAlpine, for the great job she did in editing my work. Christina Hess for the hours she spent at the Pasadena library copying newspaper articles I used in my research during the Leslie Barry investigation. My cousins Louanne Manning and Sharon Sloan; their incessant pestering to read the next chapter kept me writing. I also want to thank graphic artist Jeff Anzures for his terrific cover design and David Hathaway for proofing the proof of the proof to correct pesky formatting and typographical errors that have plagued earlier versions of the book.

"The rhythm of life is intricate but orderly, tenacious but fragile. To keep that in mind is to build the key to survival."

Judge Shirley Hufstedler

In Memory of
District Attorneys Roger Kelley and James Heins

Preface

The following report is a historical document, written over Christmas 1979, for Roger Kelley, the Chief Prosecutor in the State of California V. Angelo Buono. The only change I made when entering it to my computer was in the typeface and font size. Other than that, minus the exhibits that were attached to it, the report is exactly as it was when I personally delivered it to the District Attorney's Office in January of 1980.

The 4 exhibits attached to this report were:

Exhibit A. A photograph of suspect Dennis Cantu showing him to be a dead ringer for Kenneth Bianchi

Exhibit B. A copy of the rental applications of cousins Eddie Castillon and Tony Smith as evidence of their residency at the Monterey Rd. Apartments in South Pasadena

Exhibit C. A map of the area marked where Hillside Strangler victims were either found or lived along with markings of the previous residences of the two cousins during the period the Hillside Strangler was operating in the area

Exhibit D. A Los Angeles Sheriffs crime lab photograph of the murder weapon in the Leslie Barry murder showing a complex system of knots

I never personally discussed this report with Roger Kelley and for months, I was curious as to what he thought about my theory of the case. During the preliminary hearing, as I walked through the courtroom in line with other members of the Buono defense team, our eyes met for a split second and Kelley winked. At the end of the hearing, which lasted for nearly 6 months, he made a motion to dismiss all murder charges against Angelo Buono. With just an

Preface

ephemeral flicker of the eye, our crossing of paths in the courtroom told me all I needed to know about how he felt about my report.

INVESTIGATIVE MEMORANDUM

TO: ROGER KELLY,   January 4, 1980
        Chief Prosecutor
        Los Angeles District Attorney

FROM: Ronald E. Crisp
        Private Investigator A-7503-I

SUBJECT: HOMICIDE–Leslie   Fae   Barry;   Delores Cepeda; Sonja Johnson; Kristina Weckler; Elizabeth Cevallos

Leslie Fae Barry – Victim #4

Leslie Fae Barry was sodomized and strangled on November 20, 1978. She was 12 years old and attended South Pasadena Junior High School. Prior to attending South Pasadena Junior High, she attended Stancliff, a private school. She lived with her mother, Aina Barry, in an apartment at 400 Monterey Road, South Pasadena, California.

She was described by classmates as a moody and lonely child. She didn't have men friends and the ones she did have say she was argumentative and withdrawn. After her death a rumor was circulating around the apartments that Leslie was prostituting herself. The origin of that rumor was never determined.

THE CRIME

Leslie Barry was strangled with an electrical cord attached to a wall sconce on the north wall of the south bedroom. The cord was tied in three places (see attached photo). Two of the knots corresponded to the right and left sterno thyroid muscles evidenced by hemorrhaging to that area. The third knot was tied in front. The cord was doubled over and tied tightly with a square knot on the left side of victim's neck. A simple knot was tied on the right side of the victim's neck. The knot in front appears to be a granny knot.

Preface

PHYSICAL EVIDENCE

The only physical evidence found by police at the scene of the crime was four strands of pubic hair. The hair was described as two dark brown and two light brown hairs by investigators. Negative findings by latent prints; negative findings on acid phosphatase, and negative findings of blood. On the kitchen sink in the Leslie Barry apartment were two grocery sacks. Crisp attempted to trace those sacks to local markets, but because of the paper shortage stores were receiving various makes of sacks and never knew from one delivery to the next what type of sacks they would receive. It is believed that one of the sacks contained a Dairy product (milk) that was still in the bag when investigating officers arrived at the scene.

There are three stores within walking distance of the 400 Monterey Road apartments: Monterey Plaza Liquor, an Italian Deli, and Pronto Market. The store clerks at these stores did not recall having seen Leslie, but stated that they knew who she was and it was possible that she had been in the day of her death. It is also known that the suspects utilized the same stores as the victim. Mainly, Monterey Plaza Liquor and Pronto Market.

Steve Bialek, son of the owner of Monterey Plaza Liquor, confirmed that he knew both the victim and the suspects and that they all frequented the store.

At Pronto Market, the store manager confirmed that he had seen Leslie Barry a number of times in the store and Martin Smith had bounced a check there that he never made good.

Investigator Crisp believes that Leslie went to one of these stores on the day of her death.

WITNESSES

Aina Barry

Mrs. Barry states that she called Leslie at approximately 4:30p.m. from work. Leslie had not attended school that day due to a minor illness. The conversation was concerning whether or not Leslie had done the laundry yet. Leslie had told her mother that she had not

Preface

done the laundry, but she would have it done by the time her mother got home from work.

Mrs. Barry further states that she arrived home at approximately 5:15p.m. She could not remember if she had to use her key to get into the apartment. Mrs. Barry states that she went to the kitchen and put her purse down and then left the apartment and proceeded to the front of the apartment complex to get her mail. (Investigator Crisp timed that walk at approximately 2-1/2 minutes.) When she returned to the apartment she noticed that the door to Leslie's bedroom was open about eighteen inches and that is was dark, except for the light from the television set. The volume on the television was turned up exceptionally loud.

She proceeded to the bedroom and found Leslie with the aforementioned cord tied around her neck. Mrs. Barry stated that she went to the kitchen and got a pair of scissors, returned to the bedroom and with a great deal of difficulty, cut the cord from around Leslie's neck. She then administered CPR and called the paramedics. The paramedics arrived approximately three minutes later at 5:20 p.m.

Lisa Ballatore
Lisa stated that she called Leslie at approximately 4:55 p.m. and had a ten or fifteen minute phone conversation with her. Since Leslie had missed school that day they discussed the homework and some other things that Lisa cannot recall. At approximately 5:05 p.m. Leslie suddenly ended the conversation saying, "I've go to go now. My mother is home."

Lisa also said that she had been to Leslie's apartment on numerous occasions and on those occasions Leslie would always leave her apartment door unlocked. Lisa said that she had warned Leslie that it was dangerous to leave the door unlocked, but Leslie never paid any attention to her.

Investigator's note: The time of the above phone conversations was confirmed by Janice Fitzpatrick, a babysitter, who stated she was waiting for Lisa to get off the phone so she could take the Ballatore children to swimming lessons.

Preface

Shawn Peter Hagen

Shawn Hagen was a friend of Leslie Barry's. Because of his age and the fact that the police "leaned" on him so heavily, his father would not allow Investigator Crisp to interview him.

However, Hagen stated to investigating officers on the evening of the Barry homicide that he felt this (Barry's murder) was a "rape case." That he knew one of the Hillside Strangler victims, Dolly Cepeda. He stated that he knew Cepeda from Stancliff School.

Arthur Anzures (First Statement)

Anzures was the apartment manager of the 400 and 406 Monterey Road apartments. He and his wife Denise knew Leslie Barry very well. On many occasions Leslie would spend the night at the Anzures'. She played with the Anzures children and went places with the Anzures family.

On November 20, 1978, at approximately 3:15 p.m. Arthur Anzures was cleaning up the carport area of the 406 Monterey Road apartments, when a friend of his, Tony Barrett, stopped by to chat. While they were talking a car (white NFD) drove up and parked in the carport area of the above-mentioned apartments. Anzures identified the driver of that car to police as "Jeanne Marek's brother." He did not know the person's name. (Jeanne Marek's brothers name was later learned to be William Asper.) Anzures gave the following description, from memory, of William Asper: 6'3" tall, 220-225 lbs., 35 years of age, brown curly hair (see William Asper statement). Anzures did not see this person get out of the car, nor did he see him leave the apartment.

Mario Dare

Mario Dare stated that he had gone to the apartments at 406 Monterey Road at approximately 1:00 p.m. to see a friend, Frank Hall, who was staying with Jeanne Marek. Hall was not there at that time so he went to Squires Liquor store to make a sales call, as he is a liquor salesman. At approximately 3:00 p.m. he returned to the apartments and drove west down the alley. He saw Anzures talking to a man sitting in a pickup truck. He states that he did not park in the carport, but drove completely through the alley, turned left on

Preface

Pasadena Avenue and then left on Monterey Road, and parked on the south side of Monterey Road, across from the 400 Monterey Road apartments.

He stated that he stayed at Jeanne Marek's apartment until about 6:00 p.m. at which time he left to play handball with Frank Hall at the Pasadena YMCA.

Mario Dare is 6'3" or 6'4" tall, 240 lbs., dark wavy hair, about 40-45 years of age.

Frank Hall

Frank Hall stated that he left Jeanne Marek's apartment at approximately 3:30 p.m. and went to the Pasadena YMCA to work out. He was not at the apartments at the time of the Leslie Barry murder.

Jeanne Marek

Jeanne Marek stated that she arrived home at 4:30 p.m. She also stated that she arrived home at the time the ambulance and police arrived which was 5:20 p.m. (Jeanne Marek seems to have a drinking problem and perhaps she does not know when she arrived home.) Marek stated that on a Friday, before Leslie Barry was murdered, a person came to her door at about 8:00 p.m. and asked "How many married and single women live in the apartment?" and stated his name was Eddie. She did not open the door and did not see him but she heard him go away. (This statement was confirmed by Helen Marie Mekboub who lives in apartment "B" across from Jeanne Marek.) Neither of these women saw the person that made the above statement.

Hansford Bartley

Hansford Bartley stated that there was "odd activity" going on in the apartment next door to him (Apartment No. 14). He said he could never tell who was living there. He stated that he had passed by apartment No. 14 on several occasions when the door would be open. He could smell marijuana coming from the apartment and see boxes stacked up. The apartment was filthy. Bartley stated further that he had seen one of the men that lived there at the pool one day. This person had a pet lizard that he was leading around on a string.

Denise Anzures
Denise Anzures was the co-manager of the apartment complex. She stated that at the time of Leslie Barry's death apartment No.14 was vacant. Prior to the homicide the apartment had been rented to Eddie Castillon and Martin Anthony Smith. She stated that Smith had moved out sometime in the summer and gone back to Texas where she had heard he was a police officer. After Smith moved out Castillon took in a female roommate (NFD) for about a week. When the female moved out, another friend of Castillon's , Dennis Cantu, moved into the apartment.

Arthur Anzures (Second Statement)
In August, 1979, Investigator Crisp spoke with Anzures at the prison facility at Chino. Crisp asked Anzures if he was sure that the person who drove up in the white car was Jeanne Marek's brother, William Asper. Anzures stated that he was not sure then or now if that person was William Asper.

Anzures was asked if he knew Dennis Cantu. He stated that he knew Cantu but not very well. Anzures could remember what Cantu looked like but could not state with any certainty that the person he saw drive up in the white car was Dennis Cantu. Anzures did, however, remember that on a Saturday, approximately four weeks before Leslie Barry was killed, he had just returned from the store and ran into Dennis Cantu coming out of Leslie Barry's apartment. Cantu acted embarrassed and awkward about having been seen. Anzures further states that he does not know who, if anyone, was home at the Barry apartment when the incident took place.

William Asper
William Asper states that he did not go over to the apartments the day Leslie Barry was killed. Asper states that he was at home working in his photo lab all day on November 20, 1978. He further states that on the above date he owned and drove a red Porsche.

Preface

Delores Cepeda/Sonja Johnson – Victims #1 and #2

Delores Cepeda was raped and strangled sometime between November 13 and November 20, 1977. Her body was found, along with the body of Sonja Johnson on November 20, 1977. She was 12 years old. Prior to her death she attended Stancliff, a private school. She was friends with Shawn Peter Hagen. According to friends and family she was a very athletic person. She was physically mature for her age. The autopsy report states that she appeared to be three or four years older than her stated age of twelve.

Sonja Johnson was 14 years of age. She disappeared on November 13, 1977, and her body was found on November 20, 1977. She attended Saint Ignatius School. She was friends with Delores Cepeda. According to friends she was the wild type. She smoked marijuana as well as regular cigarettes. Gang type writings were found in her notebook. According to the autopsy report Sonja Johnson appeared to be three of four years younger than her stated age of fourteen.

THE CRIME

Little is known about how or where the crimes were committed. No ligatures were found at the scene where the bodies were discovered. There were three of four torn packages of Trojan prophylatics found at the scene, along with an old discarded mattress and an assortment of beer cans and bottles. Acid phosphatase for sperm was negative on both girls. The girls left the Eagle Rock Plaza and caught the bus at approximately 4:00 p.m. They got off the bus at the Avenue 46 and York Avenue stop. They were last seen alive by Louis Landinquin.

WITNESSES

Louis Landinquin

Louis Landinquin was the last person to see the girls alive. He was riding the same bus as Cepeda and Johnson. He told investigators that Cepeda and Johnson got off the bus at Avenue 46. The bus was headed east on York Boulevard. Landinquin saw the girls cross York Boulevard from the south side to the north side and walk east on York Boulevard. At that time a car stopped and Landinquin believes that Johnson approached the car. This is all Landinquin saw as the bus he was on pulled out and continued east on York Boulevard.

Fernando Ponce, Police artist

Police Artist Fernando Ponce made a composite of the car. From the rear view it looked like a number of 1976 model cars, including a Grand Torino and a Maverick.

Investigator's Note: Crisp would add to that list a 1976 Ford Elite which resembles a Grand Torino from the rear. Landinquin described this car under hypnosis as black vinyl top on white or white vinyl top on black.

Carlos Dela Torre

Carlos Dela Torre, a boyfriend of Sonja Johnson's, stated that he had received a phone call from Sonja Johnson on November 15, 1977. He stated that he did not know that the girls had been missing for two days at the time of the call. Dela Torre says that he felt Sonja was calling from an empty room because of the hollow sound in the background. Dela Torre said that when he came to the phone Sonja started talking "Chinese talk" a language Sonja had made up. Sonja suddenly ended the conversation saying, "I've got to go now. My mother is home." Dela Torre said that he had heard a knock at the door and a man's voice just prior to Sonja's statement about her mother being home.

Investigator's Note: The above phone conversations was verified by another person. The police have not been able to discount the above statement.

Anthony Crossa

Anthony Crossa saw the girls at the bus stop at Eagle Rock and York Boulevard. He was given a ring by Sonja Johnson and stated that she had a lot of of jewelry. He believes the ring was stolen.

Investigator's Note No. 1: In the Leslie Barry case, jewelry was found (earring for pierced ears) in her bedroom and there were various reports that she had stolen jewelry items on several occasions. This could be a pattern of the victims.

Investigator's Note No. 2: In addition to the above information on Cepeda and Johnson, it should be noted that these girls were found near Landa Street. The Cepeda family lived at 1926-1/2 Mellon Street at the time Delores Cepeda was born. Mellon and Landa Streets are about three or four blocks apart. This might indicate a familiarity by the suspects with the Cepeda family background.

Kristina Weckler – Victim #4

Kristina Weckler was 20 years of age and attended the Art Center College in Pasadena. Her Father, Charles Weckler, is a commercial photographer in New York. According to friends, Kristina was, by nature, an extremely careful person and was even more so because of the Hillside Stranglings. Her nude body was discovered on November 20, 1977, at the corner of Ramon and Wawona Streets. She had been strangled, raped, and sodomized.

THE CRIME

It is believed that Kristina Weckler was abducted from her apartment on the evening of November 19, 1977. According to the police report, Ms. Weckler's apartment was locked and there were no signs of forced entry or of a struggle inside the apartment. Her bed covers were rolled back as if she was about to go to bed and her nightgown was lying on the lavatory.

The autopsy report stated that there were fresh needle marks on both arms, but there were no signs of drugs in her system.

WITNESSES

There were various sightings of a compact pickup truck with a camper shell in the area where Ms. Weckler's body was found.

A Glendale police officer was one witness who sighted the above mentioned truck. Under hypnosis he described the driver of the truck as a male, Caucasian, short light brown bushy hair, with a mustache.

Preface

The police officer described the license plate as a California commercial plate.

Kristina Weckler's boyfriend told police that he had given a party that evening but since it was a "pot" party and Ms. Weckler was opposed to drugs of any kind, she had not been invited. The boyfriend furnished a list of the guests that had attended this party.

Investigator's Note: Most interesting to that list was the name Pat Dunn. Pat Dunn had applied for an apartment at 400 Monterey Road, South Pasadena, in late 1977. This indicates a possible connection between the apartment, the suspect and the Art Center. It is not known if Pat Dunn knows the suspects in the Leslie Barry Homicide.

On the day of her death Ms. Weckler had gone to the Eagle Rock Plaza to buy some art supplies. This indicates a pattern of the victims Cepeda, Johnson and Weckler, since all three had gone to the Eagle Rock Plaza the day they disappeared or were killed.

Elizabeth Cevallos – Victim #5

Elizabeth Cevallos was 15 years of age and attended Montebello High School. Her father, Benjamin Cevallos is from San Antonio, Texas. According to friends she had not attended school that day.

THE CRIME

Her nude body was found on March 27, 1979. It was at first thought that she had been strangled, but the autopsy revealed that she died from brain hemorrhage. Her body was found stuffed in a drainage filter in the Rio Hondo wash at the end of Beverly Road in Pico Rivera. An electrical cord was found nearby and there were marks on her neck which led police investigators to believe, at first, that she had been strangled. The acid-phosphatase was negative.

WITNESSES

Sgt. Ray Verdugo
L..A. County Sheriff's Dept.

Sgt. Roy Verdugo told Investigator Crisp that he thought she had run away from home. He stated that her boyfriend was a member of a gang in Pico Rivera.

Preface

Irene Cevallos

Irene Cevallos, Elizabeth Cevallos' mother, told Investigator Crisp that friends had seen Elizabeth on the Monday of her death at the bowling alley on Beverly and Howard Streets in Montebello. According to her mother, Elizabeth "hung out" at this bowling alley often. Irene Cevallos is now married to a Mr. Segura who operates a messenger service in Hollywood.

Mrs. Cevallos told Crisp that several years ago she had gone to the U.S.C. Dental School to have dental work done and that the dental student who had worked on her teeth (she did not recall his name) had called her on a number of occasions to encourage her to come in for more dental work. She stated that at the time she felt it was odd that a dental student would do follow-up work. She stated that she never went back to the dental school.

Investigator's Note: It is not believed that the dental student mentioned is a suspect in this case. Mrs. Cevallos could not recall how long ago she had gone to the U.S.C. Dental School, but stated that it was at least five or six years ago. However, the possibility of a connection through records to the suspects and Cevallos in this case does exist. (See suspect Eddie Castillon.)

SUSPECTS

Martin Anthony Smith

Martin Smith is currently a police officer in Laredo, Texas. He is 26 years of age, 5'10" tall, dark brown hair, medium build (no photo available).

Martin Smith was born in Laredo, Texas in 1954, to Nellie Mae Martin. Nellie Mae Martin currently goes by the name of Nell Ritterath. On November 28, 1953, according to Laredo Court records, Nellie Martin filed for a name change from Nellie Mae Martin to Maria Elena Smith. She stated that her reason for a name change was that she was pregnant and that when she signed her marriage certificate she inadvertently signed her name Maria Elena Smith. She stated in the document that she wanted the name on her child's birth certificate to be the same as her name appeared on the marriage certificate.

Preface

Edward Castillon, Martin Smith's cousin, told Investigator Crisp that Smith's parents got a divorce when Smith was about 12 years old. Castillon intimated that it was a nasty affair, resulting in Smith's living with the Castillon family.

Smith told Crisp that he came to California after graduating from high school and attended Pasadena City College and then UCLA Smith stated that he majored in police science and pre-law. He was an Explorer Scout with the South Pasadena Police Department.

Castillon said to Crisp that Smith was really "into" becoming a police officer and had applied for a position with the L.A.P.D. as a student worker. Castillon stated further that Smith knew all the police codes and the location of police officers at a given time. (He did not state how Smith knew the movements of police officers, but one might assume that Smith listened to the police band radio.)

Castillon stated to Crisp that when Smith applied for a position as a police student worker he was extremely upset over being turned down.

According to Smith, shortly after graduating from UCLA he returned to Laredo, Texas, to become a police officer. This was in August, 1978.

Sgt. Ray Verdugo of LA Co. Sheriff's Department ran a check on Martin Smith regarding arrests and warrants and learned that there is a warrant for his arrest on a Health and Safety code violation in California. Sgt. Roy Verdugo is the investigating officer on the Elizabeth Cevallos case and was extremely cooperative, sharing information with Crisp on the Cevallos case.

In the application for rent at the 400 Monterey Road apartment, dated September 25, 1977, Smith listed his present place of residence as 6421 Crescent Street, Los Angeles, from February to November. Smith did not move into the 400 Monterey Road Apartments until November, 1977.

Previous to the Crescent Street address, Smith lived at 1340 Ontario Street, Pasadena (see map). Monterey Road, Crescent Street, and Ontario Street form a half circle pattern in relationship to where several Hillside strangler victims lived or were found.

Preface

Smith is not a suspect in the Leslie Barry and Elizabeth Cevallos homicides, but is a suspect in the Delores Cepeda, Sonja Johnson, and Kristina Weckler homicides.

Edward Martin Castillon

Eddie Castillon is currently a fourth year dental student at U.S.C. Dental School. Castillon is 5'10" tall, 150-160 lbs., light brown hair, 26 years old, light complexion. A photo is available through the U.S.C. Dental School. He is from Laredo, Texas, and plans to return to Texas to practice dentistry. He currently lives with Dennis Cantu at 4420 Richard Drive, Los Angeles, California. His father, Carlos Castillon is a prominent attorney and a former District Attorney of Laredo, Texas. Eddie's mother, Betty Castillon is the sister of Nellie Mae Martin, also known as Nell Ritterath.

Investigator Crisp spoke with Eddie Castillon for the first time on April 5, 1979. At that time he was living with Dennis Cantu at 912 Victoria Street, Montebello, California. The purpose of that conversation was to gather background information on Martin Smith and Castillon. Castillon was a suspect in the Leslie Barry case at that time, but Crisp used the pretense of calling Castillon as a character witness for Anzures.

Important to that conversation was Castillon's denial that he knew any of the Hillside strangler victims. (see statement of Gessel Montiforte.)

Investigator's Note: On April 24, 1979, Investigator Crisp spoke with Martin Smith by phone. Castillon had talked with Smith about the Leslie Barry case shortly after Crisp had contacted Castillon.

In the April 5, 1979, conversation, Castillon had begun the conversation by stating that he knew who Crisp was because his aunt had called him and told him that an investigator had called. However, he pretends at first not to recognize the names Art Anzures and Leslie Barry.

On July 2, 1979, Investigator Crisp contacted Eddie Castillon by phone. Crisp stated that Anzures had been convicted and would be sentenced on July 5, 1979. Castillon began to stutter that he did not believe Anzures had committed the crime, and wanted to know if there was anything he could do for me (Crisp). Crisp stated that

Preface

Castillon might be able to help. Castillon then suggested that Crisp meet him at the dental school the next day.

Investigator's Note: Crisp noted that the nervousness in Castillon's voice was of incredible intensity. This nervousness was in response to Crisp's having called and not to anything Crisp had said to Castillon at that point in the investigation. Castillon does not normally stutter.

On July 3, 1979, Investigator Crisp met with Castillon at the U.S.C. Dental School. Crisp wanted to measure Castillon's response to some of the evidence against him in the Leslie Barry case. After going through part of the information, Castillon stated "I would arrest me now." Crisp noticed that the nervousness of the day before had vanished.

At the end of this meeting, Castillon was visibly shaken. He was most insistent upon Crisp talking to Dennis Cantu right away. Castillon tried to get Crisp to meet with Cantu that evening but Crisp declined.

Investigator's Note: During the course of the July 3rd meeting with Castillon, Crisp stated to Castillon that one of two people had killed Leslie Barry. It was either him (Castillon) or Dennis Cantu. Crisp stated further that there was something very unusual about the knots in the cord. Castillon suggested that the knots were perhaps surgical knots. Up to that point the only thing that Crisp had told Castillon about the crime itself was that it had been committed in Aina Barry's room with a telephone cord. Castillon's response indicated more intimate knowledge about the crime than was known to the public.

In October, Investigator Crisp contacted Castillon once again. The purpose of the call was to ask Castillon if he would voluntarily submit to a privately administered polygraph and submit blood samples for analysis. Castillon declined to do either.

On July 22, 1979, Investigator Crisp "tailed" Eddie Castillon for about 20 minutes. On this day Castillon stopped at the El Rancho Market on Huntington Drive. He entered the market for approximately five minutes. When he returned to his car he was not carrying anything and from all appearances he had not made a purchase. From the El Rancho Market he proceeded to the Vons market on Fair Oaks and Monterey Road where he repeated his action from the previous stop. From Vons he went south on Fair Oaks and stopped at the Safeway Store on Fair Oaks where he repeated the procedure of the previous two stops. Investigator Crisp checked these three stores to determine if Castillon had check cashing privileges and he did not. He could have been looking at magazines, but given the fact that all five of these girls could have been followed from stores (or the bowling alley in the Cevallos case), this could have been an exercise of the M.O. However, Crisp never learned of any deaths or rapes in the area on that day.

Dennis David Cantu

Dennis Cantu is currently an intern at U.S.C. County Medical Center. He is 6'3" tall, 200-210 lbs., brown curly or bushy hair, mustache, light complexion, 26 years of age (see photo attached).

Cantu is a boyhood friend of Eddie Castillon and Martin Smith from Laredo, Texas. He graduated from Baylor Medical School in Waco, Texas. His field of study in medicine is unknown.

Cantu's father died when he was a child. Precisely when or how is father died is unknown at this time.

Very little is known about Cantu's background. Neither Castillon nor Smith wanted to talk about Cantu.

Investigator Crisp has tried numerous times to make contact with Cantu, but to no avail. Crisp has had him paged at the hospital and Cantu does not respond to the pages, nor will he come to the phone at home.

On April 23, 1979, Investigator Crisp sent Gessell Montiforte to the home Antonia Cepeda to determine if the Cepeda family knew Eddies Castillon or the Castillon family. Montiforte reported to Crisp that neither Antonia nor Cecilia Cepeda were home. However, Montiforte said that she talked to a boy, believed to be about 15 years old, that was home at the time and he verified that the Cepeda family was from Laredo and that they knew the Castillon family and Eddie Castillon.

In August of 1979, Investigator Crisp went to the Cepeda home in an attempt to verify the above information from Cecilia Cepeda.

Preface

Mrs. Cepeda was cooperative and knew who Investigator Crisp was, apparently from officers Mellecker and Holder of the L.A.P.D. Task Force. She stated to Crisp that the young boy who Montiforte talked to was her 11 year old son. She stated to Crisp that her son was wrong and did not know what he was talking about. She said that she and her husband were from San Antonio, Texas, and that she did not know the Castillons and had never lived in Laredo, Texas. Mrs. Cepeda further stated that her husband was an accountant at U.S.C. County Medical Center and she worked as a counselor for a school in the area. Mrs. Cepeda told Crisp that if Tony Johnson (Sonja Johnson's father) had picked up the girls like he was suppose to, none of this would have happened. She stated further that she was convinced that Kenneth Bianchi had killed her daughter and the killings were random.

ANALYSIS AND CONCLUSION
(Suspects who knew the Victims)

Leslie Fae Barry

Both Castillon and Smith have admitted to knowing Leslie Barry. Art Anzures saw Dennis Cantu come out of her apartment and all three men lived at the 400 Monterey Road apartments. The conclusion can be made that Dennis Cantu also knew Leslie Barry.

Delores Cepeda/Sonja Johnson

The young Cepeda boy says that he knows the Castillon family and Eddie Castillon. It is the opinion of the investigator that an 11 year old or a 15 year old, unless he suffers from a mental disorder, knows where his family is from and has the ability to recognize names. A young person in some instances is a more reliable source than an adult. This is one of those instances. Mrs. Cepeda, in dealing with her grief, seems to have the need to blame Tony Johnson, for the death of her daughter.

The second indication that the victims knew the suspects is the phone call on November 15, 1977, between Sonja Johnson and Carlos Dela Torre. This phone call two days after they disappeared is convincing evidence that the girls were there voluntarily and not by force.

Kristina Weckler

From an analysis of the crime particularly the condition of the apartment (no struggle, no forced entry, bed clothes out, etc.) it is more likely than not that Kristina Weckler knew the person who killed her. However, a solid connection had not been made between this victim and any of the suspects.

Elizabeth Cevallos

Two indications that the suspects knew this victim is a non-reaction to her name by Castillon. When Crisp mentioned the names of some of the victims to Castillon, he would reply, "Who?" But when Elizabeth Cevallos' name was mentioned he did not react at all. Crisp had the impression that Castillon recognized the name. The other indication is the connections between Irene Cevallos and the U.S.C. Dental School. This connection has not been fully investigated.

COMPARATIVE ANALYSIS OF THE CRIMES

Leslie Fae Barry was killed in her apartment on November 20, 1978. The bodies of Delores Cepeda, Sonja Johnson, and Kristina Weckler were discovered on November 20, 1977. All four girls had been sodomized and strangled.

Leslie Fae Barry was strangled with an electrical cord, still attached to the lamp. The cord was tied around her neck with three knots. Two of these knots corresponded to the left and right sterno-thyroid muscle.

Sonja Johnson was strangled with an unknown ligature. However, hemorrhage to the soft-tissue of the right and left sides of the neck is consistent with knots being tied in the ligature used to commit the crime.

Leslie Barry was found in her apartment while the other four victims were found in the open. An analysis of the Leslie Barry murder reveals that the suspect was in all probability still inside the apartment when the mother of the victim came home from work. The suspect escaped undetected when the mother left the apartment to get her mail. Since the crime was interrupted it is uncertain whether the suspect intended to move the body to another location.

It is probable that Dolly Cepeda and Sonja Johnson were killed at a location other than where their bodies were found. This assumption is based upon the degree of difficulty in transporting the two live girls, undetected, through the city. This would be made even more difficult when one considers the magnitude of the search being conducted to locate Cepeda and Johnson.

Investigator Crisp suggests that Cepeda and Johnson were killed at 6421 Crescent Street, Los Angeles. This would be consistent with the M.O. of the Leslie Barry murder. Suspects Smith and Castillon moved out of the Crescent Street address shortly before the Cepeda and Johnson girls were reported missing. They kept a key to that address and returned after they picked up the girls. They moved into the Monterey Road apartments after moving out of the Crescent Street address. In the Leslie Barry case, Cantu and Castillon moved out approximately three weeks before the Barry murder. They only turned in one set of keys and their apartment was vacant at the time of the Leslie Barry homicide.

That Cepeda and Johnson were killed at the Crescent Street address is also consistent with the statement by Carlos Dela Torre that he thought Sonja Johnson was calling from an empty room. In addition to this, Johnson had told Dela Torre that she was sharing a house with Dolly and that it was near her home. (See map for location of Crescent Street)

It is fairly certain that Kristina Weckler was killed at a location other than where her body was found. The area surrounding the Ramon and Wawona Streets is fairly populated. It cannot be ruled out that Weckler was killed in her own apartment. There was no sign of forced entry and no sign of a struggle. From all appearances Weckler was preparing for bed. She had told friends that she was going to bed early.

A couple of things are worth noting here. In the Leslie Barry murder there was no sign of forced entry and no indication of a struggle. Neighbors did not hear screams in either case. There were similar bruises on the back portion of Weckler's right leg just above the ankle as appears on Leslie Barry. Weckler's pattern on the day of her death was similar to that of Dolly Cepeda and Sonja Johnson in that all three had gone to the Eagle Rock Plaza.

There are two major differences between the Weckler case and the other four cases in this report. The first difference is the age of the victims. Weckler was a grown woman at the age of twenty. The other four victims were teenagers. Leslie Barry and Sonja Johnson were undeveloped. They had no breasts to speak of and could be characterized as skinny. Elizabeth Cevallos and Delores Cepeda were very well developed, as was Kristina Weckler. Cevallos was 15 years of age and Cepeda was 12 years of age. Therefore, it is the opinion of Investigator Crisp that age and development were not a criteria in selecting the victims.

The second major difference in the Weckler case is that Weckler had fresh needle marks on both arms. Her friends all stated that she was totally against the use of narcotics. Therefore, one can assume that the person or persons who killed Weckler used the needles on her. According to the autopsy report there were no drugs found in her system.

It could be argued that anyone can get narcotic paraphernalia on the street. However, the person who killed Weckler knew her and probably knew her feelings about the use of drugs.

Dennis Cantu, as an intern, has access to syringes. Dennis Cantu also fits the description of the person the Glendale police officer described as the driver of the compact pick up truck.

The Leslie Barry case is unique for several reasons. The amount of time the crime took to complete (10-15 minutes); the knots in the cord (3), two corresponding to pressure points; the lack of physical evidence (no prints, no blood, no sperm, no screams), and the coolness of the suspect to escape undetected.

Two conclusions can be reached from the above facts: 1) the person who killed Barry had some knowledge of anatomy, and 2) the person who killed Barry had killed before.

Investigator Crisp's feelings about the Cepeda/Johnson crimes is that the girls were apparently runaways; that there was no indication from family and friends the two girls were dissatisfied with their

Preface

home life; the phone call between Johnson and Dela Torre reveals that they were there voluntarily; when Johnson ended this conversation she said almost word for word what Barry said to Lisa Ballatore; Ballatore and Dela Torre were apparently the last people to have heard their respective friends alive.

There are numerous similarities between the Kristina Weckler case and the above-mentioned cases. An important item in this case is the statement by Weckler's best friend that Weckler was extremely cautious due to the Stranglings occurring at the time. The conclusion can be reached that Weckler not only new the person that killed her, but trusted him as well.

The similarities between the above four crimes and the Elizabeth Cevallos case is less pronounced. However, the evidence of cord marks on this victim's neck and the presence of an electrical cord near the body might indicate that the suspect intended to strangle her but did not because he lost control of the victim. She did not die of massive brain hemorrhage and she had not been beaten severely indicating that she had probably been hit just once. The fact that the suspect did not proceed with the strangulation might also indicate a medical background. The suspect knew that the victim had hemorrhaged from the fatal blow.

The above facts and analysis of this report are consistent with the police department's earlier conclusion that the Hillside Stranglings were committed by two set of suspects, probably working independent of each other.

The suspects in this report fit the profile developed by the police in that the police were looking for two people: one with a medical background (Dennis Cantu) and the other with knowledge of police procedures (Martin Smith).

The suspects fit the psychological profile, in that they were all raised in the same environment. Castillon and Smith are related and Dennis Cantu is a boyhood friend of both.

The suspects lived in four areas where the five girls in this report either lived or were found.

Dennis Cantu fits the physical description of the Hillside Strangler. (He bears a striking resemblance to Kenneth Bianchi)

Preface

Castillon's car fits the description of the car described in the Cepeda/Johnson Homicide.

This report contains evidence that tends to show the suspects knew at least three of the victims and probably knew all five of these victims.

The date November 20th, is relevant to four of the homicides in this report. That Leslie Barry would be sodomized and strangled on November 20, 1978, and the bodies of Cepeda, Johnson, and Weckler were found on November 20, 1977, is more than a mere coincidence.

The last person to hear from Leslie Barry alive, Lisa Ballatore, reports that Barry stated abruptly "I've got to go now. My mother is home." The last person to hear from Sonja Johnson, Carlos Dela Torre, stated that Johnson said the exact same thing.

Dated:_____. 1980

Ronald E. Crisp
Private Investigator

Chapter 1

In its heyday, the Green Hotel was a five star hotel where the President of the United States once stayed while politicking in California. By the time Crisp and Marley moved in, the hotel was a federally subsidized housing project for elderly people living on social security. The ground floor rooms, once occupied by fancy gift shops, hair salons, and haberdasheries, were rented to small businesses like mine. A row of offices lined one side of the cavernous hallway and mine was the last one on the right, next to the violin shop and catawampus from the grand old ballroom.

With the ballroom and main lobby restored to near mint condition the Green Hotel was an attractive site for Hollywood producers filming period pieces. George C. Scott and Trish Van Devere once used the ballroom for a thirties era dance scene in a movie they made entitled "Movie Movie."

The extras camped out in the hallway, and I could watch them through the windows of the French doors of my office. Clad in Tuxedos and long, thirties era evening gowns, they looked uncomfortable and bored. Curious about my business, some of them wandered in and out of my office to ask me questions about what a real private eye did for a living. They wanted to know the difference between what I did and the private eyes in novels or on television. I joked that I didn't get beat up much and I hadn't been in a car chase since I flipped off a bunch of navy guys when I was in high school. Other than that, James Rockford and Sam Spade had nothing on Crisp and Marley.

Marley was Jacob Marley from Charles Dickens' "A Christmas Carol." Together we were Crisp and Marley, Legal Research and Inquiry. We worked exclusively for lawyers, mostly in the area of personal injury and product liability cases. Occasionally we picked up work on a criminal case, but the primary focus of the business was tort law.

I worked with my wife, Wendy. She was a highly intelligent woman with a good memory and a quick wit. An excellent writer and editor, she often expressed herself with great flair and melodrama. It was Wendy who came up with the name Crisp and Marley for our business. With a degree in English and a lifetime teaching certificate in adult education, she was a student of the classics. One of her favorite authors was Charles Dickens, and Wendy thought it would be fun to steal Jacob Marley from A Christmas Carol and make him our partner. I embraced the idea enthusiastically.

When business became too much for Wendy and me to handle on our own, we hired a secretary and instructed her to answer the phone Crisp & Marley. If I was out of the office and the caller asked for Mr. Marley, our secretary was told to quote the opening line from "A Christmas Carol," "Jacob Marley was dead seven years now." Some lawyers got it and some didn't. The lawyers that got it would burst out in hysterical laughter. The ones who didn't apologized profusely and offered their heart-felt sympathy and condolences.

When people showed an interest in what a real private investigator did for a living I would point to the wall next to my desk. I kept mementos of some of my more interesting cases there. Among other things, there was a picture of a casket with the bottom cracked and splintered. It was an emotional distress case and I was hired to find out who manufactured the faulty casket that fell apart during a funeral sending the portly, half-naked corpse rolling down the steps of the mortuary in front of all of his friends and relatives. I couldn't believe how secretive the funeral business was. They don't put serial numbers, trademarks or any identifying features on caskets. This one turned out to be a lawsuit in the making when purchased by a warehouse in San Pedro, who resold it to a mortuary in Paramount.

Also hanging in the makeshift museum was a statement taken from a witness to a slip and fall accident. When I began the case, I had nothing more to go on than a first name from the guy's grease monkey shirt given to me by the plaintiff, a man who suffered severe head injuries in a fall at a gas station. I wasn't even sure if it was the witness's shirt or if the shirt was a hand-me-down from a previous employee. The name of the guy I was looking for could have belonged to anyone. I found the man's last name and located a relative. His kin informed me that the witness had joined the Navy since the accident and I tracked him down through the Navy locater and took his statement by phone aboard a ship in transit to the Bering Strait. He told me he had tried to wash gasoline off the cement around the pumps with water. The combination of water, gas and concrete produces a surface as slick as ice. Because of that statement, the plaintiff's lawyer was able force the oil company into a six-figure settlement.

Crisp and Marley moved into Old Town Pasadena several years before urban renewal took over and turned it into the hottest nightspot in Southern California. When my detective agency was there, the area was a run-down section much like the skid row of any big city.

The Rose Parade passed through Old Town on New Year's Day, and the Tournament of Roses committee managed to keep the blight of Old Town from the millions of TV viewers by erecting grandstands in front of the dilapidated buildings. They had the TV cameras set up at a more scenic location on the corner of Orange Grove Avenue and Colorado Boulevard.

Urban renewal might have come to Old Town sooner except the wad of money and media attention the Rose Parade and Bowl game brought to the area made it sacrosanct and untouchable. With so much money at stake, TV cameras going behind the grandstands to show the public what a run-down shit-hole Old Town was would be like pissing on the parade. So, the media kept their cameras focused on the floats and stayed the hell out from under the bleachers.

The Rose Parade floats never rolled on New Year's Day when New Year's fell on a Sunday. Sunday was a day of rest and putting on a parade the magnitude of the Rose Parade was anything but restful. A local beermiester and a crack PR man, Peter Apanel, had had enough of the snobbery and hypocrisy of the Tournament of Roses committee and launched the Doo Dah Parade that marched down Colorado Boulevard in Old Town that year. The Doo Dah Parade was meant to be a one-time joke giving the public a parade on Sunday while the elitist Tournament of Roses went to church.

The Doo Dah chose as its queen the most physically objectionable woman they could find in Pasadena. With entrants like the chainsaw massacre drill team and other low life from the community, the Doo Dah Parade was more consistent with the surrounding urban blight than the Rose Parade. If you came to Old Town on Doo Dah day, you could get a hamburger at the Korean owned greasy spoon named Gil's Grill, or go around the corner from Gil's and have a beer at a dive called the 35er. Except on Doo Dah day, customers at the 35er were mostly hookers and hardcore drunks. The hookers did a good business with the horn dogs coming out of Le Sex Shoppe across the street and with men cruising the slums for sex. There was an over-priced antique shop next door to the porn store. I seldom patronized the 35er or Le Sex Shoppe, but on sunshiny mornings I had my coffee and newspaper sitting at the outside counter of Gil's Grill.

The Doo Dah entrants were so creative, irreverent, and raucously funny that the parade caught on with the media and it became a heavily controlled annual event in Pasadena during the holidays. Ironically, the Doo Dah Parade, which started out as an out of control, chaotic parody of the Rose Parade, became as institutionalized as the parade it was mocking. After the first one, it never again marched on New Year's Day and they barred the parade from having any motorized entrants. Today people can't remember how or why the Doo Dah got started. Wendy and I were never big fans of the status quo and we joined the fun and rode on a fire truck in the first Doo Dah Parade.

Skid Row is not skid row without vintage clothing stores. I was always able to find what attire I needed for undercover work and stakeouts at a shop on the northwest corner of Colorado Boulevard and Fair Oaks Avenue. Just down the street from there was my backup shop, the ghetto-requisite Salvation Army thrift store.

Across the street from the Green Hotel on Fair Oaks Avenue was a three-story brick building with a quote from T.E. Lawrence painted on the side in big blue letters. The quote read, "My people are the people of the dessert..." The owner of the building was an aspiring actor named Duane Waddell, and I always assumed he was the one who had the quote painted on the building. The quote was a point of curiosity with me because I never understood the significance of it. I thought perhaps it was the idea that a noted author had misspelled desert and made his people the people of the banana-custard cream pie. Whatever the significance of the quote it was a landmark, and when I saw it after returning from a case or vacation, I knew I was almost home.

The T.E. Lawrence building once housed the Pasadena Repertory Theater, not to be confused with the Pasadena Playhouse, which was not in operation at the time. Before we met, Wendy had been involved in the theater when it started out as an actors group in Sierra Madre. She decided, soon after we got married, that it would be fun for me to work in the theater and she introduced me to Duane Waddell at a party one evening. Wendy was right, too. It was a great experience working with such talented people as a young actor named Ed Harris, as well as Marie Peckinpah the ex-wife of famed director Sam Peckinpah. Also lending considerable talents to the theater were academy award nominated actress Elizabeth Hartman and a slew of creative writers and set designers. This assembly made the Pasadena Repertory Theater a remarkable school for developing theatrical talent.

After rehearsals, the cast and production crew would caravan down the street to Monte's Steak House for a few beers and some lively conversation about the theater and politics or just some good old-fashioned flirting. Yet, that was Pasadena and I loved it warts, and all.

At my Green Hotel office, I had just hung a new addition to my wall of odd cases, when I received a call from Mitch Molino, a Highland Park lawyer whom I had previously worked with on a couple of personal injury cases. The memento I hung on the wall was a blue nylon bridle used in the recovery of a valuable foundation line Appaloosa. The horse had ended up with the wrong party after a nasty divorce. My agency spent six months scouring the scrub brush of Simi Valley, searching without success, and my client was putting the pressure on me to find his horse. One Friday morning I announced to the office that I was going out to Simi Valley and I wouldn't be back until I found that damn horse. People in the office laughed at my bravado and one of my investigators asked me who I would be leaving the business to in the event I didn't return. But they could laugh all they wanted. I had devised a plan for finding the horse that I was certain would work.

I found an inexpensive motel for the weekend and spent all day Saturday handing out flyers offering a fifty-dollar reward and spreading the rumor among stable owners that the person who had the horse would have him gelded before she let her ex-husband get him back. I knew the reward wasn't much but the rumor about castrating a valuable stallion wouldn't play well with the horse lovers in Simi Valley.

Shortly after returning to my office from handing out the flyers, I got a call from a stable owner telling me she had the horse. The woman said she wasn't interested in the reward, although she would accept it to help defray the cost of boarding. Her main concern though, was that nothing bad should happen to the horse. I rented a rickety old horse trailer from an equipment rental company in Pasadena and got him to a safe stable with only one minor hitch. The trailer blew a tire on the freeway and the stallion nearly kicked the trailer apart. Over all though, the case turned out to be one happy trail.

I didn't know Mitch very well. He was a young lawyer with a small practice and a store front office in Highland Park. I'd done a few minor things for him like taking a statement or two and serving papers in a couple of civil cases, but other than that we were pretty much strangers to each other. When he phoned I couldn't resist telling him the missing horse story and in return Mitch did some chest pounding of his own.

He had just gotten an acquittal in Glendora for a client charged with assault on a police officer. I was impressed. Glendora had more cops per square inch than any town in California. You couldn't waltz in your living room without stepping on the toes of a cop. To get an acquittal in Glendora for an assault on a police officer would take a nifty piece of trial work and it wouldn't hurt if the jury pool were selected from residents of Monrovia or maybe some other planet.

"You ever do criminal investigations?" Mitch wanted to know when he had finished his crowing.

"I've done work on a few drug cases but nothing I would call a real investigation," I responded. "I'm interested in taking in more criminal work though. Why do you ask?"\

Mitch got to the point.

"Did you hear about the murder of the young girl in South Pasadena recently."

"Yes," I answered, "I heard about it on Saturday. Wendy and I attended a small dinner party thrown by some friends in South Pasadena. The hostess was talking about the murder of a twelve year old girl and expressed her concern that the Hillside Strangler might have struck again."

"Well, keep this under your hat," Mitch said, "I was just contacted by a man named Julian Anzures and he says his son is a suspect in the case. The son hasn't been arrested yet but the police are focusing their investigation on him. Mr. Anzures said he would come into my office tonight with the retainer. If he does, I want you to start conducting a very discreet investigation of the murder."

At this point I don't have many facts about the murder or know much about our client, Mitch continued. "I know his name is Arthur Anzures and he's the manager of the apartment building where the young girl lived. I believe the murder happened about a week ago. Apparently they've moved out of the apartments and are now staying with his wife's sister in Glendora," Mitch concluded.

Wendy had stopped work and was listening intently to my end of the conversation.

"What was that about?" she asked, after I hung up the phone.

"Remember Mitch Molino? The lawyer in Highland Park that we did a few things for a while back?" I asked rhetorically. "That was Mitch. He said there's a possibility that he will be retained on a murder case tonight and he wants us to investigate it for him if the guy comes through with the retainer."

"Who got murdered?" Wendy wanted to know.

"The young girl in South Pasadena. The one Judy Howland told us about on Saturday. Shit, the guy hasn't even been arrested yet and he's already hiring a lawyer. The cops must feel strongly that he's their man."

"Hey, what if that murder is connected to the murder of those two little girls over in Highland Park last year?" Wendy asked.

I didn't have the slightest idea what she was talking about. I read the L. A. Times every morning and tried to keep up on current events, but I'll be the first to admit my retention for news is not very good. My mind is like Teflon--nothing sticks to it. For one thing, most of the news is bad and I have a little Merry Sunshine lurking beneath the surface of my psyche to block out bad news. Wendy, on the other hand, is like a sponge soaking up everything she reads or hears. Her reference to the two girls in Highland Park went right over my head.

Mitch phoned the next day and said that Mr. Anzures had paid the retainer. After coming to terms on a fee for my services, Mitch gave me the address and phone number in Glendora where our client and his family were staying.

The thing I liked best about being a private investigator was that no two cases were ever alike. On the way to meet my newest client, I was both excited and apprehensive about getting this assignment. It was like the first time I ever jumped out of an airplane. I was excited about floating through the air but scared to death that my chute wouldn't open and I'd do an Elmer Fudd right through the roof of a barn. On my drive from Pasadena to Glendora, I wondered if I was about to meet an actual child killer.

Chapter 2

The house in Glendora was located in a solid middle class neighborhood with lots of asphalt, a few trees, and well kept lawns. It was the last place you would expect to find a murder suspect. There were no junk cars sitting on cement blocks in driveways or collapsing porches with screen doors dangling from rusty hinges. This was Norman Rockwell's America. Residents in Glendora flew the flag on patriotic holidays and ate pot roast every Sunday after church.

From the porch, I could hear a lot of activity going on inside the house. I rang the doorbell and the door immediately swung open. Hanging from the doorknob was a young kid about four or five years old. Coming up fast was a woman who looked to be in her early to mid-thirties.

"Hi, my name is Ron Crisp," I introduced myself as the woman removed the kid from the doorknob and shooed him away. "Is Art Anzures around?" I asked.

"Can I ask what this is about?" she inquired with a hint of caution in her voice.

"I'm a private investigator," I explained, "I was asked by Art's attorney to talk to him about this incident in South Pasadena."

I had not called to make an appointment before going out to Glendora. I didn't want any prepared speeches or rehearsed lines. I didn't want Art or anyone in the family discussing what they would say. Lawyers hate surprises and every lawyer tells his client not to lie to him. Yet, nearly every client lies. A big part of my job as an investigator was to cut through the bullshit so the lawyer I worked for wouldn't be surprised in court. If there were any bombshells dropped it would be on the prosecutor and not the defense lawyer.

The woman, whom I later learned was Denise Anzures' sister, opened the screen door and invited me in. I stepped inside the door and looked around. After introductions, the woman excused herself and disappeared through a doorway on the right to get Anzures. Like most middle class ranch-style homes, the front door opened into the living room. There was no foyer blocking anything from view. I stood my position at the door and took in as much as I could.

To my left, angled toward the center of the room and the TV set, was a recliner occupied by a man, thirty to thirty-five, whom, I assumed, was the head of the house. The kid who had been hanging from the doorknob was now crawling over his legs trying to get on his lap. I exchanged pleasantries with the man and learned he was indeed my client's brother-in-law. Across the living room and to my left was the kitchen. I could see a couple of women in the kitchen either cooking dinner or cleaning up after dinner. I wondered if one of them was Art's wife, Denise.

There were numerous kids of various ages running around the house, playing board games, and watching TV. The house was teeming with people and I couldn't imagine the sleeping arrangements for so many adults and kids. The house was clean and tidy with a pleasant scent of potpourri or lilacs or something that was sweet and flowery.

Religious pictures and icons decorated the walls and gave me the sense that this was a God fearing, church going family. As the wayward son of a Southern Baptist minister, I was always suspicious of religious zealots. The pictures of Jesus and the plaque of the Lord's Prayer on the wall invoked memories of my childhood and the many years I spent going to church three or four times a week. As the saying goes, "familiarity breeds contempt" and I was far too familiar with church. It was my strongly held belief that the more people went to church, the more they probably needed to go.

My Dad was hellfire and brimstone, and liked to chastise his congregation from the pulpit. With his deep, booming voice echoing off the walls and ceiling of the sanctuary he sounded like God handing down the Ten Commandments to Moses. Pounding the Bible and making grand gestures with his hands he'd shout in that evangelistic cadence, "You come to church on Sunday morning, drop a nickel in the offering plate, say amen, and sing Jesus Paid It All. On Monday you're out gossiping, backbiting, and laying with your neighbors wife."

He'd get a lot of amens out of that one and I always wondered if the amen men were agreeing because they were guilty of it themselves or if they thought everyone else was doing it. Still, playing the guilt card and singing Just As I Am usually got a good response at altar call.

Still, the religious décor gave the place a look and feel of warmth and hominess. It flooded me with a mixture of fond memories and momentary melancholia from my own childhood.

Denise's sister returned from the bedroom wing of the house and her voice snapped me out of my trip down memory lane.

"Art will talk to you in the den," she informed me. "Down the hall, the second door on your left."

I followed her directions down the hallway and tapped lightly on the closed door. A male voice told me to come in and as I opened the door, I saw Art sitting on a small sofa next to his wife. As I entered, both of them got up from the sofa and Art extended his hand and introduced himself and his wife. His hand was soft and his grip was weak. He tried hard to smile but by the time it reached his face, the expression was more of a grimace than a smile. He had the pained look of constipation. He motioned me to sit in an armchair facing the sofa.

Sitting across from him, I tried to get a feeling for who Arthur Hernandez Anzures was. Physically he was about 5' 9" or 5' 10", 150 to 155 pounds. He had medium length, jet-black hair combed to the side in a big wave. He wasn't fat by any means but his round face and thick shoulders gave away the pudginess hidden under a loose fitting shirt. He looked a lot like a teenager who hadn't lost his baby fat.

Art was not the Marlboro man but I think the girls would call him cute. He reminded me of a Hispanic Wayne Newton. Whatever else he may have been, I knew from my experience attending school in the Hispanic, gang infested area of Wilmington, California that Art was not a gang-banger or street smart. I judged that he probably played a musical instrument in the marching band and belonged to the optimist club in High School. Art Anzures' attitude and experiences were as solid middle class as his current surroundings.

His skin color was light and he could easily have passed for a regular old white boy. I figured his heritage to be heavy European Spanish rather than that of Aztec/Mexican descent. Art's face had an unnatural red tint to it and made him look as if he was deeply embarrassed. His eyes were red and swollen from crying and his forehead wrinkled from worry. He looked bone weary, like he hadn't slept for a week.

His wife looked tired and worried too. She was a pretty, reed thin, brunette just above average height. Her most noticeable physical trait was her fragility. She looked like she would break in two with one big hug. She had attractive facial features, but her skin was so pale you could see the blood vessels in her cheeks. Sitting there beside her husband, Denise, even if she didn't understand why this was happening to them, was supporting her man.

The look of confusion on their faces told me they were in denial about the gravity of Art's trouble with the police. They were not at all prepared to talk to me or even to be represented by a lawyer. Art still couldn't believe what was happening to him and he thought they could handle this problem on their own. The look on Art's face reminded me of that famous Mad Magazine cover of Alfred E. Neuman with a stupid grin and an innocent but puzzled look on his face with the caption, "What? Me worry?"

"Why do you think the police suspect you of murdering this girl?" I asked Art.

Art did not strike me as being stupid. On the contrary, I had the impression he was very intelligent. His was a book smart, intellectual, artistic kind of intelligence and not the street-smart survival of the fittest variety. He was detached and dispassionate. His thoughts fragmented and his words came laboriously. He appeared to be trying to show emotion but it just wasn't there. If he had any real emotions about the murder or what was going on with the police it was all drained out of him from hours in interrogation.

Without looking at me, he crossed his arms over both knees and rested his head on his forearms. He began to cry but the whimper that escaped from him sounded phony. Art was putting on quite a show and I didn't know if it was for my benefit or if he was trying to convince his wife of his sincerity.

"Well," Art started slowly, "the police talked to me twice and interviewed me at the station for a long time. They gave me a polygraph and said I had failed the test."

"They had him in there for nine hours the first time and the second time for twelve hours." Denise piped up in a tone both angry and incredulous over their treatment by the police.

"They wanted to know all about my sex life. I told them over and over what I had been doing on the day of the murder and they didn't believe me." Art continued.

"Why do you think the police are focusing their investigation on you, Art?" I asked hoping to get a feel for his grasp on reality.

"I guess it's because I'm the apartment manager, I had a key to the apartment and I was the last person to see Leslie alive." Art reasoned.

Art said the police had asked him about his sex life and I wanted to talk to him about it without Denise being in the room. I needed to know what kind of questions he had been asked and how he answered them. I wanted him to be frank with me. I asked Denise if she minded if I talked to Art alone for a few minutes. With what seemed like great effort, she lifted her fragile frame off the sofa and quietly left the room. Once Denise was out of the room I asked Art in a conspiratorial tone.

"What kind of questions were they asking you about your sex life, Art?"

"They wanted to know things like how often my wife and I had sex; if I had any violent sexual fantasies; if I preferred anal sex over regular sex; and things like that." Art answered.

Those were harmless questions and I suspected that Art was holding back on me.

"Did they ask you about any sexual contact you had with the victim?" I pried.

"Yes, but I told them it was all very natural and playful." Art answered in a frustrated voice like he wanted desperately to convince me, or maybe himself, of the innocent nature of the contact.

"What did you tell the police about your contact with Leslie?" I asked. I needed to find out what the police had on him. What he may or may not have done to the victim was irrelevant to me. What he told the cops could be used against him in court if he was arrested. I would have to find some way for Mitch to explain his actions or his admissions to a jury.

"I told them that I had patted her butt and joked with her about needing a bra by pinching her breasts." Art said without the slightest hint of emotion; but Denise was there many of the times when I did that and she thought it was funny."

There was a tone of finality to his answer signifying to me that he didn't wish to pursue this conversation any further. I didn't want him to feel like I was giving him the third degree or that I was interrogating him like the cops. If Art was busted I would find out enough about him and the circumstances of the murder in due time. Besides, his answer had given me some idea about what the police had on him and it wasn't good.

I had one question to ask before ending the interview. I knew before the question was out of my mouth what the answer would be but I thought I might detect something in his body language or other demeanor that might be useful to me when I knew him better.

I prefaced the question by telling him that neither I, nor anyone on his defense team, would hold his answer, whatever it was, against him. I would still be there to help him and his lawyer would still represent him no matter what the answer might be.

"Did you do it, Art?" I asked matter of fact, as if yes or no meant absolutely nothing to me. "Did you kill the girl, Art?"For most of the interview, Art had sat bent over with his head resting on folded arms across his knees. Raising his head, he turned in my direction. His eyes were red and bloodshot. Darting from side to side, he seemed to be trying to make direct eye-to-eye contact with me but his eyes wouldn't cooperate.

"No. I didn't kill her." Art responded meekly.

I asked if he could get Denise back in the room. When she came back in, I explained to them how I worked.

"You both need to be completely honest with me," I stated emphatically. "Anything you say to me is confidential and protected by the attorney/client privilege. Talking to me is just like talking to your lawyer. You both know the apartment complex, the victim and the people I need to talk to and you can be helpful to me in conducting my investigation. I need your help and cooperation to do my job. I'm sure Mitch has already told you this but I'll say it again: Under no circumstances should you speak to the police again without Mitch being present. I'm dead serious about this—do not talk to the cops without your lawyer being there."

I got up to leave and extended my hand to Art. Denise asked me in a timid, frightened little girl voice.

"Do you think they'll arrest Art?" she asked.

"I don't know," I answered honestly, "since the victim is a young girl it's a particularly sensitive case. From what I've heard and you've told me, they don't seem to be looking at anyone else. If they think they can get a conviction or for some reason want to close the books on the case, Art's their man. You have to realize that guilt or innocence is not important here. The only thing that's important is what they can prove, or what they think they can prove. You and Art shouldn't help them make their case by continuing to talk to them."

As I was about to leave nearly all the adults in the house were at the door to tell me goodbye. The look of concern was etched in their faces. No one in the house was taking this lightly.

"Do you think they'll arrest Art?" The brother-in-law asked, as I was about to walk out the door.

"Denise just asked me the same question," I said, fighting off the Miss Merry Sunshine urge to tell them everything would turn out okay. "I told her I didn't know, and I really don't."

On my drive back to Pasadena, I thought about the meeting with Anzures. I really hadn't learned much about my client and even less about the murder of Leslie Barry. I thought Art looked a little guilty with that red hue to his face and his reactions to me; the way he avoided eye contact, his false display of emotions, how he rested his head on his arms, the fragmented speech patterns. It all seemed strange to me if he was innocent; but then, I had never talked to anyone who had just spent more than twenty hours over a period of two days being interrogated by the police about a murder. Nevertheless, his reaction to the brow beating didn't seem right to me. If he was innocent, why wasn't he angry about his treatment at the hands of the cops and proclaiming his innocence from the rooftops? After about nine hours in the hot seat the first time, why did he go back for a second helping?

I didn't have any ideas about what my next move should be. Mitch had made it clear that he wanted a discreet investigation. It would not be very discreet to go over to the Monterey Road apartments and start asking questions about the murder. To get people to talk I would need to identify myself and as part of my identification, I would have to disclose the identity of my client. Telling people I was hired by Art Anzures would get back to detectives at the Sheriff's Department and they might take my presence on the case as a sign of Art's guilt and make an early arrest. I figured it was their party and I should wait for them to ask me to dance. Beyond talking to Anzures, I didn't see anything to discreetly investigate.

I had a few brief moments of self-doubt about my ability to handle the case. This was before needles became the government's weapon of choice when they wanted to kill someone and if Art was arrested the state of California would be looking to strap my client to a chair in a metal, airtight chamber, and drop pellets of gas that would cause vapors to fill the room and choke him to death. Even if a jury found him not guilty, unless he was cleared of the murder, the public would always have doubts about his innocence. That was a heavy responsibility.

From a purely business perspective I didn't know if taking the case was a good decision or not. Being successful on the defense of a child murder case is never a good thing in the public's eye. I really wanted to be recognized as an honest investigator and not that slick investigator that helped the defense lawyer get the child killer off. The only people who appreciate a good defense team are criminals and defense lawyers; but then, from where I sat, maybe that was enough reason to take the case.

Back in Pasadena, I stopped at the Sawmill on South Lake Avenue for a highball. Sitting at the bar, I nursed a Bloody Mary back to health and thought about the people I just met. The in-laws seemed like decent folks who were having a difficult time digesting the notion of their relative being a suspect in a murder. It was admirable that they were circling their wagons in support of their in-law. They obviously liked Art because if they didn't most in-laws wouldn't be supportive of the outsider. They'd encourage Denise to get rid of the bum and stand in the gallery cheering for the cops to put a spit up his ass and roast the son-of-a-bitch. After a few drinks, I decided it was time to go home.

I walked through the back door of my big old Pasadena house and stopped in the kitchen just long enough to get a beer out of the fridge then headed for the den where I knew Wendy and the kids would be watching TV and doing homework. Wendy was sitting in her favorite chair with her legs drawn up under her working on articles for the magazine she edited. She wanted to talk about my meeting with Anzures and sent the kids upstairs to bed.

"How'd it go?" Wendy asked with great anticipation as the kids scampered up the stairs.

I sat down on the end of the sofa and took a long pull on my beer. I didn't use long pauses for dramatic effect. When I had too much to drink, my thoughts became murky and I had trouble focusing on the issues up for discussion.

"It went fine." I answered not really knowing what to say or even if I wanted to talk about it.

"Well, what did you think about him?" Wendy persisted. "Do you think he did it?"

"How the hell would I know if he did it or not?" I snapped. "How would I know that?" I said softening my voice. "I thought he was a little strange but I don't know what that means yet. Maybe he was just reacting to the police being in his face for two days."

Wendy was an early to-bed early to-rise type. I hated mornings, preferring to stay up late, and sleep-in in the morning until the effects of the previous nights spirits wore off. After our short but terse exchange, Wendy went back to her editing and I sat on the end of the sofa alternating between watching TV and thinking about nothing. If someone were to say to me, "A penny for your thoughts" they'd be overpaying.

For the next couple of days life resumed as normal and I went on with my bread and butter work taking pictures of accident scenes, skip tracing reluctant witnesses, and serving legal papers on people for their negligent ways.

One lawsuit I served paper on involved a woman who was hit by a runaway shopping cart in the parking lot of the Safeway market on Sunset Boulevard in Hollywood. The cart had bumped into her leg breaking the skin and causing a bruise on her ankle. The lawyer sued for fifty-thousand dollars and settled the suit out of court for seven thousand. Upset by the frivolous nature of the complaint, I suggested to the plaintiff's lawyer, a friend and my biggest client, that maybe the woman should've watched where she was going. These are the cases, he retorted, that make it possible for us to work on the big important ones. He was right of course, and the irony of the insurance companies financing the big lawsuits against them gave me a good laugh.

I stayed busy with work and apart from taking a few drive-bys of the murder scene, I pretty much forgot about Art Anzures and his problems. Until the police decided what they wanted to do with him there wasn't much I could do.

Of all I'd heard thus far about the Leslie Barry murder, the most interesting comments were the references to the Hillside Strangler murders. Judy Howland, when telling us about the young girl recently murdered in South Pasadena had expressed her concern that perhaps the Hillside Strangler had struck again. Wendy's first reaction was that maybe the murder was connected to the disappearance of the two young girls in Eagle Rock implying the murder was the work of a serial killer.

Those comments were understandable. The atmosphere of fear, particularly among women in Los Angeles, was palpable. The so-called Hillside Strangler had been terrorizing Los Angeles for nearly two years and the police didn't have a clue about the identity of the killer or killers. The fact that many of the victims were either kidnapped, or their bodies dropped in the immediate area of the Barry murder made these concerns even more understandable. Still, I wasn't jumping to any conclusions.

If they busted Art Anzures for the murder, I would investigate the crime objectively without any preconceived notions about who murdered Leslie Barry.

However, if the issue of the Hillside Strangler were to come up during my investigation, I didn't have any reason to dodge it, either. Unfortunately, not far down the road, I would learn that others involved in the case couldn't say the same thing.

Chapter 3

Art and Denise had been the apartment managers at 400 and 406 Monterey Road in South Pasadena for just under a year. They had lived there for a little longer, but when the Howard Jarvis property tax initiative passed, and Art lost his job with the City of South Pasadena, they took the position as managers in exchange for rent. Denise got an outside job at Slavic's Jewelers in Arcadia to pay food, clothing and other expenses.

Each had their areas of responsibility as co-managers. Denise handled the books and rented the apartments while Art kept the outside area clean and did minor maintenance work around the apartments.

Art didn't mind the work and actually took pride in his position as manager. He and his wife got their apartment free and that took a big expense off the family budget. The only thing that really bothered him was staying at home doing childcare while Denise went off to work for the paycheck. It was a threat to his masculinity to be doing what he considered a woman's job while his wife brought home the bacon.

November 20, 1978 was a day much like any other for the Anzures family. Denise went to work at the jewelry store in Arcadia and Art stayed home, took care of the kids and the apartment complex. Until a little past five o'clock, the only event that stood out in an otherwise ordinary day was when Art sold an old car he owned to one of the tenants for five hundred dollars. With a little money jingling in his pocket, he called Denise at work and informed his wife he would be taking the family out to dinner to celebrate their good fortune. He told Denise he would have the kids ready for dinner by the time she got home from work.

After talking to his wife and putting the kids down for an afternoon nap, Art went outside to clean up around the apartment buildings. The apartments at 400 and 406 Monterey Road in South Pasadena are mirror images of each other. Each building has sixteen apartments separated by a common sidewalk. The buildings face each other and each has its own laundry facility, carport, and swimming pool.

The apartment buildings are perpendicular to Monterey Road and built on three different levels. The street level, the carport level, and the ground floor level where the apartment entrances are located. Partially Supported by stilts, the buildings were designed to conform to the hilly terrain.

The main entryway into the complex from Monterey Road is slightly higher than street level and has five concrete steps stretching across the front between the two buildings and leading up to a landing on the apartments ground level. There's a small, well-manicured yard area on both sides of the steps and landing. The yards have rounded embankments that gradually slope from the top of the steps to the sidewalk. Exotic plants and shrubs lined the front of the building. Colored floodlights highlight the decorative foliage and the landing, and light the entryway for tenants and guests at night.

Art took his job as apartment manager seriously. He felt like he owed it to the apartment owner, to himself, and to his tenants to provide a clean, safe environment for his kids and his tenants. Living close to a high crime area made the residents in that area of South Pasadena particularly nervous. They were even more on edge since the abduction and murder of two young girls from just across the freeway in Eagle Rock a year earlier.

The knowledge that a serial killer, known as the Hillside Strangler, was on the loose had every woman in the area buying small handguns to carry in their purses or taking self-defense classes to learn how to defend against this vicious serial killer. As the apartment manager, Art was always on the lookout for trouble and people who didn't look as if they belonged. A year earlier, he had chased down a purse-snatcher who accosted one of his tenants. He caught the petty thief and held him until police arrived to take the man into custody.

With the kids down for a nap, Art began sweeping up the eastside carport area when a friend, Tony Barrett, drove down the alley and stopped to chat for a bit. Art knew Barrett from his days working for the City of South Pasadena and enjoyed visiting with him when he would stop by in his city truck.

Leaning on his broom next to the driver side, Art visited with Barrett making small talk, when a white car drove up and parked in the carport under the eastside apartment building. He didn't think much of it. It was just the brother of Jeanne Marek, one of his tenants.

Barrett told Art that he had a leaf blower in the back of the truck and he could blow the debris away easier and faster than Art could sweep it up. Barrett took the leaf blower out of the city truck and began blowing away the trash. The chore took ten to fifteen minutes and when all the trash around the carport area had been blown across the alley and into the weeds at the side of the railroad tracks, Barrett got into his truck and went back to work for the city of South Pasadena.

It was 3:30 in the afternoon by the time Tony Barrett left and Art still had some cleaning to do in the carport area. Donette Walker came up to him while he was finishing his clean up and said his son was looking for him. Tony Anzures was only five and Art didn't like leaving his kids alone in the apartment for long and figured he'd better go and see what his son wanted and check on the other kids.

After getting the kids settled down in front of the TV, he went back outside to finish his cleaning job. Art wanted to get the front of the building swept up from the sidewalk to the steps and landing area before quitting time. Since the time change in October, the days had gotten shorter and while it wasn't dark by any means, by four in the afternoon the sun had disappeared behind the hills to the west leaving the front of the apartment building awash in twilight and shadows.

While sweeping the landing area in the front of the building, Art noticed a person sitting in a dark colored Lincoln Continental parked on the street in front of the apartments. Ever since chasing down that purse-snatcher, he was extra cautious and wary of strangers around the apartments. Art had never seen this car before and made a mental note that the person, who appeared to be a man, was slight of build and wore dark horn-rim glasses.

After finishing his sweeping, Art put the broom away and went back to his apartment to bathe and dress the kids for dinner. It was a rare occasion these days for Art to be able to treat his family to an outing and he wanted it to be special. After bathing the kids, he went in search of something to dress them in for dinner. He discovered that all their good clothes were dirty, but it was only four o'clock or thereabouts and since Denise wouldn't be getting home until around 6:30, it gave him plenty of time to do a load of laundry.

House cleaning was not Art's forte and Denise was usually too tired after working at the jewelry store all day to do much housekeeping. Consequently, dirty clothes were piled up and strewn all over the kid's room. Rather than take the time to find the clothes they specifically needed for dinner he scooped up everything around the room and leaving the kids in the apartment went to the laundry room located next to his apartment to do a load of wash.

When he entered the small laundry room, Leslie Barry was standing at the machine putting her clothes in the washer. Jokingly, and with mock anger he said, "You'd better be finished." Art knew she didn't like doing the laundry and he could tell when she scowled at him that she wasn't in any mood for joking around.

Leslie had had a fight with Art's daughter over some childish thing and when she was mad at any member of the Anzures family, she was usually mad with all of them. Art thought it was mostly her prepubescent hormones causing the mood swings and making her angry at the world. At any rate, she wasn't in any mood for joking around and Art wasn't going to mess with her. He took his clothes over to the laundry room in the 406 building. After putting the clothes in the washing machine, he went back to his apartment and watched TV with the kids.

From inside his apartment Art heard the washing machine Leslie was using click off. He had put his clothes in some five minutes after Leslie so he waited a few minutes before checking his wash in the other building. Leaving the apartment, he peeked into the laundry room to see if Leslie had moved her clothes from the washer to the dryer. The lid was still down on the washer and the dryer was not turning.

The dryer in the other building was not working efficiently and it usually took two cycles to dry a load of clothes. The dryer in his own building, where Leslie was doing her wash, worked better and Art would much prefer to use it. He wasn't in a hurry to tangle with Leslie again, but there was no telling how long it would take her to move her wet clothes from the washer to the dryer.

He walked down the sidewalk towards Leslie's apartment to see if she was on her way out to put her clothes in the dryer. If not, then he would sneak his clothes into the dryer before she got to it. He stopped about 10 feet away from her apartment and craned his neck to see if there was any activity going on inside the apartment. He saw that her door was closed, the drapes drawn, and the apartment was dark. From the way the apartment appeared, Art thought she must have gone out with her mother, probably to dinner.

Feeling like this was his lucky day all around he returned to the laundry room in the other building, gathered up the wet clothes and carried them over to the dryer in the other building. After setting the timer and pushing the start button, he went back to his apartment and sat down in front of the TV set with the kids.

It wasn't long after getting comfortable in his favorite chair that he heard sirens and became aware of red lights flashing through the front window of his apartment. The red and blue lights from the emergency vehicles were lighting up his living room and Art could hear people running past his apartment and down the center sidewalk of the apartment complex. He stepped outside to see what was going on. The apartments had suddenly become overrun with paramedics and uniformed police officers. They ran past Leslie Barry's apartment and then, apparently realizing they had overshot their target, turned around and went back to apartment #6.

Art was curious about what was going on but he couldn't leave his kids alone while he went outside to investigate. He was afraid they might wander outside and get in the way. He went back inside, sat down, and tried to concentrate on the television. He thought Leslie must have gotten sick or had a minor accident or something. There was no way it could be anything serious, he thought. He'd just seen her less than an hour ago at the laundry room. Yet, there were so many emergency people running around and why were the cops here?

The continuous commotion outside the apartment was getting to him and he couldn't stand the suspense anymore. Admonishing his kids to stay put, he stepped outside to see if he could find out what was going on. Walking to the center sidewalk, Art saw many of his tenants standing in front of Leslie's apartment and from his position, he could see Leslie's mother inside the apartment along with paramedics and police officers. He watched as Aina Barry walked from Leslie's bedroom to the living room and paramedics prepared to transport the young girl to the hospital.

When the paramedics wheeled Leslie out on a stretcher with an oxygen mask over her face, he knew that this was no minor illness or accident. He desperately wanted to find out what had happened to her but for the time being he would have to wait. He went back inside his apartment to check on the kids. Sitting there in front of the TV set, he worried about his young friend and wondered if she would be okay. The apprehension and nervousness made him antsy. Soon his apartment was filled with other tenants talking about what they knew, or thought they knew, had happened in apartment #6.

Denise came home shortly after the ruckus and found her home filled with tenants. It was going to be a long night, so she decided to make coffee for her friends and neighbors as they held a vigil and prayed for Leslie. As long as she was making coffee, Denise figured she might as well make enough for the detectives and police officers milling around Leslie's apartment.

While Art and Denise considered taking coffee to the police a simple act of consideration, investigators, looking for a possible child killer viewed the act with wariness and suspicion. They wondered why the apartment managers were trying so hard to ingratiate themselves with the cops. Were they just nice people or was there a more sinister explanation? Maybe, they thought, rather than being nice, Anzures was trying to get back to the scene of the crime to make sure he hadn't left anything behind that could point the finger of suspicion at him.

Chapter 4

It was Monday morning, three days before Thanksgiving, and Leslie was getting into the vacation mood. She wanted to ditch school and just hang out around the apartment. Complaining to her Mom of having a sore throat and faking a little cough, her mother, although knowing she wasn't very ill, reluctantly agreed to let her stay home.

On the cusp of puberty, a lovely girl with blond hair and soft, delicate features, Leslie didn't like the immature boys in her seventh grade class at South Pasadena Junior High School. It bothered her when they stared at and teased her about her developing body. That's not to say that she didn't love attention from males. Maybe it was the alienation she felt from her father since her parent's divorce, but Leslie thought of herself as being older and more mature for her age. She had started to wear lipstick and dress to look older than her twelve years to attract the attention of the older more mature boys and young men around the apartment complex.

Leslie and her mother, Aina, had lived in apartment 6 at 400 Monterey Road in South Pasadena for several years. It was a pleasant apartment complex with two swimming pools and other kids to play with, including her long time friend and classmate, Shawn Hagen. Besides Shawn, Leslie had spent a lot of time with the apartment manager's family. Art and Denise Anzures had three kids and because they were much younger than Leslie, she often baby-sat them. It gave her a sense of maturity and responsibility to watch their kids for a few hours while Art and Denise did other things.

Her closest friend, Shawn Hagen, lived in the apartment building across from hers. He was a little older than she, and was more like an annoying older brother than a potential romantic interest. Instead, there were other older guys around like the ones living in the apartment a few doors down from hers that Leslie enjoyed flirting with when she ran into them at the pool or saw them hanging out around the apartments. When she saw them at the swimming pool, she would horse around trying to get them to notice her. Like the time she was in the pool with Art and his kids and she jumped on Art's back just to show off and attract some attention.

Leslie was aware that one of the young men living in that apartment had moved out in the middle of the summer; but another one, just as cute, had moved in. She didn't know much about them except what Shawn had told her. They were college students or something like that, and she enjoyed flirting with them by giving them a lingering look and a big smile. On many occasions, she had caught them checking her out as well.

She liked it when the Anzures' would include her in family outings on picnics and to Magic Mountain or Disneyland. Generally, she liked Art and the attention he paid to her, but he could sometimes be a pain in the ass. He was worse than the kids at school when it came to teasing her about her budding body. On occasion, he would pinch her breasts and make crude comments to his wife about her needing a bra. It embarrassed Leslie and made her mad. She often got irritated at the Anzures kids as well for treating her like a peer. She was older and more mature than they were and she thought they should respect that.

At first, it was fun staying at home lying in bed in her pajamas and watching soap operas, but after a few hours, Leslie was getting bored with daytime TV and curious about what was happening at school. It might have been more enjoyable watching the television had the volume knob on the portable black and white TV Set in her bedroom worked properly. The on and off volume knob had been broken for quite a while and the sound kept jumping from too loud to too soft. She was tired of messing with it every time it went out of whack. Continually getting up from her comfortable bed to tap the knob and adjust the sound was irritating. It wasn't long before she wished she had gone to school after all.

It was well into the afternoon and Leslie was hungry. She hadn't eaten since morning when all she had was a bowl of corn flakes and part of a slice of coffee cake. The coffee cake didn't satisfy her taste buds and she just took a couple of bites of it before putting it aside. Getting up from bed she went to the kitchen to find something to eat. The box of cornflakes from breakfast was still sitting on the counter and she decided more cereal would suit her just fine. She took another bowl down from the cupboard and going into the refrigerator for milk found an empty milk carton. She then remembered that she had used most of the milk for her breakfast bowl of cereal.

Leslie thought walking to the store would give her a good excuse to get out of the house for a while and if her mom called to check on her she could use the excuse that she was hungry and needed milk for her cereal. She wanted to avoid running into Art on her way out. If he saw her, he might say something to her mom and cause a big hassle and Leslie didn't want any hassles. Besides, she didn't feel like talking to Art and she didn't want him to know she had stayed home from school.

Slipping on her flip-flops, Leslie left the apartment and was careful to look around to see if she could see Art anywhere. He was nowhere in sight and she figured he must be either in his apartment with the kids or cleaning up somewhere outback in the alley area. It was perfect timing for her to sneak out the front way and walk down the sidewalk of Monterey Road. The liquor and convenience store was just half a block away at the corner of Monterey Road and

Pasadena Avenue. It wouldn't take her long to get down there and back.

While standing in line to pay for the milk, Leslie struck up a conversation with an acquaintance, one of the young men she once flirted with at the apartment complex. He was one of the college students who shared the apartment down the way from her and had moved out just a week or two before. Leslie was surprised and happy to run into him at the store. During the conversation, the young man asked her why she wasn't in school and Leslie told him she had stayed home because of a cold. Casually, he inquired if her mother had stayed home with her. Leslie told him her mother had gone to work as usual. Desiring to pique his interest and let him know how grown up she was, she added that she was staying home by herself.

On her walk home, Leslie was in higher spirits and less lonely after having had the short conversation with her former neighbor. He seemed like a nice man and it didn't hurt that he was cute too. Arriving at the apartment complex, she still needed to sneak back in without Art seeing her. From the landing in front of the apartment building, she could hear the annoying whine of a leaf blower in the back of the buildings so she hurried up the front steps and ran down the center sidewalk and into her apartment. Safely inside, she put the sack containing the milk on the kitchen counter and fixed herself a bowl of cereal. Relieved that no one saw her, she took her bowl of cornflakes back to her bedroom and turned on the TV.

It was getting late in the afternoon when Leslie remembered that she had promised her mother that she would have the laundry done before she got home from work. Quickly removing all the dirty clothes from the hamper Leslie gathered up dirty clothes strewn around her room, put it all in a laundry basket, and went to the laundry room located at the front of her apartment building.

While putting her laundry in the machine, Art stuck his head in the door and made a smart aleck crack to her about wanting to use the machines. Leslie was annoyed that he had finally discovered she was home. She was hoping not to run into him at all today and when she snarled at his sarcasm, he disappeared fast.

It was about 4:30 and Leslie was lying on her bed watching TV and eating her second bowl of cereal when the phone rang. Jumping up from her bed, she went into her mother's bedroom, next to hers, and answered the phone. Hoping that it was one of her friends from school, either Lisa or Shawn, she was disappointed when it turned out to be her Mom calling to check up on her. Aina wanted to know if she had done the laundry like she promised.

Leslie said that she had started the laundry but was not done because Art was doing his laundry too. Using Art as an excuse for not having the laundry done seemed to work. Her Mom told her that she would be home at a little after five and wanted the laundry done by then. Leslie started to argue but caught herself and instead told her Mom she would try to get it finished by that time.

Hanging up the phone, Leslie went back to her bedroom to the screwed up TV and her bowl of cornflakes. No sooner had she gotten comfortable than the phone rang again. Thinking it was her Mom calling again, Leslie was irritated at having to get up from her comfortable position to answer it. She wished her mom would just leave her alone. Leslie left her bowl of cereal on the bed and hurried to her Mom's bedroom. She was somewhat relieved to hear the voice of her friend, Shawn Hagen.

Shawn was calling to give her the math homework assignment due for the next day in school. Leslie could hear Shawn's radio playing in the background and the music he was listening to was irritating. She put the phone down, went to her room and turned up the volume on her TV set to drown out Shawn's music. After getting her math homework from Shawn, she hung up.

It was getting close to time for her Mom to get home and Leslie wanted to talk to her friend Lisa Ballatore while she was still alone. A few minutes after hanging up on Shawn, Leslie called Lisa to get her English homework assignment and gossip about school.

Lisa gave Leslie the homework assignment and filled her in on the events of the day at school. They talked about their plans for the upcoming Thanksgiving holiday and Leslie expressed her disappointment that she would not be able to spend it with her dad.

The two girls chatted for ten minutes and Leslie could hear the babysitter in the background urging Lisa to hang up so they could leave. The front door of the apartment was not visible from her mother's bedroom, but Leslie heard the door squeak open and then latch closed. She didn't want her Mom to catch her talking on the phone to Lisa when she was supposed to be sick and had chores to do. Quickly and softly, almost in a whisper, she told Lisa. "I've gotta go now" and put the receiver on the hook.

The phone back in place, Leslie hurried to the bedroom door. As she entered the small hallway she expected to see her Mom standing by the kitchen table looking tired and haggard after a long day of work. She started to say, "Hi Mom," but what she saw stopped her in her tracks. A man was coming at her from across the living room. He wasn't running but he was moving fast and taking very long strides. She turned on her heels and ran into her bedroom to the farthest corner in a vain attempt to evade the intruder.

Chapter 5

Being a single Mom was difficult for Aina Barry. She worked long hours as a bookkeeper at the Boys Market Office on Arroyo Parkway in Pasadena and more often than not she was too tired when she wasn't working to do much with her daughter. It was a big help having the Anzures family there to look after Leslie and include her in their family outings. Knowing that Leslie had a few friends nearby to keep her company filled the void of not having a father around and gave Aina a measure of peace. It was also comforting to know that an adult was there in case of an emergency. Still, Aina hated leaving Leslie at home by herself all day.

As she approached puberty Leslie was becoming more sullen, argumentative, and withdrawn. What bothered Aina the most was this recent phase she was going through--trying to act and dress older than her 12 years. Leslie was trying to grow up too fast and it was a source of many bitter arguments.

Aina was having marital problems when Leslie was conceived and when she found out she was pregnant she tried everything she could to reconcile her marriage.

Because of her failed marriage, Aina felt guilty after an emotional blowup with Leslie. In some ways, she blamed herself and her divorce for Leslie's mood swings and mild depression.

Aina often over compensated for her guilt by allowing Leslie to get away with many things she might not otherwise allow. Sometimes she was just too tired to fight about it. When Leslie woke up on the morning of November 20, complaining of having a cold, Aina knew that she was probably faking it, but she was in no mood to argue with her.

Throughout the day, she called home to check on Leslie to make sure she was doing okay and not getting into trouble. Knowing that her daughter wasn't all that sick, Aina had given Leslie a few chores to do in hopes of keeping her busy and out of trouble. Doing the laundry was at the top of the "to do" list and at around 4:30 PM Aina called home to find out if Leslie had finished her chores.

Leslie told her Mom that the laundry was not done yet, but that she had started it and having a 12 year-old's sense of time, she assured her Mom that the chore would be done before she got home from work.

At five o'clock sharp Aina cleaned up her desk and headed for home. It was a short distance between her job on Arroyo Parkway and her apartment on Monterey Road. From door to door and without traffic, the drive took less than ten minutes.

It was dark when Aina turned off Monterey Road onto a side street and made a left turn down the alley to her apartment building. She didn't want to park her car on the street. The city of South Pasadena aggressively enforced the overnight ban on street parking and since she wasn't planning to go out again she headed for her carport parking space. A left into the driveway, and then another left into her parking space under her apartment building and she was home. Grabbing her purse, Aina kept her keys in her hand as she got out of the car and headed for her apartment.

The Barry apartment was in the center of the building on the ground floor. The subterranean tunnel, leading from the carport to the common area of the complex, came up to ground level under and next to the Barry's porch. A short flight of steps led from the tunnel to the common sidewalk in the middle of the complex. The apartment porch was partially enclosed by a four-foot solid cinder block wall opposite the front door. Exotic trees and potted plants partially blocked the view of the front dining room/kitchen window from the center sidewalk. The entry to the porch was on the south side of the apartment door with a short walkway leading from the sidewalk to the porch.

As Aina walked through the tunnel and up the steps to the center sidewalk, she felt tired and happy to be home. Approaching the porch, she could see that the apartment was dark. She walked around to the short sidewalk, past her dining room/kitchen window and up to the door. She entered her dark apartment and turned on the light in the dining room located on the wall to the left of the front door. As she put her purse down on the dining table, she didn't see Leslie or hear any noises coming from her bedroom. Aina figured Leslie was either asleep or at the laundry room doing the wash.

With keys in hand, Aina left the apartment and went to the mailboxes at the front of the apartment complex to check her mail. The mailboxes were located near the laundry room, across from the manager's door at apartment #2. While getting her mail, she heard the dryer in the laundry room turning. Thinking that Leslie might be in the laundry room, Aina stuck her head in the door. The room was empty. She must be asleep, Aina thought, returning to her apartment and entering for the second time.

When she walked through the front door, Aina noticed that the door to her daughter's bedroom was slightly ajar and the room was dark except for the flickering light from the little black and white TV set sitting on Leslie's chest of drawers. The volume on the TV was turned up louder than necessary and Aina headed to her daughter's bedroom to let her know she was home and to tell her to turn it down.

As Aina pushed on the door, it bumped against something lying on the floor. In the dim light from the TV, she could see the silhouette of her daughter's body. Her mind didn't immediately grasp the situation. She wasn't sure what was going on. Was Leslie hurt or just fooling around? She hadn't flinched a muscle when the door hit her and that didn't seem right.

In the darkened room, it was difficult to see and she couldn't imagine anything life threatening happening to her daughter in such a short period. She had just spoken to Leslie thirty minutes ago and she was fine. Yet she sensed something wasn't right. As her mind cleared, Aina began to feel fear and dread that some horrible and inexplicable thing had happened between now and the time she last spoke to Leslie. The surroundings seemed surreal. It was as if she had suddenly gone into a dream world and everything was cloudy, out of focus, and moving in slow motion.

Aina knelt beside her daughter and in the flickering light from the TV set, she could see that something was tied around Leslie's neck. It was a cord or a rope of some kind and it was tied unbelievably tight. Aina was on automatic pilot now. She tried desperately to untie the ligature and free it from her daughter's neck so Leslie could breathe.

"How could this have happened?" she thought as she struggled to release the cord from around her little girl's neck.

Several seconds of struggling with the knot and getting nowhere was enough. Aina jumped up and ran to the kitchen. First looking on the counter top then rapidly rummaging through drawers, she searched desperately for the scissors. By now, she was frantic and felt faint. It took her a minute or two to find the scissors, but a minute in an emergency seemed like forever. She rushed back to the bedroom where Leslie lay on the floor beside her bed.

With the cord tied so tightly around Leslie's neck, it was difficult for her to slide the blade of the scissors under the cord so she could cut it. She had to be extra careful not to cut Leslie's throat while getting the scissors into a better position for cutting the cord. Aina got the tip of the blade between the neck and the cord and squeezed down hard on the handle of the scissors. She hadn't gotten the scissors under the cord far enough to give her leverage to cut through the plastic coating. She spread the blades of the scissors as far as they would go and laid one blade flat against her daughter's neck. Getting the blade under the cord a bit further, she was able turn the blade up and saw through the hard plastic coating cutting a lock of Leslie's curly blond hair in the process.

With the cord removed, Aina began CPR. Overlapping her hands, she began the rhythmic chest compressions, stopping frequently to blow breath into her daughter's lungs. After a few minutes without a response, Aina hurried to the phone in her bedroom and called 911 then returned to continue CPR until help arrived

After the mayhem from the weekend, Monday's are customarily slow days for paramedics everywhere. It was shortly after 5:00 PM and the paramedics, stationed at the South Pasadena fire department less than a mile away, were not busy. Upon receiving the emergency call of a child choking, they jumped into action. The rescue unit took just 3 minutes to get to the apartment complex at 400 Monterey Road and after locating the right apartment found the victim in a prone position on the bedroom floor. It was dark in the bedroom, so while one paramedic retrieved a lamp from another room the other medic began administering emergency treatment on the still warm body of Leslie Barry.

Chapter 6

When paramedics arrived, they didn't waste any time getting to work on the victim. The young girl was not breathing, but her body was extremely warm. Except for the light from the TV the room was dark. While one medic got a lamp from another room the other medic applied CPR and worked intensely to get oxygen to the victim and to set up a saline fluid IV.

Uniformed police officers from the South Pasadena Police Department arrived shortly after the paramedics and began assessing the situation. Officers Modica and Ridley noted that Leslie was nude from the waist down, and her pink pajama pants were in a heap at her feet. Her panties were across the room at the foot of her bed. A clear plastic electrical cord lay near her head. The officers noted that the cord had been cut through two strands and had several knots tied in it. A clump of blond hair was entangled in one of the knots. From the condition of her clothing and state of undress, the officers concluded that the girl had probably been sexually assaulted. If she didn't survive, this case would go down as a murder/rape investigation.

South Pasadena had a homicide maybe once every ten years, so there was no need to maintain a murder cop. Major crimes like murder were turned over to larger police departments with the resources and experience to investigate those crimes. Normally they would call in the Pasadena Police Department for a case like this. If Pasadena was too busy or couldn't conduct the investigation for some reason, they would ask the LA County Sheriff's Homicide Bureau to investigate. Whatever department was going to handle the Leslie Barry investigation, they needed to get started on the crime scene immediately. The condition of the body indicated a "hot" crime scene, and the proximity in time between discovering the body and the commission of the crime could give investigators an advantage they didn't often get in these cases.

The big city cops from the LA County Sheriff's Homicide Bureau swaggered onto the scene at 6:45 PM. Upon their arrival, they had to push their way through the crowd of curious tenants who had gathered on the center sidewalk in front of the apartment. By now apartment #6 had been cordoned off with yellow crime tape, and Detective Sergeant David Kushner strutted around the small apartment shaking his head at the mess left behind by the paramedics and South Pasadena Police Officers. The paunchy and balding detective had been in homicide for 16 years and was considered a competent and able investigator. It was going to be a challenge to separate the obvious evidence from those traces left behind by the rescue team.

Kushner could understand the need of the paramedics to try their best to revive the victim and even to rush her to the emergency room for further resuscitation efforts; but too many people had trampled over the crime scene, and it might be hard to separate potential evidence left by the killer from the traces left by emergency personnel. Mentally he ticked off the list of people he knew had been in the apartment: There was the mother, two paramedics, three firefighters, and at least four South Pasadena cops.

It was disconcerting that the South Pasadena Police, while sealing off the apartment, had not thought to seal off the surrounding area. The hope of finding evidence like a footprint or perhaps something dropped by the killer during his escape was all but gone by allowing the dozens of spectators to walk all over the immediate area outside.

Kushner told an idle officer standing nearby to disburse the crowd of tenants in front of Leslie's apartment and tell them to stay in their own apartments until they were interviewed. He knew the stairwell leading to the carport area, and the carports themselves should have been cordoned off before the crowd of curious people had a chance to destroy potential evidence. It was too late for that now.

The Paramedics, fire department personnel, and police had left their mark on the crime scene for sure. Their hair, fingerprints, and fibers were all over the place. In their efforts to save Leslie's life, they had moved things around in the room and brought items in from other rooms; there were wrappers from medical supplies strewn on the bed and on the floor. Kushner ordered an officer to compile a list of all the emergency personnel and anyone else who might have been inside the apartment and the victim's bedroom. He would need this information later to distinguish official fingerprints and other potential evidence from what might have been left behind by the killer.

Not having the victim' body at the crime scene complicated things. Detectives would have to rely on the visual observations of patrol officers, and there was a good possibility that the less experienced officers from the South Pasadena Police department had missed something in their inspection of the body at the scene. The victim had not been officially declared dead, and while paramedics were attempting to revive her, police could not interfere with that process to collect evidence for a murder investigation. One officer, Kathleen Ridley, was a reserve police officer with the South Pasadena Police Department. In giving her oral report to detectives, because of her lack of experience, she might have left something out-- something that could prove to be vitally important to the investigation. Without a body to observe and inspect, detectives would have to depend on these oral reports from officers at the scene. Considering the stressful situation, those reports could be as accurate as idle gossip.

There was precious little to indicate that a heinous crime had occurred in the small apartment just a short time ago. There was no body. There was no blood. Evidence left behind by the killer was trampled, hidden under, or contaminated by the police and paramedics who had worked to revive the young victim. All that remained as a testimony to the last moments of Leslie Barry's life and the way she had succumbed were a few of her things. Her pajama pants, her panties, a few dirty dishes lying about the room, a poster of a rock star lying in a heap on the floor. The murder weapon, an electrical cord, was still attached to a wall lamp, the plug end lying on the floor between the bed and the bedroom door. It was not much to go on, and Kushner was unaccustomed to not having a body, or at least a chalk outline of a body, at the scene of a murder.

He looked around and took in the scene all at once like drawing in a deep breath of air. What were the things that made this room uniquely Leslie Barry, and what had the killer disturbed or left behind that could possibly identify him, or at the very least, tell him something about how the crime was committed?

There was a clothes hamper against the wall at the head of the bed. The victim used the hamper as a nightstand. Two glasses, a cereal bowl with a spoon in it, a fork lying by itself, and a stack of playing cards lay on the hamper. Next to the hamper was a three-shelf bookcase. The bookcase was cluttered with stuffed animals, a textbook, notebook paper, and several board games: Monopoly, Life, Booby-trap, and checkers. On top of a game box on the second shelf lay a saucer with a half eaten portion of coffee cake or some other pastry. A wall lamp was mounted on the wall a few inches above the hamper.

An electrical cord, still attached to the wall lamp, stretched across the hamper between the two drinking glasses, across the edge of the cereal bowl, and over a stack of playing cards. The playing cards, the right height to be two decks, were askew but still in a stack. Kushner thought it interesting that the cord had not knocked over the stack of cards as it was being tied around the victim's neck, or when the mother cut through it in a frantic attempt to free it from her daughter's neck.

Paramedics had brought a table lamp into the room from another room so they could see to do their jobs. The lamp, sitting on the bed near the pillows, was plugged into the electrical outlet behind the hamper. It was the only electrical outlet on that wall, and the plug for the wall sconce had been plugged into that socket before the killer unplugged it and turned it into a murder weapon. Kushner wondered if anything on the hamper had been moved, disturbed, or replaced by emergency personnel. If nothing had been changed, it was odd that the killer could unplug the cord, tie the knots, and strangle his victim without disturbing any of the items on the hamper.

After a few minutes of studying the crime scene, Kushner wanted to check the outside of the apartments. As he stood on the porch surveying the layout and talking to other investigators and police officers, out of habit, he reached inside his suit jacket and took out a pack of cigarettes. Without thinking, he removed a cigarette from the pack and lit up.

Finishing his conversation on the porch, Kushner went back inside the apartment. He forgot to extinguish his cigarette before reentering the crime scene and as the smoke filled the room, he became aware that he was polluting the air. Looking for the nearest place to extinguish his smoke, he went to the victim's bathroom and tossed the butt into the toilet. Kushner didn't realize the photographer had not yet photographed the bathroom and was one step behind him taking pictures of everything.

To an experienced and competent detective, odors in the air, like after shave, cigarette smoke, or particularly bad body odor can foul the air and become a clue that can lead police to consider a certain individual as a suspect. Before DNA testing of human secretions, a cigarette butt could still be vitally important in solving a crime. Crushed out in an ashtray of a nonsmokers apartment, absent-mindedly tossed on the floor, or ground out on a sidewalk, it could be used to determine a blood type; show that the killer was a non-secretor; or tell an investigator that the perp smoked and what brand of cigarettes he smoked.

Kushner knew that strong colognes and bad body odor could leave a scent at the scene of a crime that lasts long after the crime was committed. Extinguished cigarette butts have solved many crimes over the years and it was a major blunder for him to be smoking inside the scene of the crime. He knew he had screwed up; but as messy as this crime scene was anyway, a little cigarette smoke and a butt swirling around in the toilet wouldn't make much of a difference. He clearly hadn't counted on the crime scene photographer taking a picture of his mistake.

Agent Louis Hatfield of the South Pasadena Police Department had taken charge of the initial investigation and had dispatched

Officer Munoz-Flores to Huntington Memorial Hospital to collect evidence and keep police at the crime scene informed about the condition of the victim. Until Kushner heard from Officer Munoz-Flores that the victim had expired, the investigation would not be officially listed as a homicide. Nobody expected Leslie Barry to survive, and unless he heard differently, Kushner would treat it as he would any other homicide.

After checking out the inside of the apartment, he went outside to check the layout of the complex. He instructed his crime photographer to take pictures of the porch area from different angles. The photographer took pictures of the porch from the sidewalk leading up to the porch and the front door. He took pictures of the porch straight on from the main sidewalk running down the middle of the complex. Then he took pictures from the north side showing the proximity of the tunnel to the porch.

While Kushner walked around the area scenarios flashed through his mind like pictures from a slide show. He looked at possible escape routes and made a mental note that there were several good possibilities. Given what he already knew about the crime, some were more feasible than others. Like any good homicide cop, Kushner kept his theories to himself.

The mother, Aina Barry, had told officers that she got home from work at a little after 5:00 PM. She came right home and didn't stop at the store or anywhere else. She could remember using her keys to open the door, but she didn't remember if the door was locked or not. She had entered the apartment, put her purse on the dining table, and left the apartment to check her mail at the mailboxes in the front of the building next to the manager's apartment. When she returned to her apartment from the mailbox, Aina noticed that the door to her daughter's bedroom was ajar. It was dark in the room, and the volume on the TV set was up louder than normal.

Kushner was accustomed to putting facts together fast. He quickly deduced that the killer was inside the bedroom when Aina Barry first entered the apartment from work. The killer had escaped undetected when the mother left to get her mail. The perpetrator could not have gone out the front way to the street without running into Aina Barry coming back from the mailbox. His escape route had to be somewhere in the other direction, and the escape had to be a hasty disappearing act. Similarly, if the killer took the center sidewalk as an escape route to the alley, he would've needed to do the 40 in 2.5 seconds or the mother would have seen his back as he disappeared into the darkness of the alley. Aina Barry hadn't seen anything out of the ordinary.

That left only two other possibilities: either he escaped through the east side tunnel of the 406 building, or he escaped through the west side tunnel of the 400 building directly beneath the Barry's front porch. The east side tunnel of the 406 building presented the same problem as a frontal escape to the street or a rear retreat to the alley. He couldn't make it without being spotted by Aina Barry. Even if she couldn't identify him, it would not have been a clean escape and she would've told police about seeing someone running from the scene. The mother hadn't seen anything, including the back of someone streaking for the east tunnel or the back alley.

The west side tunnel in the 400 building had its own set of problems, but it was the quickest, and for pulling off a hasty disappearing act, the most feasible route. The tunnel was accessible by vaulting over the corner of the porch and directly into the stairwell. Kushner made a mental note that the jump would cover about four feet laterally then a drop of about seven or eight feet to a precarious landing on the steps leading into the tunnel. It would not be an easy jump to make without incurring some injury. The son of a bitch must have nearly broken his fucking leg getting out of here, Kushner thought to himself.

He inspected the stairwell carefully for any evidence that might prove his theory. It was dark and he had to use a flashlight to see. Kushner could see nothing on the South wall of the stairwell or on the steps of the stairwell that indicated the killer had made the jump. If he vaulted over the porch at an angle from south to north, the momentum of the leap would carry him toward the North wall of the stairwell. Kushner inspected the north wall very carefully.

Three-fourths of the way up the wall, he saw a round red spot about the size of a quarter. There were small streaks of red going in a downward direction, and the red marks appeared to be blood. It was possible that someone could've left the mark by falling against the wall going down the stairs. The red spot was probably blood, but he wasn't going to bother the lab people with it. There was no proof of the source of the blood, nor a direct connection to the murder scene. He made a mental note that when he came up with a suspect to check for injuries to the right hand or arm and to observe if the suspect walked with a limp.

Kushner had to worry not only about capturing the killer but getting a conviction later. So-called Genetic fingerprinting was still about 10 years into the future, and in 1978, a good defense lawyer would make easy work out of discrediting evidence found in a place away from the actual crime scene and accessible to the general public.

Nevertheless, Kushner was convinced he had found the killers escape route, whether he could prove it or not. Now the question was, "Did the killer disappear into the dark carport area where he had parked his car, or did the killer live nearby and escape on foot to the safety of his own home?

As he continued through the tunnel to the carport area, he thought about the jump and how it tended to indicate that the killer was athletic, or at the very least, quite fit. The walk by Aina Barry from the mailbox back to the apartment would've taken so little time that the killer's vault into the stairwell was most certainly instantaneous. An automatic leap of that magnitude might indicate that he had planned his possible escape routes before committing the murder. To the seasoned detective it looked as if the killer had, at the very least, a minor familiarity with the apartment complex. Maybe he lived in the apartments, visited frequently, or lived nearby. Maybe he was an ex-tenant who had returned to the apartment specifically to kill the girl. The killer could've been stalking Leslie for weeks before killing her.

Using his flashlight, Kushner walked from the carport area of the 400 Monterey Road building to the alley, then east down the alley to the carport area of the 406 building. He didn't find anything out of the ordinary or of an evidentiary nature on his walk and reemerged to the crime scene area through the tunnel of the east building.

Before checking the outside of the apartment building, Kushner had looked at the murder weapon but had not really studied it. By the time he got back to the crime scene the electrical cord had been put into a clear plastic bag and marked as evidence to be photographed later. Kushner would study it closely when he got back to his desk at the Hall of Justice.

After canvassing the apartment building for witnesses, Officer Kathleen Ridley gave Kushner a rundown on what she had learned. Referring to her notes she told him there had been a number of people home at the time of the crime, but no one had seen or heard anything out of the ordinary.

The apartment manager lived in apartment #2 and was home at the time of the murder. He had spoken to the victim at the laundry room just shortly before the police and paramedics arrived. His name was Arthur Hernandez Anzures, a twenty-seven year old Hispanic male. He had been doing his laundry in preparation for going out to dinner with his wife and kids. He was not aware of anything happening until he saw the lights and heard the sirens from the paramedics and police units.

Continuing her run down of the canvass for witnesses, Ridley told Kushner that no one was home in nine of the sixteen apartments in the 400 Monterey Road building, and the ones who were home saw nothing at, or around, the time of the murder. There was, however, one young boy, Shawn Peter Hagen, who had made an interesting statement.

Shawn Hagen lived in Apartment B of the 406 Monterey Road building. He had been home since school let out and had spoken with the victim by phone at around 4:30p.m. Shawn and the victim were good friends from school and hung out together around the apartment complex. The victim had called him to get the homework assignment for the next day.

Hagen had known the victim since they attended Stancliff School, a small private school in South Pasadena, and told Officer Ridley that he thought this was a Hillside Strangler case because he knew one of the Hillside Strangler victims. At the time he made this statement, Hagen had no idea what had happened to Leslie Barry.

Kushner listened attentively to the report from Officer Ridley on her canvas of the apartment complex. He knew he would have to re-interview all the tenants, but the purpose of the canvas was to turn up any eyewitnesses that might enable them to make an early and immediate arrest. It was also good to get pure statements from people before they knew what had happened or before rumors and misinformation colored what they really saw and heard.

It was too early to come to any conclusions, but of all the people Officer Ridley and Officer Modica had interviewed, the apartment manager, Arthur Anzures, sounded the most promising to Kushner. The apartment manager knew the victim and had seen her shortly before her mother discovered her body. There was no evidence of forced entry into the apartment and the manager had a passkey. He lived nearby and would be able to get back to the safety of his apartment without being detected by Aina Barry. If he intended to make an early arrest Arthur Anzures would be the logical place for him to begin his investigation.

At just past 8 P.M. Officer Munoz-Flores called from Huntington Memorial Hospital to inform officers at the crime scene that the victim, Leslie Fae Barry, had been pronounced dead at 8 O'clock. Leslie Barry was officially a homicide.

Chapter 7

To their family and closest friends, Art and Denise seemed sincerely upset by the murder of Leslie Barry. Like everyone else who knew the victim, they wanted to find out what had happened to their young friend; but every time one of them inquired about the murder, it brought more suspicion on Art. Their emotions were becoming a jumbled mass of fear and confusion about what had happened to Leslie and what was happening to them in the aftermath of her murder. They needed to get away from the apartments to reflect on the recent turn of events in their lives and seek solace in the support of family members.

Without fully understanding it, Art had become a suspect in the murder. His inquiries to the police about the specifics of the crime had been sternly rebuked and met with a suspicious eye. He felt thoroughly chastened for his display of curiosity. If grief, depression, and Art being suspected of murder wasn't enough reason to get away, Denise was frightened out of her wits that the killer could be stalking her or one of her children, and that, in itself, made getting away from the apartments a necessity if she were to keep her sanity.

Then, there were the two long interrogations of Art by the homicide detectives investigating the case.

In the early evening hours on the Saturday following the murder, Detective Kushner phoned Art to ask if he would mind coming down to the South Pasadena Police Department for an interview. Art considered the request odd because he thought he'd already told them everything he knew when he was interviewed on the night of the murder. Detective Kushner said it wouldn't take much of his time and gave him the old cliché, "We just have a few routine questions to ask you. You'll be back home in an hour or so," Kushner assured him.

The detective sounded friendly on the phone, and Art considered this an opportunity to finally get a few details about the murder. Art would tell them what he knew, and in return, they would give him some facts about what had happened to Leslie. Nervously he consented to the interview, saying he wanted to do anything he could to help them solve the case.

Remembering his previous, less than friendly encounters with detectives at the apartment complex, Art was pleasantly surprised to be greeted at the station by detective Kushner who was smiling and offering an extended hand. Kushner took him by the arm, and gently guided him to a small, drab interrogation room. The two men were joined by Kushner's partner, Deputy Jerome Beck. The detectives were cordial and went out of their way to make him comfortable. They offered him coffee and sodas and spoke to him in soothing tones. Art was curious about the change in their attitude from previous sessions, but he liked it and they made him feel relaxed.

Detective Kushner began the interview by going over Art's previous statements about his activity on the day of the murder: cleaning up the outside of the apartment complex, Tony Barrett stopping by for a visit, selling the old car to his tenant Richard Querio, meeting Leslie at the laundry room while preparing to go out to dinner, etc. It was natural, Art thought, for them to be interested in the specific timeframe of each activity.

After talking him through the details of his activity on the day of the murder, Kushner said they wanted to get a better feel for the relationship he had with the victim. By this time the pressure Art felt was not so much from their questions as the tone and direction the investigators were going. As the apartment manager, he expected to be questioned thoroughly about his activities, but he wondered if they weren't leaning a little too heavy on him.

In an objective, dispassionate monologue, Art told detectives that Leslie was an argumentative and troubled child, but she seemed to be feeling better about herself and a little more communicative in recent days. Art told them that he had never had a real in-depth or comprehensive conversation with her, and he didn't see himself as a father figure or substitute man-of-the-hour. Nor did Leslie have any unusual affection toward him, Art added.

"And how did you feel about her?" Kushner asked.

"I loved her," Art replied, "she was like my daughter,"

"How do you feel about her death?" Kushner probed.

Art broke down and began sobbing uncontrollably. He hated such an open display of emotions in front of these tough cops, but he had been under so much pressure with the murder and the move and everything going on in his life, that he couldn't help himself.

"I feel awful about her death," Art replied between sobs. "I feel like I lost a member of my family."

He was hoping the interview was about over. Sniffling and drying his eyes on his forearm, he assured Kushner that he couldn't be more than a few minutes off on the timeframe of his activities on the day of the murder.

After regaining his composure, the detectives questioned him in detail about his military service. The change in subject matter was a relief. Art was embarrassed by his display of emotions and it was a relief to be changing the subject to a manlier, less emotional topic. Besides, the detectives were probably veterans like himself, and he felt the interview was changing direction to a more buddy-buddy-bullshit-war-story swapping tone.

Art was not a demonstrative person; but with a little more animation and zest than he had when talking about Leslie, he told the detectives that he had served for three years in the army as an airborne trained military police officer. Most of his time in the service was spent in Germany. While there, he explained, he had done some things that in retrospect, he regretted. He was embarrassed to go into any details about what "those things" were but the implication was that it involved sex with prostitutes.

Kushner was itching to delve deeper into his background, but he had to be subtle about it. Feigning mild curiosity about the subject, Kushner asked him what kind of killing techniques he had learned in military police and airborne training schools. Art told him the only ones he could recall involved strangleholds. The chummier they got with him the more open and relaxed he became.

"Why didn't you pursue a career in law enforcement when you were discharged from the army?" Kushner inquired in a friendly tone.

The old detective sensed that Anzures' military service was a point of pride with him, and Kushner felt that if he could get his suspect talking about a subject comfortable to him, he might just slip up and say something useful to the investigation. Getting Anzures to relax was not the only reason Kushner had for asking that question.

The detective had been intrigued by Shawn Hagen's statement about knowing one of the Hillside Strangler victims. Expert profilers in the Hillside Strangler investigation, after studying victim drop sites and other evidence, came to the conclusion that the killer was probably a cop or someone with knowledge of police procedures, or a person who might be a disgruntled employee of one of the downtown police departments. They might be looking for a cop who was fired or someone turned down for employment with the LAPD or the County Sheriff's Department. One victim had been found on a hillside overlooking the downtown area and intentionally positioned with her crotch facing the Parker Center. By placing his victim in such an obscene pose, the profilers thought the killer was taunting or showing his disrespect and contempt for the LAPD.

"When I got out," Art explained, "I applied to the Los Angeles Police department. When I went in for my pre-employment polygraph, the personnel investigator asked me some embarrassing questions and I didn't want to answer them."

"What kind of questions did they ask you?" Kushner pushed.

"They asked me questions about knob polishing and other sexual shit," Art answered, "so I just got up and left."

Kushner' sixteen years in homicide had sharpened his sense of timing in interrogations. He was happy with the information he had already extracted from his only suspect. The statement by Shawn

Hagen about knowing one of the Hillside Strangler victims had been of intense interest to the detective. Now his prime suspect in the murder had admitted having a police background and to having been rejected for employment by the LAPD. Both of those facts fit with the profile of the Hillside Strangler.

Kushner had kept Art in the hot seat for several hours, and he could tell that Anzures was getting tired. Kushner knew he had taken him about as far as he could for the day. He had elicited some good statements from him, and he didn't want to spook his only suspect into asking for, or retaining, a lawyer. The lab reports were not yet completed, and he didn't have the physical evidence or eyewitnesses to make a murder charge stick. Too, he needed to run this new information by his superiors to see what they thought about pursuing the Barry murder as a Hillside Strangler investigation.

Nevertheless, Kushner wasn't going to allow Art to just walk out of the station with a thanks-for-coming-down and a pat on the ass. He wanted Anzures to leave a piece of himself behind and another reason to come back for an encore performance. Kushner thought he was guilty as hell, at the very least, of the Barry murder; but he wasn't ready to call him a suspect yet. At least not out loud. It might've been the Christmas season but the old detective wasn't going to play Santa Claus and put a lawyer under his tree. To call him a suspect at this point would require reading him his Miranda rights, and that would end any chance the detective might have of getting a confession. He'd have a hell of a time getting anything out of his suspect with a lawyer in the room.

While explaining to Art that he was under no obligation to do so, but impressing on him that it would be to his benefit to cooperate, Kushner asked if he would voluntarily supply samples of his head and pubic hair. Tired and hungry and wanting nothing more than to get out of there as fast as he could, Art pulled a few strands of hair out of his head and put them in an envelope being offered to him by deputy Beck. Without asking for privacy or even turning away from the rest of the room, Art shoved his hand down the front of his pants and pulled out a few strands of his pubic hair. Beck put those in a separate envelope.

During the interrogation, Art talked about his fear of taking the pre-employment polygraph at the LAPD because he feared disclosing certain sexual proclivities that included his fantasies during masturbation. To most young men masturbation was no big deal, and they often joked around about spanking the monkey. Considering his suspicions about Art's involvement in the murder, Detective Kushner sensed there was something more behind Art's fear of the polygraph than met the eye. Sexual repression was a common characteristic in serial killers and unless his fantasies contained perverted acts, he wondered why Art would be so fearful or embarrassed by a few questions about his sexual fantasies.

Before letting him leave, Kushner asked if he would voluntarily take a polygraph. Again, the detective reminded him that he was under no obligation to take the test. Art was afraid that his refusal to take the test would be taken as a lack of cooperation and reflect poorly on his claim of innocence. In spite of his fears, Art said he had nothing to hide and would be more than happy to take a lie detector test.

Art was antsy to get the hell out of there and retreat to the safety of his home and the comfort of his family, but there always seemed to be one more thing the detectives wanted to ask him.

"Have you told us everything we should know about your involvement in the case?" Kushner asked. "Have you been truthful with us Art?" He added with just a tinge of disbelief in the tone of his voice. Wearily nodding his head, Art said he had told them everything he knew and had been truthful about everything they asked him.

Kushner couldn't resist taking one more shot at him.

"You're sure there's nothing else you want to tell us?" Kushner jabbed.

Art shook his head and walked out of the station.

On the short drive home, exhausted from the hours of interrogation, Art thought about the interview and considered the implications of the questions he had been asked and the tone the detectives had taken with him toward the end of the interview. It was obvious to Art that they considered him a suspect. He had been at the station for nearly nine hours and much of that time was spent in the interview room completely alone. Throughout the evening, when detectives were out of the room, he had thought about just getting up and going home. The only thing that stopped him was the feeling that if he walked out the cops would think he was hiding something. They might even try to stop him. So, he complied and stayed in the room left to his own thoughts about what was going on outside in the detectives' room and what was going on at home with his wife and kids.

Denise had waited patiently for Art to return home from the police station, and she was worried sick by the time he walked through the door. She was at the door to greet him with a hug, a peck, and a lot of questions about what took so long. She wanted to know everything that had transpired at the police station and if he had found out anything about the murder. They sat up all night talking about it.

When Art had finished telling his wife about the interview, the type of questions the police had asked him, and how frightened he was at the prospects of taking a polygraph, Denise urged him to tell his Dad about what was going on. Art didn't want to alarm his family at this stage. He was certain he could straighten out any misunderstandings or wrong impressions the police might have that caused them to suspect him of the murder. He knew they were on the wrong track and that the cops would eventually come to that conclusion and focus their attention elsewhere. Art believed in the fairness and honesty of the system and that the truth would win out.

The next day Detective Kushner called to tell him they were ready to administer the polygraph at the Sheriff's Department crime lab. Art didn't argue or show any resistance to the request and arrived at the lab at around 3:00 PM and was introduced by detective Kushner to the polygraph examiner, Sergeant Benedict Lubbon.

Lubbon began the test with a pre-examination interview. The pre-examination interview is necessary in order for the examiner to get to know his subject. A competent polygraphist will try to expose any guilt complexes that might cause a false physiological response to questions not germane to the subject of the examination. To prevent a physiological response by way of surprise, before being given the test, the examiner will give the subject a list of questions that he will be asked during the test. The polygraphist will only ask questions that can be answered with a simple yes or no.

The polygraph machine is seen as an uncanny instrument in discovering deception; but the machine is only as good as the man sitting behind it, and sometimes, when the man sitting behind it is a cop, the lie detector, as it's commonly called, is used as a bad cop in a game of good-cop, bad-cop.

Kushner and Beck were standing nearby listening and tape recording the pre examination interview. Sergeant Lubbon began by asking a couple of control questions. Control questions are neutral facts like name, age, and address that are used to calibrate the machine to make allowance for natural nervousness, heart rate, and that sort of thing.

While polygraph tests are not admissible in court; the polygraph is still a powerful investigative tool. Everyone is nervous about being hooked up to a machine, and no one can read the graph but the examiner. The examiner can imply, by asking the same question several times, or changing the tone of his voice, that the machine is showing deception. Thinking he's been caught him in a lie, a suspect might change his story or start trying to explain his answers, which is a sure sign of deception. An examiner might also give several practice tests that shake a suspect up and produces a confession or an incriminating statement that borders on being a confession.

After Art gave Lubbon his full name, age, and address, Lubbon asked him about his college experience. Art told him he had gone to East Los Angeles Junior College after being discharged from the Army and majored in police science. Lubbon moved on to other, more benign topics, and each time, in a quiet voice, he implored Art to make sure he was always truthful. Throughout the test, Lubbon continually assured Art that the machine could tell if he was lying or telling the truth.

Lubbon could see that Art was getting tense. It would be a perfect time to delve deeper into his personal life. He wanted to know how often Art and his wife had intercourse. Did he prefer anal sex to other sexual activity? How did he feel about masturbation? What was the nature of his sexual fantasies? Did any of his sexual fantasies involve violence? Who was the initiator when he and Denise had sex?

He told Lubbon that he and his wife had had a good sex life until he lost his job. Recently though, Denise didn't desire sex as frequently as he would've liked. She was tired after working all day at the jewelry store and was rejecting his advances most of the time these days. He said that while he was curious about anal sex, it was not something he obsessed about. Art told Lubbon that he initiated the sexual activity most of the time, but he wished Denise would take the initiative more often. Sometimes, Art said, he would masturbate in front of his wife, and she seemed to enjoy that particular sex act a lot.

Lubbon reviewed the statements Art had given investigators about his activities on the day of the murder. Art repeated for Lubbon the time and specifics of his activities leading up to the discovery of Leslie's body by her mother. His story never varied from what he originally told detectives. Lubbon asked Art if he wanted to add anything before being given the test. Lubbon told him if there was anything he was hiding now was the time to get it off his chest. There was a definite finality to Lubbon' comment. Art sat in silence for a few seconds. He had to talk now or the machine would find out the secrets he was hiding. Lubbon said this was his last chance and if he didn't talk now they would know he was covering up and think he was lying about everything. They would surely think he had killed Leslie Barry.

Art had gotten himself into a pickle this time. He could wait until the poly showed him to be a pervert or he could come clean and tell the truth before he was put on the machine. His guilt about Leslie was eating at his insides, and he needed to get some of those things out in the open. Maybe if he told the whole truth about his fantasies and contact with Leslie, they would believe him when he said he didn't kill her.

Sheepishly and on the verge of tears, Art told the polygraphist that he had been touching Leslie over the last year and a half. He said he started subtly by patting her head, then progressed to patting her on the butt from time to time. Wanting to take it to the next level, he began rubbing and tweaking her developing breasts and rubbing her legs and thighs. He told Lubbon that the last time he touched Leslie was a few months before her murder when she jumped on his back at the apartment swimming pool and he rubbed her crotch through her swimming suit.

He swore to Lubbon that he had not murdered Leslie, and he didn't know anything more about the crime than he had already told detectives. Lubbon hooked Art up to the machine and began the mechanical part of the test.

"Did you see Leslie Barry on the day she was murdered?" Lubbon asked.

"Yes," Art replied.

"Did you murder Leslie Barry?"

"No."

"Did you go into Leslie Barry's apartment on the day she was murdered?"

"No"

Lubbon threw in a couple of control questions.

"Is your name Arthur Anzures?

"Yes."

"Do you live at 400 Monterey Road, South Pasadena?

"Yes."

Lubbon went back to the purpose of the polygraph exam.

"Do you have any knowledge about the murder of Leslie Barry?"

"No."

"Did you molest Leslie Barry on the day she was murdered?"

"No."

"Do you know who murdered Leslie Barry?"

"No."

Lubbon administered the mechanical aspect of the test several times, and each time he rephrased the questions just slightly. He finished the mechanical part of the test and removed the wires from Art. They sat in silence for what seemed like a long time while Lubbon studied the test results. After a bit the silence became deafening.

"I hope you find the fucking creep who killed her" Art said, suddenly breaking the silence.

Lubbon looked up from the chart.

"Are you sure there's nothing you've been holding back during the test?" Lubbon asked, again looking down at the chart.

Art was disappointed. When Lubbon unhooked him from the machine, he felt relieved that the ordeal was over. Was the examiner now telling him he had flunked the polygraph? He knew he wasn't lying about the murder questions. He must be giving a physiological response to something else he felt guilty about.

"Well, there is one thing that I didn't mention because I didn't want anyone to think I was a fucking creep," Art said bowing his head in shame.

"A couple of times," he said, "when Leslie was in my apartment playing with my kids, I would take a shower and come out of the bathroom wearing a short robe with no belt on it. Sometimes, I would intentionally bend over and let the robe fall open and expose myself to Leslie and my kids. Both times I had a partial hard-on, and it really turned me on to show Leslie my half erect penis."

Lubbon, after jotting down a few notes, left the room with the printout. Art watched as the polygraphist talked to Detective Kushner and deputy Beck. It was obvious that Lubbon was giving them the test results. When he saw their expressions change, fear, dread and embarrassment caused his face to flush crimson red. He felt dizzy and the room was spinning around ever so slowly. He fought back the queasiness in the pit of his stomach by telling himself that everything would be okay. He had finally found the courage to be honest and open with them, and they should let him go home now.

Lubbon told Kushner and Beck that his official opinion would be that the test was inconclusive. Nevertheless he still thought Anzures had shown deception during the polygraph, specifically when he was asked about his contact with the victim and his involvement in her death.

Having listened and tape-recorded the whole interview, Kushner and Beck were delighted by the job Lubbon had done for them. They had their suspect right where they wanted him, and now they could go after him with everything in their arsenal. He had made incriminating statements about his illicit contact with the victim, and the polygraph examiner reported that Art showed deception to questions about his involvement in the murder.

Kushner informed Art he had failed the polygraph, and asked him if he would mind going with them back to the East Los Angeles Sheriff's substation for further questioning. Art told them he would be more than happy to go with them. He too, wanted to clear up any problems they had with his information.

It was early evening, and Art had been at the Sheriff's crime lab for nearly four hours. The polygraph exam had drained him physically and emotionally. Art and Denise had left their children with Denise's sister in Glendora so that she could accompany Art to the Sheriff's station. She couldn't believe how long it was taking to administer the lie detector, and the longer it took the more apprehensive she became. She was relieved when she saw Art come out of the secure area of the station. She had been waiting anxiously for the whole thing to be over with so they could go home.

Approaching his wife, Art handed her the car keys and told her that he had to go with detectives to the East Los Angeles Sheriff's station to answer a few more questions. He told her he would see her at home in a short while. Denise couldn't imagine what information Art could possibly have that would warrant such intense interest.

At the East Los Angeles Sheriff's sub-station, he was ushered into an interview room and told to have a seat. Kushner and Beck left the room, and he was left alone to his own thoughts. When they returned 30 minutes later, Art was surprised when one of the detectives read him his Miranda rights. He said he understood his rights and would speak to them without an attorney present. To cover themselves legally, they put a SHAD card on the table in front of him, and handed him a pen so he could sign the card. A SHAD card is a formal acknowledgment that the police have advised a suspect of his rights, and the suspect has voluntarily waived his right to have an attorney present before questioning.

It had been a week since the murder and much of the lab work had been completed. Kushner knew he had little or no chance of getting a conviction against Anzures based on the physical evidence. Anzures' fingerprints had not been found in the victim's apartment or on any of the objects taken from the apartment. Furthermore, lab tests on the vaginal smears had failed to turn up any traces of sperm or other secretions. They had no eyewitnesses that could testify against him. The detective knew if he was going to make a murder charge stick he would have to get a confession.

Kushner and Beck started the interrogation by hammering away at the statements he had made a few hours earlier during his pre and post polygraph interviews. Playing the good cop-bad cop game they alternated between Kushner thundering at him, and Beck taking a tone of cooing, cajoling, and pleading.

Art, drained of all emotion, dispassionately told the detectives what he had already admitted during his polygraph. He began touching Leslie about a year and a half ago. He started by patting her head, then running his fingers through her hair. When he had the opportunity he would rub her legs, pat her butt, and touch, pinch, and rub her developing breasts.

Art added to his earlier admissions that he had also kissed Leslie on the lips a couple of times. He told the detectives that he did these things to arouse the sexual passions in himself and Leslie. Art explained that his touching was done in such a way that if she ever complained to anyone, he could deny it claiming they were just an innocent display of affection.

As detectives continued to pound away at him, Anzures added new admissions to his initial statement to Lubbon. He admitted having sexual fantasies about Leslie. Art felt that at some point in the future, when Leslie was older, he would eventually have sex with her. He told Kushner and Beck that he had done the same things with his seven-year old stepdaughter and his wife's twelve-year old niece.

It had been more than seven hours since Art left home to go to the Sheriff's crime lab for the polygraph, and he was getting giddy from fatigue. In a giggly voice, like a teenage girl, he told detectives about how he fantasized having oral sex with Leslie.

Detectives decided to change the subject for a bit, and see if they could find any discrepancies in his previous statements about his activities on the day of the murder. He was rock solid about the order and timing of what he did that day. They asked him pointedly if he had murdered Leslie, or if he had sexual contact with her on the day of her murder. Art was firm in his statement that he did not have sex with Leslie on the day of her murder, nor did he have anything to do with her death.

When detectives switched back to the subject of sex, Art told them that a few months ago, when Leslie had started to develop breasts, he would tweak her nipples and tease her about needing a bra.

"She was so pretty and I just enjoyed touching her," Art said. "I never did anything to her with the notion of hurting or harming her in anyway." he added.

"Everything I did was done in such a way that she wouldn't even know it was sexual."

"In the swimming pool," Art explained, "I was playing with Leslie and my own kids and Leslie jumped on my back to ride me piggyback. I reached behind her with my right hand and rubbed her crotch on the outside of her bathing suit."

"Well, how do you feel about the acts of molestation you've confessed to?" Kushner asked.

"I don't think I've done anything wrong." Anzures replied innocently. "I do these things with my own children, and even when I change the diapers on my year and a half old daughter, I playfully pinch and bite her little butt. It's just a show of love, that's all. I loved Leslie like a daughter."

"I can see why you guys are asking me these questions. After all, I am the manager, I was there all day, I have a key and I was the last person to see her alive." Art volunteered.

"Why didn't you tell us about these sexual contacts you had with the victim before now?" Kushner asked.

"Because I didn't want you to think I was a fucking creep." Art answered.

Kushner asked him what kind of tools he owned and used in his job as the apartment manager. Anzures instantly rattled off his tools: Hammers, saws, channel locks, needle nose pliers, vice grips, a pipe wrench, and several screwdrivers.

"You don't own a regular set of pliers?" The detective inquired with astonishment in the tone of his voice.

"No." Art answered weakly, feeling inadequate as a maintenance man without a regular pair of pliers.

Kushner clearly didn't believe him. A pair of pliers, found on the dresser in the victim's bedroom, was analyzed by the crime lab and material removed from the jaws of the pliers were compared to plastic from the off and on volume knob on the broken TV set. The material didn't match, but Kushner was still certain that the pliers belonged to Anzures.

In addition, no fingerprints were found on the handles of the pliers, or from the TV set itself. Nevertheless, Kushner was ready to hang his whole case on the theory that those pliers belonged to the killer and that the killer was the apartment manager. He had to place Anzures inside the victim's apartment on the day of the murder and the pliers might be his best opportunity. Still, to avoid potential embarrassment, the detective had to be certain that Anzures didn't have a pair of pliers stuck away in his tool closet.

"Would you voluntarily allow South Pasadena Police Officers to search your apartment for the tools you just mentioned?"

Art readily agreed. He had told the police he didn't own a pair of pliers and they wouldn't find a pair in his tool closet and that would be the end of it. Then maybe they would move on to other things and other suspects. He told detectives that he kept his tools in an outside storage chest next to his apartment. Art called Denise and told her that South Pasadena police officers would be coming by and to allow them to search the apartment where he kept his tools.

South Pasadena police officers, Sergeant Terpinitz and Agent Hatfield, who had been standing by observing the interrogation, were told to conduct a search of Anzures' apartment giving special attention to the areas where Art said he kept his tools.

After searching Anzures' tool chest, the two officers returned to the East Los Angeles Sheriff's station and advised Kushner that they had found the exact tools Art told them he had.

"Did you find a regular pair of pliers?" Kushner asked.

"Nope," Agent Hatfield replied, "nothing but the tools he specified."

Art had remained calm throughout most of the interrogation. The only emotion he showed was when he was asked how he felt about Leslie's death. When they asked that question, he would lay his head in his hands and cry. During one crying jag, Deputy Beck thought he caught him peeking at his watch when he was supposed to be in great emotional turmoil. After checking the time, the suspect went back to crying.

"How do you think your wife would react if she knew you were molesting little children?" Deputy Beck asked.

"I don't think she would like it," Art replied. "but Denise was in the room many times when I would tweak Leslie's breasts and kid her about needing a bra. She would laugh and giggle and she thought it was funny."

"Let's go over your activities of the day a little more," Beck said. "What if I were to tell you that I checked and you couldn't possibly see Leslie's door or window from 10 feet north of the laundry room?" Beck pushed.

"Well, that was just an estimate" Art answered, "it could've been more like 20 feet closer to her apartment. In fact, I think I may have walked right up in front of her porch and saw the lights were off and thought she must be out."

"What if I told you it was impossible to see her front door and window even standing right in front of the porch?" Beck baited him.

"I think I went up the sidewalk and stood in front of her porch while the paramedics were trying to resuscitate her." Art stated again more uncertain of what he was saying.

"So you're now changing your story after maintaining that it was true through all the other interviews?" Beck asked. "What else in your initial story did you lie about?

Kushner knew that Art's fingerprints had not been found in the apartment but Art didn't have that information. Kushner decided to bluff. If he could convince Anzures that they had evidence pointing to him as the killer they might be able to get him talking. After getting him to waver slightly on his story, now was a good time to push.

"You're absolutely certain that we won't find your fingerprints inside the apartment." Kushner asked. There's no way your fingerprints could be inside that apartment?

"No." Art said. "I was not inside the apartment for at least two weeks before Leslie's death. That was when I was in there to fix a leaky faucet for her mother.

"Everything else, the time frame of when Leslie put her clothes in the washing machine and when I moved mine from the washer to the dryer was accurate and true." Art said weakly. "I'm certain of that because of the lighting of the sky as the sun went down."

Anzures had been with the police for over twelve hours. It was getting late, and he wanted this interrogation to end so he could be with his family and friends and get some rest. He had spent hours telling total strangers embarrassing things about his feelings, fantasies, and activities to convince them he was not the killer. Over the long hours of interrogation, he had taken such an emotional beating that at times he had trouble distinguishing fantasy from reality.

While they had gotten some incriminating statements from him, Kushner had failed to get a confession to the murder. They had, for the second time, pushed him as far as they dared.

"One more thing," Kushner said. "We heard reports that you recently went into the victim's apartment without the permission of Mrs. Barry. Is that true?"

"Yes," Art replied, "my wife and I wanted to get a small, wallet sized school picture of Leslie as a keepsake, so we used our pass key to go in and get it."

"You know," said Kushner, "by entering the apartment without permission and taking those pictures without permission, you committed the crime of burglary, don't you?"

"Yes," Art said, "I know we shouldn't have gone in and taken the pictures without permission but Leslie had promised to give us one before she died, and we didn't think her mother would mind. We have the pictures at the apartment if you want to get them."

As the interview was about to end, Art asked the detectives if they thought he should get a lawyer.

"You have a constitutional right to one as you acknowledged earlier and said you understood per the Miranda warning we gave you." Kushner said, "And if you feel you need a lawyer then you should retain one."

"Well," Art said, "I have nothing to fear or hide and I'm not going to get one"

The detectives ended the interrogation and drove Art back to his apartment. As they drove up to the curb, they asked Art if he they could come into his apartment and get those stolen photographs. When they entered the apartment, Art told Denise what they wanted. She took one picture out of a family photo album and then retrieved the other from her own wallet.

Detectives noticed that on the back of each picture was written, "December 1, 1978," followed by the word "taken" then below that, "died, November 21, 1978." The detectives took the pictures and left. It didn't escape their eye that the Anzures' had gotten the date of the murder wrong on the back of the school pictures.

Once Kushner and Beck were gone, Denise took a good look at her husband. She had never seen anyone look so exhausted and emotionally drained. It had been nine hours since he had handed the car keys to her at the Sheriff's crime lab, and it looked like Art had gone through hell and back on a slow moving escalator. What in the world had happened to the man she had gotten out of bed with that morning?

Denise was worried about Art and called his family to come over to the apartment and talk to him. When Julian Anzures saw the condition of his son and heard about Art's lengthy interrogations with the police, he was extremely concerned. Over Art's protests that he didn't need a lawyer since he hadn't done anything wrong, Julian told Art that he was going to get him a lawyer just the same.

Like most women in Los Angeles, Denise Anzures was frightened by reports of the Hillside Strangler. For the past twenty months young women and girls were being abducted, raped, and murdered and their nude bodies left on hillsides around Los Angeles.

While she felt more of an abstract fear over the Hillside Strangler murders, the murder of Leslie Barry was so close to home it struck real terror in her. Fear and grief are conflicting emotions, and when both are present at the same time, a person doesn't know whether to run and hide or start bawling. While trying to grieve for Leslie Barry, Denise felt sheer terror for the safety of herself and her children. Now, suddenly, there was another fear factoring into the equation. She feared that her husband would be arrested for murder and taken away from her as suddenly as Leslie's short life had been snuffed out.

A week of thinking and talking about the murder of Leslie Barry had exacted a heavy toll from the Anzures. The sadness over the loss of a friend, plus the dark cloud of suspicion hanging over Art's head convinced them of the need to get away for at least a few days. After Art's first interview at the South Pasadena Police department, Denise called her sister in Glendora and asked her if she would mind putting them up for a few days. Just until everything blew over at the apartments, Denise said.

When the Anzures clan left, Art and Denise packed a few things and headed for Glendora where their children were already staying. It would just be for a few days until things blew over, and their lives could return to some degree of normalcy. "Normal" could never describe what lay ahead for the Anzures family.

Chapter 8

Detective Kushner knew about child murder cases. It was the consensus and general profile developed over the years by experts that the killer would most likely be someone the victim knew and trusted. It would be a step father, an uncle, a boyfriend of the mothers, or maybe a surrogate father; someone who had stepped in to fill a void left in the victim's life by a divorce, death, or neglect of the biological father. Sometimes it was even the biological father.

If the killer was someone close to the victim, Art Anzures was the best suspect. For one thing, his behavior on the night of the murder was bizarre. He seemed to be going out of his way to get into the crime scene. Because of the lax security during the initial stages of the investigation, when police, paramedics, and fire personnel were entering and exiting the apartment, Art had wandered into the victim's apartment without being challenged. A uniformed officer informed agent Hatfield that Anzures had come into the apartment, and Hatfield ordered him to leave immediately. Art readily complied with the order, but a while later he raised an eyebrow or two when he and Denise returned to the crime scene with coffee for the investigators.

Under the circumstances, detectives wondered why Art was trying so hard to ingratiate himself with the police. It could've been idle curiosity, or maybe, rather than trying to be helpful, Art was merely trying to check out the crime scene.

Being so nosy brought attention and suspicion to the young apartment manager. Snooping around and trying to get closer to the investigation was bad enough, but what he and Denise did the next day was considered by some as macabre. Without considering the possible consequences of entering an apartment that wasn't theirs, and the crime scene of a murder still under investigation, Art and Denise used their passkey to enter Leslie's apartment to get two wallet-size photographs of Leslie. There was nothing special about the photographs. It wasn't a picture of Leslie camping with the Anzures family, or attending an amusement park with them or anything like that. They were just recent school pictures that Leslie promised to give to them a week or so before she was murdered. Again, investigators thought that Art might be trying to get back to the scene of the crime to see if he had left any incriminating evidence behind.

Having the school pictures as mementos of their young friend may have been comforting to Art and Denise, but to investigators looking for someone close to the victim to pin the murder on, entering the apartment without permission seemed, among other things, to show a consciousness of guilt. If nothing else, it displayed a willingness to use his passkey to break and enter a tenant's apartment without permission.

That there was no forced entry into the apartment on the night of the murder was an important factor to investigators, and Art's use of his passkey gave detectives the idea that maybe he had used it on the night of the murder to enter the apartment and strangle the victim. Whatever the inference drawn from Art and Denise entering the apartment, detectives thought it was suspicious behavior.

Art's unusual behavior did not stop at entering the crime scene without permission, or God forbid, serving coffee to the cops. As detectives began interviewing other tenants the focus of their questions were about Art and his relationship with other tenants, particularly the females. Investigators were interested in other instances of Art trying to find out about the specifics of the Leslie Barry murder, as well as any sexual contact he may have had with female tenants.

In the second week of their investigation, Kushner and Beck focused their efforts on getting evidence against Anzures for the murder. Kushner knew his case, even with the admissions about having improper contact with the victim, was weak. In spite of their best efforts to break him down with a couple of long, tough interrogations, they were unable to get a confession out of him. Kushner had no eyewitnesses, or even circumstantial evidence to place his suspect at the scene of the crime or otherwise prove his guilt. About all he had was a gut feeling that Anzures was the killer and he knew that gut feelings were a poor substitute for evidence as far as the District Attorney was concerned.

While Anzures was his best suspect, Kushner didn't share his partner's fervor in making a premature arrest. Beck had wanted to put the cuffs on Anzures after the admissions he made during the last interrogation. Because it was Beck's first Homicide, the older, more experienced detective needed to give his new partner as much leeway as possible to learn how to solve murders. Still, Kushner had to watch him carefully. Being the ranking detective on the case, it would be his ass if anything went wrong and the DA ended up with egg on her face.

Kushner noticed that at times Beck was rash and tended to jump to conclusions. He wanted to solve the case quickly too, but it bothered him that his partner was so zealously after Anzures for the murder. He might've written Beck's fervor off to first murder case jitters, had it not been for the reaction he got every time he mentioned that the Barry murder could be related to the Hillside Strangler case.

In spite of his partner's eagerness in going after Anzures, Kushner was concerned about the weaknesses in the case. The District Attorney's Office would never file charges against Anzures based upon the evidence they had thus far. If he didn't turn up something soon, his suspect might walk, and the case would remain an open, unsolved homicide.

Art and Denise had admitted breaking into Aina's apartment to take the wallet sized school pictures of the victim. If the DA wouldn't indict for murder, Kushner could go after Anzures for burglary and put him on ice for a few days. With Anzures in custody and an informant strategically placed in his cell, maybe the informant would come up with a confession. Stranger things had happened. Informants were uncanny at coming up with confessions when you needed one. It was amazing, Kushner thought with a smile, how much suspects talked once they were behind bars. As far as the detectives were concerned, Art Anzures was going down for the murder of Leslie Barry and there was no doubt about that.

On Wednesday afternoon, eight days after the murder, Kushner and Beck re-interviewed the victim's mother, Aina Barry. They began the interview by showing her the school pictures of Leslie that Art and Denise had taken from her apartment. Aina began to cry. "How could anyone be so morbid?" she sobbed.

"Concerning the photographs," Kushner asked after she had regained her composure, "did you ever give anyone, including the apartment manager, permission to enter your apartment when you weren't home?"

"No." She snapped angrily, "I've never given anyone at anytime permission to come into my home without me being there."

With the statement from Art and Denise about entering the apartment without permission and taking the pictures corroborated, Kushner moved on to a topic more directly connected to the murder case he was investigating.

"Was the TV set in Leslie's bedroom working on the twentieth?" Kushner asked.

"No," Aina answered quietly, "the on and off knob on that TV set has been broken for some time now." She explained. "The only way we had of turning the TV set on was by plugging it into a wall socket. We had to unplug it to turn it off. Also, with the on and off knob broken like that, it was impossible to adjust the volume."

"What would you say if I told you that we checked the TV set the day after the murder and it was working fine?" Kushner asked.

"Well," Aina answered, "I've been trying to think of a reason why those pliers would be in Leslie's bedroom. Maybe someone came in and fixed it while I was at work. That would explain where the pair of pliers came from."

"Who would you call if you needed someone to do repairs inside your apartment?" Kushner asked.

"The only one I ever called to do small or large repair work inside my apartment is the manager, Art Anzures." She answered.

Kushner and Beck were putting in overtime collecting data and writing up the reports to take their case to the District Attorney in hopes of persuading the DA's office to file murder charges. At 10:00 PM Wednesday evening, Harley Segura, a Sheriff's Department Criminologist, phoned from the crime lab and informed the detectives of the test results on the hair found at the crime scene. As near as he could tell, Segura reported, the strand found on the bed was a head hair and the two found on the victim's vaginal and anal area were pubic hairs. All three strands, Segura said, were similar to hair supplied by Art Anzures.

While putting together the arrest reports Kushner could see many of the flaws of the case. Even with the admissions by Anzures of exposing himself to the victim, the improper touching and the hair analysis from the crime lab, the case was weak. The major weakness as he saw it, was his failure to place Anzures at the scene of the crime. Without fingerprints or any other credible evidence to prove he was inside the apartment, Kushner felt that the pair of pliers found on the dresser in Leslie's bedroom was his best chance of placing Art inside the apartment on the day of the murder.

Mentally the detective ticked off what he had on the case: First, he could show that Anzures had a propensity to use his passkey to enter apartments without the permission of the tenants who lived in those apartments. This was important because there was no evidence of forced entry into the victim's apartment. Furthermore, the television set had been fixed sometime between the morning of the murder and the day after the murder. That raised the question of who had entered the apartment to fix the TV when Aina wasn't home. While Aina said the only person she would ever call to fix things was Art Anzures, it was insufficient to place Anzures in the apartment at the time of the murder. Moreover, the motive of the crime was sexual gratification and he had the admissions by Art of having been sexually attracted to the victim. While these facts strengthened Kushner' resolve that Anzures was the killer he was still a long way from a prosecutable case.

The lab report on the hair samples was interesting but inconclusive. Before DNA, the only way to determine the source of hair was by analyzing the pattern of hair. A proper hair analysis would take a minimum of twelve hair samples from both the suspected source and the crime scene for a comparative analysis. Even with twelve hair samples, a criminologist could only determine the possible source and not the probable source of the hair. In the Barry murder, there were only three strands of hair booked into evidence, and the hair could've come from any of the many emergency personnel at the crime scene or the hospital staff during medical treatment. His case against Anzures needed to get a lot stronger before it could be taken to a jury, Kushner thought. He had to find a way of placing Anzures at the scene of the crime.

On Friday, Kushner and Beck were at the South Pasadena Police Department cleaning up paperwork and trying to tie up loose ends. While waiting around killing time and joking with his fellow cops, Agent Hatfield took a phone call from a reporter at the Pasadena Star News. The reporter was calling to verify the eminent arrest of a suspect in the murder of the young girl in South Pasadena. The reporter said she had information from a reliable confidential informant of the newspaper that there was going to be a big break in the case. The informant had told the reporter that the suspect had made a statement to an attorney in Highland Park, and that the suspect was currently living in the city of Glendora. The informant said the suspect would either surrender or be arrested later that day. The Star News reporter was looking for confirmation of her information and a statement by the police concerning the impending arrest. The department refused to officially comment on the reliability of the statement.

After lunch, Beck phoned Anzures at his relatives in Glendora.

"We'd like for you and your wife to come down to the South Pasadena Police Station and clarify some statements you've made," Beck told Anzures when he came to the phone.

"I've obtained the services of an attorney." Art replied, "Do you think I should bring him with me?"

"You have a constitutional right to bring your attorney." Beck told him with a trace of disappointment in his voice; "but your cooperation would go along way in helping us solve this case. You do want to help us solve this case, don't you Mr. Anzures?"

This attitude was beginning to wear thin with Art. He had already told the police everything he knew about the murder. He had been as honest and forthright as he could, revealing stuff about himself that he had never told anyone else, and still they wanted more. In the off chance that they'd leave him alone after one last interview, and wanting to fully cooperate with the investigation, Art agreed to go down to the station with Denise to clear up any discrepancies there might have been in his previous statements.

At around three in the afternoon, Art and Denise arrived at the South Pasadena Police station, and upon their arrival they were immediately separated. Art was ushered into a small interview room, while Denise was told to wait in the lobby. Deputy Beck and Detective Kushner initiated some light conversation and a little joking, but this time Art was not amused or relaxed. He knew something was up and he didn't have a positive feeling about it.

A few minutes into the third interrogation, Kushner walked out of the interview room, leaving Beck alone with Anzures. It made Art uncomfortable being alone with Deputy Beck. There was something in Beck's eyes or demeanor that was crazy or hateful about him. He had a bad attitude that instantly invoked resistance. Once Kushner was out of the room, Beck began asking Art about his sexual feelings toward young children. Realizing he shouldn't have come in without his lawyer, Art stood up and announced that he would not answer any more questions without his attorney being present.

"You're under arrest for murder, rape, sodomy, and child molestation." Beck said angrily, taking out his handcuffs and slapping them on Art's wrists tighter than they really needed to be. Beck pushed Anzures roughly to the booking room at the station.

While Beck was making the arrest and handling the booking, Kushner went to the waiting area and escorted Denise into an interview room.

"Your husband has been arrested for murder, rape, sodomy, and child molestation." He advised her.

Denise started to tremble. Her worst fears about coming down to the police station had been realized. She suddenly saw her whole world crumbling around her. Her face paled, her hands shook, and she felt faint. Nothing seemed real to her.

"He didn't do it." She screamed, "I don't know what you people are doing, but he didn't do it, and he told me you said you were going to put him in jail so that he would be butt fucked by the other prisoners, and he said it would be better for him to commit suicide than to be put in state prison."

"We never threatened him." Kushner replied softly. "If you want proof, we have the tape recorded interviews right here, and you're welcome to listen to parts or all of it if you want to.

Did Art ever make admissions to you about his sexual activity with children?" Kushner asked.

Denise flinched at the question.

"The things he did with Leslie were normal and innocent and were no more than he did with his own children." She said in defense of her husband.

"I don't see anything wrong with the things he did. It was just a display of love. I saw him pat our own children on the butt from time to time, and I know it was just an innocent display of affection."

"Do you think feeling Leslie up in the swimming pool is normal and innocent?" Kushner pressed.

"How about when he came out of the shower and intentionally exposed himself to Leslie and your own children, or feeling up your 12 year old niece. Is that normal and innocent?"

Denise didn't know if she was going to faint, throw up, or both.

"I don't believe you." She said recoiling from the question as if she'd been slapped in the face, "He wouldn't do that."

"We have the tape recordings right here." Kushner baited her. "We have the tape set at the point where he made those statements if you want to hear it we can play it for you."

"I don't want to hear any of it." Denise fired back. Denise was struggling to save her world from total ruination. "I love him no matter what he's done."

"What time did you get home on November 20?" Kushner asked changing the subject and trying to get her to calm down.

"I got home at about 6:30." Denise spit out the answer. "When I got home the kids were cleanly dressed and ready to go out to dinner at Carrows just like we had planned on the phone when Art called me at work earlier in the day. Art told you this already. Why don't you believe him? And no," she added anticipating the next question

"I didn't see any dirty laundry laying around the apartment."

"Did either you or Art go out and check the washers or dryers for laundry at any point during the evening?" Kushner pushed.

"No. There was no reason too. The laundry was done before I got home." Denise answered agitatedly.

Kushner had been keeping a pair of pliers out of sight during the interview. When it was time to move in for the kill, he brought the pliers out and shoved them across the table toward Denise.

"Where are these pliers normally kept in the house?" Kushner asked.

It was a "when-did-you-stop-beating-your-wife" question, and, if Kushner wanted to catch her off guard, he couldn't have done a better job than asking that question then and in that way. When Denise's eyes saw the pair of pliers, her mind translated it into a tool that she instantly associated with Art and his maintenance work around the apartment. She knew where Art kept his tools and told the detective.

"In the closet." She answered quickly.

The memory of the search of their apartment and Art's tool closet suddenly came back to her flooding her mind with confusion. What was the question he had asked? Did he ask her where Art kept the tools or did he ask where Art kept the pliers? Was it the same question? She realized she had fallen for a trick question and tried to recover. Denise knew the police had been asking questions about the pliers. Their friends, the Woodbury's, who lived in the apartment above theirs, stayed in close contact with the Anzures' and told them about the police coming around asking questions about the ownership of the pliers, and if they knew whether Art owned a regular pair of pliers. Donald Woodbury had told the police that he didn't think Art owned any regular pliers, because Art had borrowed his a while back and had returned the pliers to him.

"Art doesn't own any pliers like that." She stammered trying to correct her mistaken answer. Denise was getting herself deeper in the hole than she could handle.

"You just gave two different answers." Kushner shot back, "Which one of them is true?"

"Art has never owned any pliers like that," she said, uncertain now whether she got the answer right.

"Can you give us a list of tools Art owns?" Kushner asked, figuring that Denise probably didn't know channel locks from a can opener.

She tried to focus her mind on the tools that she knew Art owned but couldn't think of any. Denise was so rattled, upset, scared, and confused by this unexpected turn of events, that she couldn't have named her own kids. Kushner ended the interview and told her she could leave. On the drive back to Glendora, painfully aware that Art was not with her, Denise felt so lost and alone. As the emotions welled up inside of her she burst into tears sobbing and shaking so hard she had to pull over to the side of the road.

I was having dinner on Friday night when the phone rang. Mitch had my home phone number in case anything developed over the weekend and he needed my help.

"Art's been arrested." He said when I picked up the phone. "I'm at the South Pasadena Police station and I just finished talking with Art. They're moving him to the men's central jail and I cautioned him to keep his mouth shut while he's in custody. I've had the police place him out of the general population and told them to put him on suicide watch.

"His arraignment will be on Wednesday, but I'll file a discovery motion on Monday. In the meantime, the detectives said they'd give us any information they have ready tonight. I want you to meet me at the homicide bureau on the eighth floor of the Hall of Justice at nine o'clock."

Mitch sounded excited, like he was on an adrenalin high, and I listened in silence as he gave me more information than I really needed know. I told him I would meet him at the Hall of Justice at nine o'clock sharp.

Most cases I took on I knew from experience what to expect. Others were like jumping off a cliff blind folded. I knew the bottom was there, I just didn't know when I would hit it.

Filled with anticipation and more than a little trepidation, this was going to be a long sleepless night.

Chapter 9

When I got off the phone Wendy wanted all the details. I repeated what Mitch had told me, and she could see I was having some reservations about taking the case.

"It's a feather in your cap that you got this case." Wendy said in her usual upbeat way. "You'll do a great job, and this could open some doors for you," she encouraged.

I phoned Mark Sutherland, my most trusted investigator and a newly admitted member of the bar. Mark thought I was nuts for taking the case, and he was reluctant to get involved. His main objection was our lack of experience in handling criminal cases. If Wendy hadn't just reassured me that taking the case was the right thing, Mark might've been able to talk me out of it. Instead, I turned the tables on him. I argued that he could gain some valuable experience from working a murder case with me and he relented. I told him to be at my house at eight o'clock.

Mark Sutherland had worked for me for a little over a year. I met him one October day of the previous year after I mistakenly buzzed him in through the security door of the Green Hotel. He found his way to my office shabbily dressed in torn jeans, a stained white T-shirt, tennis shoes, and with three days of beard shadowing his face. He stood silently in the center of the office for what seemed like a long time. When I asked how I could help him, he didn't answer. He was standing closer to Wendy' desk than mine, and I could see a look of concern on her face. After several minutes of not answering me or saying anything, Wendy ask him if there was something she could do for him. He didn't speak. I was beginning to worry that he might be a mentally deranged lunatic; a squatter from up the street on Colorado Boulevard.

He appeared to be confused and disturbed. Not just one of the many bums in the area who had wandered in looking for a handout but a full-blown psychopath. His silence was beginning to make me uncomfortable. It was an eerie silence. Like a gentle breeze blowing just before a tornado rips through your trailer house.

"What do you want man?" I asked raising my voice for emphasis.

Watching him closely the man seemed about ready to speak. When he finally broke the silence I was relieved that his words weren't garbled and didn't contain phrases like, 'the wrath of God' or 'my space ship is out of gas'.

"What kind of business is this?" He asked haltingly and not looking directly at anyone.

"Well," I answered, "we do two things here. I run a legal research and inquiry firm, and Wendy is in advertising and public relations."

"What do you do in legal research?" He asked looking in my direction but not directly at me.

By now, I had reached the conclusion that he was mentally retarded and probably not dangerous. He hadn't done anything even remotely aggressive. If anything, he was timid.

"What is it that you're looking for?" I asked with the edge still in my voice.

My question obviously stumped him because he went silent again. After another long pause, he decided to rephrase the question.

"What kind of research and inquiry do you do?" His voice was stronger, with a little more confidence to it. This was the first sign of intelligent life the man had given me. I didn't think he would understand even if I told him; but I took a shot.

"We do two different things," I answered, "in the legal research department I use law students to search case law and prepare minor documents for lawyers. The inquiry side of the business is legal investigations for lawyers. We do chores like locate defendants and witnesses, take witness statements, photograph accidents and accident scenes, we serve summons and complaints and subpoenas and we work mostly for plaintiff's lawyers in civil cases."

I still hadn't asked the man's name and I wasn't sure I wanted to know it. There was another long pause but I could tell he was considering what to say next. I was kind of hoping that after telling him what Crisp and Marley did he would leave, but he stayed and later I was glad he did.

"I graduated from Western State law school and I just took the bar exam for the third time." He said.

Yeah, right I thought. How could this bum I initially thought was mentally retarded, be a law school graduate? I had gone to law school myself and having taken the Baby Bar, I knew what kind of dedication and commitment it took to pass the California State Bar. The Baby Bar was just like the Bar exam except that it had fewer questions and only took a day and not three. After cramming for days on end, and then withstanding the pressure of taking the examination, I was a zombie for a week. This man was beyond zombie. He was comatose.

"I'm Ron Crisp," I introduced myself extending my hand to him.

"I'm Mark Sutherland," He said taking my hand.

Nice to meet you, Mark. Why don't you have a seat?" I offered indicating I wanted him to sit in the chair facing my desk.

"Would you like a cup of coffee or something else to drink?" I offered while he was getting comfortable.

"No thanks." He answered politely.

I leaned back in my chair and lit up a cigarette. Mark asked if he could bum one, and I slid the pack across the desk.

"Are you interested in a job, Mark?" I asked exhaling a stream of smoke and trying to blow smoke rings. Blowing smoke rings was not one of my talents, but I kept trying anyway.

"Yes," Mark answered, "I'd like to do something in the legal field while I wait on the Bar exam results."

"Having finished law school, you would probably like to do legal research then, huh?"

Mark looked at me like I was nuts.

"I would like to do anything but open a law book for the next six months." Mark said, "I've had enough studying for a while."

"Okay." I responded. "One of the things my attorneys and clients like about using my services is that not only am I a resourceful investigator, but I also have a good working knowledge of the law. I know the elements of a tort action and what the lawyers are looking for when I take statements. Having a law degree, you should fit right in with the services Crisp and Marley offers.

"I can't pay you much, but there are other benefits to working for me. Should you ever pass the bar," I jibed, "you'll make contacts and meet a lot of lawyers who might be able to help you set up your own practice. Furthermore, you'll gain some valuable practical experience in handling court cases."

Mark was ready to go to work as a private investigator the minute he walked through the door. He just needed to verify for himself that we were, indeed, a private investigation firm.

Over the next several months, Mark not only became a competent and trusted coworker with Crisp and Marley, but a good friend as well. He would often stop by the house for dinner, or to knock back a few beers while discussing cases or watching football. Mark was always surprising me. I guess the third time was a charm for him, because he passed the bar, and was notified of that a few months after coming to work with me. I figured he would be moving on to better things after passing the bar, but to my surprise, he stuck around and continued to work with me.

Eventually he opened his first law office at the Green Hotel just down the hall from Crisp and Marley. When the Anzures case came along, I was happy I hadn't thrown that bum out of my office. I needed his help, his friendship, and his insights.

Mark showed up at my house at eight, and by eight-fifteen we were on the Pasadena Freeway headed to Downtown Los Angeles to meet Mitch Molino and the detectives who arrested Anzures. I'm a fanatic about being on time, and I wanted to meet Mitch in the lobby and take the elevator ride up to the eighth floor with him.

Mitch and I arrived at the Hall of Justice at the same time. We greeted each other at the door and shook hands. Mitch introduced his lawyer friend, John Neece, as his paper man. Neece would be handling all the motions and appeals that would inevitably come up before and during the trial. I introduced Mitch to Mark and gave him a short bio of Mark on the way up to the Homicide bureau.

"Mark is one of my best investigators and a newly admitted member of the bar." I said. "He'll be helping me with the investigation."

I felt confident that things were going well so far and that Art Anzures would be well represented in his legal defense. Mitch had associated another lawyer on the case to help with the myriad details of paperwork the system required during a murder trial and I had someone I felt comfortable with to assist in handling the investigation.

When we stepped off the elevator Mitch asked a detective passing by where we could find Detective Kushner or Deputy Beck. We were directed to Beck's desk on the ninth floor. We walked up a short flight of stairs to the ninth floor. The ninth floor of the Hall of Justice was an attic. It looked as if it were used primarily for storage of files and to accommodate an overflow of detectives.

Deputy Beck was sitting at his desk located to the side of a narrow aisle and detective Kushner was standing next to the desk. Mitch had already met the two cops at the South Pasadena Police Station and he made the introductions. While Mitch was making the introductions, I was giving the detectives a once over. Detective Sergeant David Kushner was friendly and didn't seem threatened by us in the least. As we were being introduced, he shook my hand and repeated my name. I felt like I could at least stay in the same room with him for 10 minutes without wanting to kick him in the nuts.

Kushner was about my height and weight and had a protruding gut that lowered his belt line a good ten inches. He looked like he could just as easily have been a plumber or a sheet rock man as a homicide cop. Take away his badge and give him a tool belt and he'd show enough butt crack to get a journeyman's card. His thinning hair didn't cover much scalp and with his wrinkled tie and sports coat, he looked to be a man with some substance and character. Furthermore, he seemed to understand that he had his job to do and we had ours.

Kushner's partner, deputy Jerome Beck, was nearly the direct opposite of the more senior and ranking detective on the case. Even before we said anything, he was already scowling at us. It was like we were invading his territory by coming down to the station. To Beck, we were the enemy no better than our child molesting, murdering client. We were there to question his authority and make him look like a fool if we could. We would attack his character and distort everything he said.

When he begrudgingly stood up to shake hands, I estimated him to be an inch short of average height with a stocky build. Unlike Kushner, Beck had a full head of curly hair. It looked almost like an Afro and I wondered if it was natural or if he'd had a permanent. His face was elongated with a square jaw line. Beck was dapper Dan, dressed for success, with his tie hanging straight and his shirt and sports coat as smooth and unwrinkled as if they had just come from the dry cleaners. His instant defensiveness towards us told me he was exceedingly judgmental and reacted from things on the surface without giving anyone the chance to show who they really were.

After introductions, Kushner excused himself saying he had to go and check on how the tape duplications were going. While Kushner was away, we tried to make small talk with Beck and the chitchat seemed to make him nervous and uncomfortable. He fidgeted in his chair, first leaning forward in his seat and putting his elbows on the desk, then leaning back in his chair and putting his hands behind his head. He avoided eye contact with us and from time to time nervously dilly-dallied with a paper clip. It was like he was afraid he might say something that we would use against him in court. I could tell that Mitch didn't like him anymore than I did. He was acting guilty about something and I almost felt like reading him his Miranda rights. Anyone who squirmed like that was sure to be hiding something.

When Kushner returned he told us the tapes would be ready for us shortly. He handed Mitch a copy of the investigative and arrest reports and said the autopsy and crime scene photographs should be ready at the arraignment. Mitch asked him if he could make a couple of copies of the reports and Kushner, taking the reports from Mitch, said he would be happy too. He disappeared down the narrow aisle and into a room at the back.

Kushner was gone for what seemed like a long time, and we stood in awkward silence at Beck's desk. While we shuffled impatiently from foot to foot and whispered back and forth, I could see that Beck was more comfortable with the silence. Mitch didn't want him to get too comfortable.

"I hope you aren't planning on putting a snitch in with my client." Mitch said breaking the silence."

Beck didn't say anything. He leaned back in his chair and put his hands behind his head. An angry expression crossed his face, and he glared at Mitch. Old Mitch had some stones, I thought to myself. This could get interesting.

Kushner returned with copies of the reports Mitch had given him and the duplicate tapes of the police interviews with Art. He handed all of it to Mitch, who in turn gave me my copies of the police reports. Handing me the interrogation tapes Mitch ordered me to listen to them over the weekend. Divvying up the reports in front of Kushner and Beck was a smart ploy. It told them we were going to be on top of this case and they'd better watch their step.

Once we were back out on the street, I asked Mitch about the snitch comment. I told him he really hit a nerve with Beck and wondered how he knew they'd be using snitches.

"They almost always use snitches in murder cases where they don't have a confession." Mitch responded. "It's about the only way they can build a case without evidence."

I was impressed by Mitch's knowledge of how things in the system worked and I was looking forward to working with him. This could be quite a learning experience.

Chapter 10

O ver the weekend Wendy, Mark, and I read the police reports and listened to the interrogation tapes. The reports were a disappointment to me. They didn't contain the detailed information about the murder I was hoping to get. The first one I read was a handwritten narrative of the observations made by South Pasadena Police Officers at the scene of the crime, and a few general statements taken from tenants on the night of the murder. It looked as if most of the tenants were not home when the police stopped by to interview them.

I was curious to know if there was a witness, not yet deposed, or perhaps a statement I had not yet seen, that might provide insight into who committed the murder. One statement in the handwritten report caught my attention. Shawn Hagen's statement about knowing one of the Hillside Strangler victims floored me. Wendy suggested for the second time that this murder could be connected to the disappearance of the two girls in Highland Park.

This time her remark didn't fly by me. Most people didn't know one murder victim, let alone two, and this young man, barely fourteen years old, had two friends that had been sexually assaulted and murdered by ligature strangulation.

"What do you think the odds are that someone could have two friends murdered by strangulation, with rape or attempted rape as the motive for both murders, who lived a short distance from each other and that those murders would not be related?" I posed the question to Wendy and Mark.

"Probably astronomical." Wendy responded. "You should go to the library on Monday and get some details on those two girls."

I put talk to Shawn Hagen and research murders at the library at the top my growing list of things to do before Art's preliminary hearing.

The other report was the arrest report. The arrest report contains the evidence of probable cause that justifies arresting the suspect. In the Anzures case, probable cause was a written synopsis of the statements he made during the interrogations. I thought the report should have contained more specifics about the crime than it did, but it was short on specifics of any kind, including evidence pointing to Anzures as the killer.

The three of us listened to the interrogation tapes together. Wendy hated confrontations of any kind, and the tapes were painful for her to listen to. Throughout the playing of the tapes, she commented that they reminded her of stories she had heard about the methods used by the Viet Cong to interrogate American POW's. The brow beating, cooing, pleading; then, the sudden switch back to threatening the young suspect for hours on end, made her queasy.

"You can't trust anything Art says under that kind of pressure," she observed at the end of listening to the first tape.

I agreed with Wendy. Under intense stress, Art was confusing fantasy with reality. He didn't get it that to the cops, a jury, or the courts, whether his statements were true or false wouldn't make much difference. If he could think or fantasize about something, he could do it and it could all be used against him in court. He sounded scared and tired when detectives yelled at him and threatened him, and he seemed so relieved and disarmed when they switched to a friendlier tone. He told them whatever they wanted to hear when they were making nice to him to avoid the threats and brow beatings that scared the shit out of him. Overall, his statements sounded like he was just trying to please his interrogators.

It was difficult to understand why, after the severe grilling he took during the first interrogation, Art would subject himself to more of the same the next day and then during the polygraph. I figured it must have something to do with not wanting to appear guilty by invoking his rights. It's ironic, I thought, that the laws we have to protect the innocent always make them appear to be guilty. Why do you need a lawyer if you're innocent we ask? Why would he invoke his fifth amendment right against self-incrimination if he didn't have something to hide? People who don't understand how seemingly innocent and innocuous things can be twisted around to give the appearance of guilt, ask these questions because they want to believe, or convince others, that the person being accused is guilty. Innocent pictures of baby in the bathtub found in the family photo album can be presented as definitive evidence of child molestation when the owner of the album is suspected of being a pedophile. A stack of Playboy Magazines found under the bed is a cache of pornography to a man suspected of a sex crime like rape. It's a no win situation for the innocent, but it reinforces the notion that if you find yourself under suspicion of a crime and you value your freedom, you should retain the services of a good lawyer. If you're unfortunate enough to become involved in a high profile case, your good name and reputation will be irreparably damaged anyway.

With deputy Beck, cooing and cajoling, making him think they were on his side and it was perfectly normal to have sexual urges and fantasies about young girls, Art relaxed and went into more detail concerning his sexual fantasies or experiences with Leslie Barry. It was hard to tell where Art's reality stopped and fantasy took over. It was clear he wanted to please and impress the cops.

The interrogation by polygraphist Lubbon was the worst of all. From the way Lubbon handled the pre-interview questions it didn't sound like he intended to give Anzures a legitimate polygraph. Art had told Kushner and Beck about his fear of taking the LAPD pre-employment polygraph, and they wanted to exploit his fear of the lie detector and hopefully get a confession or at least some admissions out of him. I noted that most of the incriminating statements about his sexual contact with Leslie Barry came during the pretest interview before being hooked up to the machine.

While talking to Lubbon, Art began to open up, telling his inner most thoughts, secrets, and fantasies and once he started talking he couldn't stop. The tone and quality of his voice was filled with fatigue, and after hours of answering the same questions repeatedly, the pressure was taking an emotional and physical toll on him. The cops didn't believe anything he said, and after trying different things, ranging from real to imaginary, Art couldn't distinguish fact from fiction. The tapes were turned off a number of times during the interrogation, and I could only imagine what was happening during these breaks. It was my guess that without the intrusiveness of the tape recorder more severe and direct threats were being leveled at him. Yet, through twelve hours of nonstop grilling, Art had not broken down and confessed to the murder.

At one point during the interrogation, Kushner noticed a scratch on Art's hand and wanted to know how he got it. Art told him he must have done it while punching the heavy bag without wearing his gloves when he was working out. Kushner didn't seem to be satisfied with that answer, and I had to admit it did sound a bit contrived. Still, it was a curious question, and I wondered why Kushner was asking about cuts. Had they found some skin particles under the victim's fingernails or blood at the scene of the crime?

The first thing Monday morning, when the Pasadena Library opened its doors, I began my research on the two girls from Highland Park. I quickly learned that their names were Delores Cepeda and Sonja Johnson and that they were listed by the LA Times as the seventh and eighth victims of the Hillside Strangler. The girls had disappeared during their return home from a shopping trip at the Eagle Rock Plaza. Delores Cepeda was twelve years old and went by the name of Dolly. Her friend, Sonja Johnson, was fourteen years old. The bodies of the two girls were found on November 20, 1977, in a ravine near the police academy in Elysian Park.

It was interesting and productive research. I now had a few more things to add to the similarities of the Leslie Barry murder. Dolly Cepeda and Leslie Barry were both twelve years of age at the time of their murders and the date November 20 was significant to both murders. Leslie had been murdered on November 20, 1978, and

Dolly Cepeda had been found on the same date a year earlier. I had other cases under investigation and didn't have more time to spend at the library. Besides, I needed to let what I had learned percolate a bit.

Two days after my research, on Wednesday, December 6, 1978, in Division 3 of the Pasadena Municipal Court, Arthur Hernandez Anzures was arraigned for the murder of Leslie Fae Barry. Judge Mortimer G. Franciscus presided over the arraignment, and after a few minor preliminaries the charges were read: Penal code section 187, Murder in the first degree; Penal code section 261.3, Rape; Penal Code Section 286, Sodomy; Penal code section 288, Child Molestation.

The formality of stating for the record the attorneys representing both sides followed: Deputy District Attorney Marilyn Porges for the people, and Mitchell Molino representing the defendant. The minor preliminaries out of the way, Judge Franciscus asked for a plea.

Mitch entered a plea of not guilty on behalf of Art and made a motion for bail. He knew given the charges against Anzures, bail was not likely to be granted but he had to make the argument anyway. Mitch ticked off the points in his argument: Art had a clean arrest record; he was deeply rooted in the community; he had not been convicted of the crime with which he was being charged; he was not a danger to himself or the community; and he was not a flight risk.

DDA Marilyn Porges argued that by statute, bail could not be set for a defendant charged with capital murder and asked that the defendant be remanded.

Everyone was taken aback when Judge Franciscus asked Mitch for recommendation on bail. Mitch, arguing that the family had limited financial resources, told the court that setting bail any higher than $25,000 would be tantamount to denying bail altogether. Judge Franciscus denied the bail motion, but noted the defense argument for the record and said the court would revisit the issue of bail at the end of the preliminary hearing.

I arrived at the Pasadena courthouse late and on my way to Division 3, I passed two Anzures brothers assisting Denise Anzures down the hallway. She was dangling between the two young men like a limp rag doll. Her lips were a dull shade of green and her face was pasty white. Her legs were so rubbery she couldn't stand by herself. Supported on the shoulders of the Anzures brothers her feet barely touched the floor. She looked like an injured football player being carried off the field. The brothers didn't look much better. When I saw the trio, I stepped up my pace a little.

As I approached Division 3, I saw Mitch and Mark standing in the hallway just outside the courtroom door.

"I just passed Denise down the hallway. I see it must have gone well," I said sarcastically.

Mark was nonplussed by my attempt at levity and Mitch ignored me completely. By the grim looks on their faces, I guessed that the proceedings had gone about as well as a botched execution.

Mitch handed me a pile of new police reports and told me to come by his office that afternoon for a strategy meeting. Without going into details, he told me Art had confessed to the murder. I was blown away by that revelation and responded in amazement.

"Oh, right, bullshit." I nearly yelled.

After withstanding twenty-one hours of intense interrogation over two days and not confessing to the murder, Art had suddenly, and without provocation, confessed to the crime? I couldn't imagine under what circumstances he would be compelled to do that at this point. With what I had learned about the similarities between the Leslie Barry murder and the Dolly Cepeda/Sonja Johnson murders, the revelation about Art confessing to the murder was discouraging to me. Something didn't sound right about this case, and I was eager to read the reports and find out what was going on. I put them in my briefcase and told Mark to meet me back at the office.

As I pushed the French doors open and entered my office, Mark was right on my heels. I settled in my desk chair and told Mark about passing Denise in the hallway. I asked him to give me the low down on what had happened during the arraignment.

Mark told me that the Anzures family filled the front row of the courtroom. Until the reality of the arraignment set in, this ordeal had been like a bad dream. Having one of their family members charged with such a heinous crime was not something they could have imagined in the deepest regions of their minds. With the reading of the charges and the taking of the plea, the graveness of the situation hit them hard. Art's mother let out a mournful wail. His father, Julian Anzures, buried his head in his hands and wept silently. The siblings, Richard, Mario, and Robert were crying and visibly shaken.

Hit the hardest of all was Denise Anzures. When the charges were read her face paled and she began to sway from side to side. It was nothing short of a miracle that she made it through the whole arraignment ceremony without totally losing it. As Art was being led out of the courtroom in handcuffs and leg irons, Denise stood up to leave and fainted in the aisle.

After Mark had finished telling me about the courtroom drama I could do little more than shake my head in sympathy. A young girl was dead. Her life snuffed out almost before it began. And now, Art. A young man with no criminal history, with a family, a mother and father, brothers and a sister, wife and kids, was on trial for his life. Even if he were eventually acquitted, nothing would ever be the same for any of them. Again, I felt the enormous weight of responsibility that had struck me when I first got the case. To put a family through something like this, I thought, the state had better have a lot better case than I'd seen so far. I assumed that police reports, autopsy reports, and the crime scene photographs, things I had not yet read, would contain substantial evidence proving Art's guilt. Otherwise, I thought, asking for the death penalty in a case without evidence was nothing short of attempted murder on the part of the State.

Before my meeting with Mitch, I had a chance to scan the reports. These reports were more detailed than the previous crime reports. One was a type written report containing more in-depth statements by tenants at the apartment complex. Besides the police report, there was a detailed list of the items taken into evidence by the criminologist at the scene of the crime, and the test results completed on the evidence. Putting them back in my briefcase in preparation to leave for my meeting with Mitch, I thought, "I'll have some interesting reading material tonight."

It was near dusk when Mark and I pulled up and parked in front of Mitch's store front office on Figueroa Boulevard in Highland Park. Highland Park was like something straight out of West Side

Story except the gangs weren't singing and dancing in the streets like the Jets and the Sharks. It was a high crime area with marauding Hispanic gangs, and I was concerned about whether my car would still be there and in one piece by the time the meeting was over. Not that I had any choice in the matter. I left my Datzun 260Z on the street and walked into the building.

Mitch shared an office and secretary with an old semiretired lawyer who used the office once in a great while. In fact, Mitch got many of his clients from the old man, who, at one time, had been a busy real estate and probate lawyer.

We entered the office directly into the reception area, and I noticed it was fairly cluttered with file boxes, cabinets, copy machines, and a scattering of paperwork. It was late in the afternoon, and Mitch's secretary looked as if she was cleaning up in preparation for going home. I cleared my throat to announce our presence and she buzzed Mitch on the intercom. Mitch came out of the back, shook our hands, and we followed him in to his office.

The office was small, but tastefully furnished, with two vinyl armchairs in front of Mitch's desk and one in the far corner of the room. The one in the corner was already occupied by John Neece, the lawyer with whom Mitch had associated on the case to handle law and motions and appeals. Mark and I took the empty chairs in front of Mitch's desk and I checked out the office while Mitch was scanning notes in preparation for our meeting.

It was a modest, wood paneled office, with a typical lawyer décor. Bookshelves containing West's Annotated Codes, and what appeared to be the complete Martindale-Hubbell directory of attorneys, lined one wall. There was a file cabinet in one corner, and various degrees framed and hanging on the wall.

After we got settled, Mitch looked up from his reading material, and we made small talk for a bit before getting down to business. Mitch began by telling us that on the night he was arrested, Art met an inmate by the name of George Winn. According to Winn, he and Art had struck up a fast friendship after Winn, who was a trustee, assisted him in getting settled into his cell. Mitch didn't want to spend much time on the details, since it was all in the report, a copy of which, he handed to me. He said that sometime between the night he was arrested and the following Monday, Art had made a statement to Winn about the Leslie Barry murder. The essential element of the statement was that he had tearfully confessed to Winn, "I didn't mean to kill her."

As Mitch was telling us about the jailhouse confession, I recalled the remark Mitch made about the snitch at the Sheriff's Homicide Bureau, and the reaction Deputy Beck had to it. No wonder Beck was nervous. Mitch's comment about putting a snitch in with Art had hit home.

Mitch concluded by saying he wanted me to do a thorough background on Winn. I told him I would get a rap sheet on the con and check him out and try to find out if he was one of their often used jailhouse informants.

Mitch wanted to know what kind of plan I'd put together for investigating the case. I told him I had a lot of reading to do tonight, and then the next day Mark and I would go to the apartment complex and start conducting our own interviews of tenants. I told him we had gone to the apartment complex over the weekend to familiarize ourselves with the layout. We hadn't talked to any of the tenants because we didn't have enough information about the murder to ask pertinent questions.

I told him I had spoken briefly with Denise Anzures and gotten some preliminary information from her. I didn't tell Mitch about what I had learned in my research at the library. I wanted to keep that to myself until I'd had a chance to read all the police reports and study the crime scene photographs. I told Mitch that I had asked Denise to provide me with the rental applications they had on file for the apartments.

As the meeting was coming to a close Mitch asked if there was anything anyone needed to do their jobs. I reiterated that I needed to get copies of the autopsy and crime scene photographs as soon as possible. Mitch said he had already ordered them, and they should be ready tomorrow or Friday at the latest.

It was dark when Mark and I left Mitch's office, and I was delighted to see that my car was still in one piece. On the drive back to Pasadena, Mark and I discussed the meeting with Mitch and John Neece. Mark was a positive, upbeat, kind of person and rarely critical of people. I placed a high value on his criticisms when they were offered.

"What do you think of Mitch's state of mind? I asked.

"He's really tense compared to the other night at the Sheriff's department when we first met him." Mark answered.

"I'm pretty tense myself." I said.

"I know," Mark chuckled, "I was meaning to tell you to lighten up."

"What did you think of John Neece?" I asked.

"Well, he really didn't say that much during the meeting." Mark replied. "I just hope he's good at law and motion."

"What did you think of him?" Mark threw the question back at me.

"I don't know. Like you said, he didn't say much during the meeting. I just had this feeling that he was kind of uppity; kind of like, because he's a lawyer, he's better than us." I answered truthfully.

"Well, maybe he is." Mark joked.

"I also have the feeling that he thinks Art did it, and that worries me at this stage of the game." I added.

"Yeah, I had the same feeling." Mark agreed.

The arraignment and meeting with Mitch had been a full day, and by the time I got home, dinner had been served and the clean up was underway. I wasn't hungry so I grabbed a beer and took my homework into the living room, where I could have some peace and quiet, and started reading the police reports.

I began with the jailhouse confession. The report was dated December 6, 1978, and since it was December 8, I knew that the alleged confession was hot off the presses. It was a luxury for a private investigator to have this kind of a jump on a murder case, and I was appreciative of the head start Mitch had given me.

According to the report, Sergeant Sams called detectives from the men's central jail at around 6:00 PM on Monday evening. Sams informed Kushner that he had an inmate that had some information the inmate wished to relay only to homicide investigators.

Kushner and Beck went to the Men's Central Jail to speak with inmate, George Winn. The report went on to say that George Winn had been convicted on four counts of burglary and was awaiting sentencing on the convictions. He had been in custody since August, and he worked nights as a trustee in module 3300 of the Men's Central Jail. As a trustee, among other things, it was his job to help inmates get settled in and to do general clean-up work. Another chore he had, mopping the hallway floors, gave him the freedom to move from cell to cell.

Winn stated to detectives that on Friday night, December 1, 1978, he was present when the defendant was brought in, and as he did with all inmates who came into his section of the central jailhouse, he assisted Anzures in getting a mattress, bedding, toothpaste, soap, and any other basic things the new inmate might need. He saw that the defendant was extremely upset and crying, and he asked him what he was in for. Art told him he was in for the murder of a woman. Winn tried to calm him down and get him to quit crying. The snitch asked him how he felt about being in jail for murder and Art replied that he felt bad. According to Winn's statement, Art told him that they came and got him at 4:00 PM and arrested him. Winn said the defendant began to cry again and started babbling about Jesus and asked if he could see a chaplain and get a bible.

As I read the report, I could feel the hair on the back of my neck bristle and my skin get hot. Were they asking me to believe that this trustee, George Winn, went around to every inmate who came to jail crying and offered them his comfort and friendship? That this was just a random act of kindness on his part and, oh and by the way, the suspect confessed to me while I was chatting with him? "What a civic minded burglar to be reporting the confession to detectives," I thought.

It was obvious that George Winn was a plant, and it struck me as odd that the police would be so transparent about it. This guy had motives for snitching. The cops were going to get him a lighter sentence in exchange for his testimony against Art. Mitch would make mince meat out of this shit-head on the stand. I felt outrage that they would insult my intelligence with this sort of evidence. I guzzled the rest of my beer, put the report down, and went to the refrigerator to get another one. When I returned I'd cooled down enough to finish the rest of the report.

According to Winn, Art ended the conversation by saying, "I'll be here for a long time, and not even Jesus can help me now." Art indicated he was tired and had a lot on his mind. He also added that he was sorry he had to put his wife and family through all of this, saying, " I know they're not going to understand."

On Sunday, December 3, 1978, Winn had another conversation with Art, and again Art asked him how he would go about seeing a chaplain. Winn took out a Bible he carried with him and immediately turned to a scripture that read something to the effect that confession was good for the soul.

Replying to the scripture, Art said, "Yeah, I didn't mean to kill her. I didn't know what I was doing." Winn told him he should talk to his attorney and ask if he could enter a plea of insanity. This snitch was a piece of work. He was both a chaplain and a jailhouse lawyer.

By the time I had finished reading the short report, my anger had turned to hysterical laughter. I didn't know if I was laughing at the absolute absurdity of Winn's statement, or the image of this squirrelly ass petty criminal mopping the jailhouse floor with a Bible sticking out of his hip pocket, stopping at cells just long enough to take murder confessions. Then, he sells the confession to an unsuspecting, bewildered, but delighted homicide cop for a lighter sentence? What kind of moron could possibly believe this bullshit?

The answer to my question came in the last paragraph of the report. DDA Aaron Stovitz, lead district attorney in the Pasadena Municipal Court, after reviewing the whole file, issued a felony complaint charging Anzures, with one count of murder in the first degree during the commission of a child molestation and alleging special circumstances.

I still had a lot of reports and other information to study; but, notwithstanding George Winn' statement about the jailhouse confession, the state of California was a long way from proving a case of murder against Art Anzures. I hadn't seen any evidence placing Anzures inside the victim's apartment on the day of the murder, let alone at the time of the murder.

It was the beginning of the case, and I didn't have any strong convictions one way or the other about the reality of Art's guilt or innocence. I thought it was just as likely as not that he did it; but the next report I picked out of the pile was one I would read many times over in the next few months. Yet, every time I read it I missed the connection between a statement by two of the tenants in the report and a clue given to me by Denise Anzures when she provided me with the rental applications a few days after Art's arrest. Connecting these dots hooked me on the case and gave my investigation an entirely different direction. Linking the two facts reinforced, in a powerful way, my belief that Leslie Barry was another victim of the Hillside Strangler, and in spite of the lack of media reports of more murders, these urban terrorists were still at large and still killing.

Chapter 11

A week after getting the case, Mitch phoned to tell me he had received the crime scene photographs, and I should come by his office and pick them up. During the call, Mitch informed me that he had called another client of his, Tony Johnson, to ask Johnson how he would feel about him taking the Anzures case. Tony Johnson, Mitch explained, was the father of Sonja Johnson, one of the victims of the Hillside Strangler. Mitch told me that he worked for Mr. Johnson on a few legal matters unrelated to the murder of his daughter, but felt, as a courtesy to his client, he should let him know about being retained on the Anzures case. Tony Johnson told him that as long as Anzures hadn't killed his daughter, he had no objection to Mitch representing him.

Getting approval from one of his clients to take the case didn't bother me at all. From what I'd seen thus far, Mitch was doing a stellar job of representing Anzures and a conflict, or even the appearance of a conflict of interest, never occurred to me. Despite being the fourth time in two weeks that someone had brought up the subject of the Hillside Strangler case in regards to the Leslie Barry murder, I wasn't concerned about any connection to the Hillside Strangler case. It was more likely that paranoia was the controlling factor in such statements, and without evidence to the contrary, I wasn't going to take those references too seriously.

Before leaving the office to pick up the photographs, I handed Mark the new police reports, including the alleged jailhouse confession from George Winn. I told him to read the reports, and stop by the house tonight for dinner and we would discuss it. We needed to start talking to the tenants soon, and I wanted him to be familiar with the facts of the case before we started our interviews.

I drove to Mitch's office and went right in to see him. Once in his office, he handed me a good size envelope that felt like it contained thirty or more photographs. I asked if he had a chance to look at the pictures, and he said he had thumbed through them, and they were gruesome and upsetting. He said I could keep the pictures because he had seen all he wanted or needed to see of them.

On my drive back to Pasadena, I thought about Mitch's reaction to the photographs. By the time detectives, photographers, and crime scene investigators arrived at the scene, the victim's body was gone and I couldn't imagine what could be so disturbing about the photographs that they would upset the defense lawyer.

When I got back to my office, I removed the photographs and started to look through them. I was mesmerized. As I looked at her living room, the kitchen, her bedroom, I tried to hone in on what activities the victim was involved in just before she died. The will to survive is the strongest of all human instincts, and I wondered what this young girl did to evade, or escape her inevitable death. I wondered what the killer did to counter those very instincts. How did he subdue her, and in the end, take her life?

The décor of Leslie's bedroom was what one might expect to find in a typical teenager's bedroom. Posters of teen idols and pop icons decorated the walls. One of the posters had come off the wall and was lying in a heap in the corner of the bedroom farthest from the bedroom door. The bed faced north and south and sat against the west wall under a large sliding glass window. The drapes covering the window were closed.

The chest of drawers faced perpendicular to the bed, so that the drawers would be easily accessible without the bed being in the way. On top of the chest of drawers sat a 13 inch black and white TV set.

The position of the TV set slanted toward the window and not centered on the bed so the victim could watch it while lying down.

Being on the opposite side of the room from where the murder occurred, I couldn't imagine what possible reason the paramedics would have to move the TV set while trying to save the victim's life. I surmised that with the poster on the floor and the TV out of position that a minor struggle had taken place in the corner of the room. It may have happened when the killer was undressing her.

Across the room on the east wall, to the left of the bedroom door, was a dresser with shelves. A combination radio/record player sat on one corner of the dresser. In front of the record player lay a regular pair of metal pliers. On a cardboard backed book, next to the record player, was a small black jewelry box. Little dolls, stuffed animals, and other knickknacks decorated the shelves.

The bed was a wooden, doublewide platform bed with a headboard and drawers on the side at the bottom. A half eaten bowl of cereal sat on the quilt nearest the window side of the bed. It looked as if the victim had been lying on her stomach watching TV and eating cereal at some point just before her death. Hanging on the wall next to the headboard was a wall lamp with an extra long plug-in cord.

At the head of the bed and against the wall, a clothes hamper doubled as a nightstand. On top of the hamper were two glasses, one a water glass, the other a stemmed wine glass, both partially filled with liquid. There was another cereal bowl with a dab of milk covering the bottom of the bowl. Next to the bowl was a deck of cards, still stacked, but slightly askew.

The murder weapon was the wall lamp electrical cord. It lay across the hamper between the two glasses, over the cereal bowl, and across the edge of the deck of cards. I was unable to see the electrical wall outlet, but by following the cord of the lamp the paramedics had brought in from another room, I could see that the electrical socket was located directly behind the clothes hamper. I was astonished that with all the activity surrounding the hamper; the killer twisting the cord around and tying knots in it; the mother cutting the cord from around her daughter's neck; the paramedics working to save the victims life; nothing on top of the hamper had been disturbed. The glasses were still standing and the cereal bowl was still in place. That none of the items displaced or fell over during the commission of the murder, and even the slick deck of playing cards stayed stacked, caused me to shiver. This killer moved with the grace and precision of a cat.

I moved on to other photographs. The mother's bedroom was next to the victim's bedroom. The door was at a right angle to the victim's bedroom and faced the hallway wall. The only part of the apartment visible from inside the mother's bedroom was the bookshelf standing against the hallway wall.

The color yellow dominated the room. Smooth and unwrinkled, the bedspread was yellow and the bed neatly made. Obviously, no one had sat or lain on it since the mother made it that morning. Above the headboard was a framed painting of yellow flowers. Two round nightstand tables draped and skirted with yellow tablecloths sat on either side of the bed. The headboard was against the west wall, and a large table lamp with a white, dial type telephone sat on the nightstand nearest the window. In the corner, under the window and between the nightstand and a dresser, was an antique wooden rocking chair. There was a collage of family pictures framed and hanging on one wall above the nightstand. The only thing that looked out of place in the room was a man's black pocket comb lying under a table standing against the east wall. I was curious about the comb and wondered if it might have something to do with the murder. Was it dropped by the killer and somehow kicked under the table during a struggle?

I shuffled the picture of the mother's bedroom to the bottom of the stack and studied the picture of the bathroom. Hosiery hung from the towel rack on the glass shower door. Cosmetics and other feminine items cluttered the area around the double washbasins located against the wall of the bathroom. Shuffling the next picture to the top, I focused on the commode. My heart raced a little when I saw a non-filtered cigarette butt stuck against the side of the bowl at water level. The toilet water washed the nicotine and tobacco out of the butt, turning the water at the bottom of the bowl urine yellow. Maybe it was just an oversight, but the police reports did not mention the cigarette butt, and I made a note to find out if my client smoked and, if so, what brand he smoked. In addition, I would need to find out if the forensic lab had tested it for saliva or other possible evidence.

The living room was large and well furnished. An end table with a lamp and a framed photograph sat in the northwest corner of the room between matching sofas. The sofas formed an L shape with one against the north wall and the other against the west wall. It looked like a clever decorating maneuver to form a homemade corner sofa set. Landscape paintings hung at eye level above and centered on each of the sofas. A large, glass top coffee table was positioned in the middle of both sofas. A live plant, a couple of magazines, and a sculpture of a mother holding a baby adorned the coffee table. The overall condition of cleanliness and the tasteful décor of the living room demonstrated the pride and effort Aina Barry had put into making a home for her and her daughter.

Against an interior wall, separating the living room from the kitchen, was a long record player cabinet. At the end of the cabinet sat an empty laundry basket. On top of the record cabinet, at the same end as the laundry basket, were several coins. The police reports said the victim had been doing the laundry just before the murder. This picture appeared to confirm that fact.

The dining nook, located off the living room just to the left of the front door and connected to the kitchen, was furnished with a round oak or walnut table and four high-backed chairs. A detective sat at the dining table taking notes.

Apart from a few dirty dishes in the sink, the kitchen was organized and clean. On the kitchen counter, nearest to the dining room, were two grocery bags. A large bag, the sides closed at the top and curling downward looked as if it contained some items. Police reports had not said anything about the grocery sacks when describing the apartment, and I thought the omission might be something more than an oversight by the police. The larger bag had to contain an item or two to keep it standing in the upright position. What was in it, and why had the police failed to mention the grocery sacks in their report?

The more disturbing question was how did the sacks get there? The mother hadn't stopped at the store on her way home from work.

I was curious to know what was in the sacks and if the police had any idea about how they got there. The other bag was a small sack like the kind store clerks use for candy and other small items. If Leslie had gone to the store sometime during the day, the possibility of suspects was opened to the entire world.

Separate from the photographs of the victim's apartment were a series of pictures of the murder weapon. Unlike the depiction of the knotted cord in the crime scene photographs, these pictures were close-ups. I had read the newest police reports the previous night so they were fresh in my mind. One of the reports contained a description of the cord and described the knots as being preexisting. I didn't know what they meant by "preexisting" knots. Were they preexisting to the photographer, as in the police didn't tie the knots so they could pin it to the board, or were they "preexisting" to the murder as opposed to being tied at the time of the murder? Whatever preexisting meant, the pictures depicted a confusing and dramatic murder weapon.

The wall lamp cord was cut from the lamp by the sheriff's crime lab and pinned to a board. The crime photographer took pictures of it in both its original state, the way it appeared when used to kill the victim, as well as laid out and unwound. At first, it looked to me as if the killer had wrapped the cord twice around the victim's neck and tied it in front with a figure eight knot. However, the other two knots in the cord held the most intrigue. I was amazed at how tight they were.

Laying the photographs side by side, I compared the two different versions of the close-ups to the crime scene version of the cord stretching across the hamper. In the unwound version, five ends showed cuts but I could not determine from the picture how they fit together. One end, severed well above the noose, was the cut made by the crime lab when they booked the murder weapon into evidence. Just right of the murder weapon part of the cord, was a rolled up portion with an inline off and on switch so the lamp could be conveniently turned on and off without reaching to the lamp base.

That part of the cord held no relevance to the murder, but I supposed it was better to take too many pictures than not enough pictures.

The plug end of the cord was used as the murder weapon. Two of the ends were long and nearly even and straddled either side of the figure eight knot. The other two ends stuck out about an inch from a knot tied so tightly I wasn't sure what kind of knot it was. It appeared in the unwound version to be a square knot. In the photograph depicting the cord in its original condition when used as a murder weapon, the crime lab had loosened the knot and I could see that it was a hitch knot of some sort. I traced a strand of the cord several times in an attempt to see how the killer tied the knot, but the middle of the knot ended at the edge of the photograph and I lost track of the strand. The four cut ends that fit neatly together were the cuts made by the mother when cutting the cord from around her daughter's neck. Mrs. Barry stated that when cutting the cord, she had to cut through two strands to free it from her daughter's neck. That bit of information assisted me in analyzing how the killer tied the knots.

The hitch knot reminded me of a knot a person might use for tying something off when it was extremely important that the knot wouldn't slip or come undone--like a suture knot used by surgeons to tie off a bleeding artery. It took me a while but I finally figured it out. This hitch knot on the side of the loop and across from the simple knot attached the cord to the victim's neck, and could not have been tied before the murder. I deduced that it would require much practice to tie and adjust the hitch knot tight enough to cause death. A plastic cord is stiff and inflexible and can be easily untied just by pushing on either side toward the center of the knot. Yet, the mother had not been able to untie the cord. The pictures of the murder weapon intrigued me. It was apparent that this killer was skilled at tying knots. In addition, it must have taken a great deal of physical strength to tie it so tightly that it couldn't be loosened by hand.

What implications did the murder weapon hold for learning something about the killer? If there was no message in the murder weapon, why not simply use the cord as a garrote? He didn't have to tie knots in it. Was the killer trying to say something about what he did or why he was killing? At the very least the knotted cord told me that the killer was adept at tying knots and possessed exceptional upper body strength. That was a lot more than I knew before studying the crime photographs.

I wondered why Kushner and Beck weren't paying more attention to the murder weapon. Had it been a gun, they would've been all over it doing tests and obtaining evidence from the testimony of ballistic experts about the caliber of the weapon and the spirals of the slug that matched the bullet to the gun. Were the murder weapon a knife, a pathologist would measure the width and length of the blade and how the knife matched the type of wounds and the angles of entry into the victim's body. The murder weapon usually told detectives something about the crime: how it took place, the positions of the parties during the commission of the crime; and sometimes it unmistakably identified the killer. It struck me as odd that other than asking Art a few questions about the methods of killing he had learned while in the Army, the police had not bothered to have the murder weapon analyzed by experts.

The crime scene photographs illuminated statements in the police reports. According to statements from two of her friends, they had spoken on the phone to Leslie shortly before the murder. The photographs showed that the only phone in the apartment was located in the mother's bedroom. From that position, Leslie could not have seen the front door or any other part of the apartment. The statement from Lisa Ballatore, the last person to ever talk to her, indicated that they were on the phone at around five o'clock; the time when Leslie was expecting her mother to get home from work. Suddenly she said she had to go and hung up. While Leslie could not see the front door from the mother's bedroom, she could hear it open, and it would be natural for her to assume that it was her mother.

The scenario developing in my mind was that Leslie came out of her mother's bedroom, and when she saw the killer coming at her, ran to the farthest part of the apartment, the corner of her bedroom, to escape. She cowered in the corner between the dresser and the wall knocking the poster of the rock idol to the floor. While attempting to get the young victim under control and undress her, the killer bumped the chest of drawers knocking the TV set toward the window. Grabbing Leslie by the ankles, he carried or dragged her to the other side of the bedroom, put her on the floor, and told her if she screamed he would kill her. He then unplugged the lamp cord, and with certain and deft speed, he tied the cord around her neck and took her life.

Aina Barry stated to police on the night of the murder, that when she first entered the apartment she had not seen or sensed anything out of the ordinary. According to her statement, she entered the apartment, put her purse down on the dining table, and left the apartment to get her mail. When she returned to the apartment from the mailbox, she noticed the door of her daughter's bedroom was slightly ajar, and the only illumination was the light from the TV set.

Did this mean that the killer was still inside the apartment when Aina came home?

I read the autopsy report to see what the coroner had to say about the crime. I had to read it several times, because I was having trouble understanding some of the medical terminology in it. There was one statement in the report, that even though I didn't totally understand the terminology, I knew what it meant because it made sense on its own. The pathologist had held the cord up to the victim's neck and noted in his report that two of the knots, the hitch knot and the simple knot, corresponded to the left and right sterno-thyroid muscle. In other words, pressure points on the neck.

After studying the knots, I thought that the murder weapon itself might corroborate the fact that the killer was still inside the apartment when the mother came home from work. The simple knot tied on the right side of the neck and the hitch knot on the left side of her neck corresponded to pressure points. The cord, tied tightly enough to stop the flow of blood from the brain, was not so tight that it would crush the larynx causing a quick death. From my examination of the knotted cord, I deduced that the killer intended that his victim die slowly while he raped her. This killer was a quick thinker, a good improviser, and there was little doubt that he had killed before.

When he heard the front door open, he knew the mother had come home and he waited patiently, in dead silence, ready to pounce on her if she entered the bedroom to check on Leslie. He listened at the bedroom door and was relieved to hear keys jangle and the front door close. Perhaps he had stalked her and knew her habits, or maybe he just assumed that she was leaving her apartment to get her mail before checking up on her daughter. The killer knew enough about anatomy to know the importance of the sterno-thyroid muscles, then he must also know that the victim could be revived. With deft speed, he tied a figure eight knot in the front of her neck to cut off all oxygen to her brain. He then fled the apartment disappearing into the darkness. How did he escape undetected?

Looking at the photographs of the outside of the apartment building, there was only one logical avenue of escape without detection. He had to vault over the porch wall of Leslie's apartment into a stairwell and flee through the tunnel out to the carport area. To take any other route his escape would've been witnessed by the mother returning to her apartment from the mailbox.

In reading the most current police reports, I had been able to establish a time line of the murder. The statement of Aina Barry about the time she had gotten home from work put the time of the discovery of the victim's body between 5:10 to 5:15 PM. The statement by Leslie's friend, Lisa Ballatore, concerning what time she had been talking with Leslie on the phone established that the victim had been alive at 4:50 to 4:55 PM. Fifteen to twenty minutes was not much time for the killer to commit a sexual assault on the victim, murder her and make a clean get away.

These photographs raised a multitude of questions that were not satisfactorily answered by the police reports nor the arrest of Anzures. Witnesses established the time line of the murder at ten to fifteen minutes. Why did the killer tie the knots in the cord? What would the killer need to know and what skill would he need to possess to tie the knots and adjust them to pressure points on the neck? How cool and calm would he have to be to stay inside the bedroom when the mother came home? Did his daring and athletic escape in jumping over the wall of the porch indicate a familiarity with the layout of the apartment complex? Did the method of the murder imply experience? Had he killed before? If he had killed before, who were his previous victims?

The statement on the night of the murder by Shawn Hagen may have held the answer to these questions. Asked by police investigators why he felt that the Barry murder was related to the Hillside Strangler case, the young boy replied, "Because I knew one of the Hillside Strangler victims'."

After discussing the facts of the case, Wendy, Mark and I decided to reenact the murder. Wendy loved the theater and was a good actor. Casting her in the role of the victim was a stroke of genius. I thought about casting Mark for that role but he didn't have the right look. Using the crime scene photographs as a guide, Mark played the part of the killer and I was the director.

I narrated the facts and put them in various positions to see if the scenario looked feasible. First, I directed Wendy to lie on the bed. We used the sofa in the den as the bed. She lay there watching TV like Leslie and eating a bowl of cereal; she gets antsy and decides to call her friend Lisa to gossip about the goings on at school that day. As far as I could see from the photographs, there was only one phone in the apartment and that was on the nightstand in the mother's bedroom. The bedding on the mother's bed was not wrinkled or messed up so we assumed Leslie talked on the phone while sitting in the wooden rocker next to the nightstand.

At 4:55 P.M, Leslie hears the front door open. She isn't able to see the front door from her mother's bedroom, but it's close to the time for her mom to be getting home from work. Leslie had been watching the clock carefully while talking to Lisa, and she figured her mom might have gotten home a little early. She didn't want to get caught talking on the phone when she was supposed to be doing the laundry. Suddenly, telling Lisa. "I've gotta go now" she hung up the phone.

We were using the hallway between the dining room and the den as the mother's bedroom. The front door of the apartment was the big sliding oak door leading from our den to the living room. I directed Wendy to walk out of the bedroom and for Mark to be standing across the room at the door.

When Wendy came out of the bedroom and saw Mark she ran to the farthest point in the room and cowered in the corner. Mark ran after her and towering over his prey, reached down and grabbed her by the ankles. I stopped the action. Wendy's reaction probably explained why the poster had been knocked off the wall and maybe why the TV set was facing in the wrong direction for viewing.

"Why didn't you scream?" I asked Wendy.

"Because," Wendy replied, "I was frozen with terror."

"What was your plan Mark? Were you going to drag her across the room to kill and rape her?"

"Yes," Mark said, "she was found on the other side of the bedroom and she had to get there some way. I figured she must have been dragged or carried to the actual spot of the murder."

"Okay," I said, "now let's kill her"

I wasn't certain of how the knot was tied, but I knew it wasn't tied in a single strand of the cord like a square knot. To demonstrate that it wasn't a square knot, I unplugged a lamp and tied a square knot in the cord. I told Wendy and Mark to compare the knot I had just tied with the one in the photograph. They could see the difference immediately. Another thing I wanted to demonstrate about that knot was how tight it was. The police reports said, and photographs confirmed, that the mother had to cut the cord from around her daughter's neck. It was extremely difficult, and probably impossible, for the average Joe to tie a knot in an electrical cord that isn't easily untied. In the photographs I could see how tight one of the knots was. At 6 feet and 220 pounds, I was a big guy, and although most of my muscle development was from bending my elbow at the bar, I still had some good upper body strength. I tied a knot and pulled on the cord as hard as I could. Handing it to Mark I told him to untie it. Mark pushed the cord on both sides toward the center of the knot and it loosened with ease. I commented to Wendy and Mark that the killer had to be damn strong to pull the knot that tight.

I instructed Wendy to lie down in front of the sofa, and told Mark to use the lamp cord I had used earlier for my demonstration on how the knot was tied, as the murder weapon. After a few inept attempts to kill Wendy with the lamp cord the way Leslie had been killed, we gave up. We just weren't very competent killers. Our biggest problem was tying the knots. Neither I, nor Mark could fold the cord over and tie the hitch knot the way it had been tied around the victims neck in a reasonable time.

After we moved the furniture back in place and got comfortable in our chairs, I wanted to review what we knew.

"The police made a big deal about the TV set being fixed and the fact that Art Anzures didn't have a pair of pliers. They found a pair of pliers in Leslie's bedroom and they think those pliers belong to Anzures. Art said he didn't own a pair of pliers. Kushner and Beck couldn't believe that an apartment manager and maintenance man wouldn't own a regular pair of pliers. Apparently, it was their contention that Art went into Leslie's apartment under the pretense of fixing her TV set; molested her, and when she threatened to tell on him he killed her.

Does that sound right to you guys?" I asked

They both nodded in agreement.

"So," I continued, "Art says that early in the day he sold a car to one of the tenants, Richard Querio, for five hundred bucks, and he was preparing to take his family out to dinner that night. His kids didn't have clean clothes to wear for dinner, so Art does a load of laundry. It's shortly after 4:00 PM, and while washing laundry, he runs into Leslie Barry and exchanges words with her.

Is there any reason not to believe any of this?" I asked.

"I can't see any reason not to believe it." Wendy said. "The fact that he sold the car is verified by Richard Querio and if he's telling the truth about that he's probably telling the truth about everything else. He has a few bucks in his pocket and he wants to treat his family to dinner. Makes sense to me. Besides, Denise backs him up on the dinner outing. Those don't sound like the actions of someone planning to commit a murder. Did anyone check to see if the laundry was still in the machines after the murder?" Wendy asked.

"Yes," I answered, "I think the report said Hatfield checked the laundry and there were clothes in the washing machine, but not the dryer. The clothes in the washer belonged to the Barry's. I don't know why they're making such a big deal about the laundry. Can somebody enlighten me?"

"I guess," Mark said, "that the police don't think Art was doing his laundry at the time, but instead was inside Leslie's apartment molesting and killing her, and he's just using the laundry as his alibi."

"So what do you think they think Art was doing while Leslie was eating cereal and talking to her friends on the phone? I asked sarcastically,

"Jerking off?"

Mark smiled and shrugged his shoulders.

"Art Anzures may have killed Leslie Barry," I continued, "but if he did, it didn't happen the way the police seem to think it did." I stated with finality. "Whoever killed Leslie went into her apartment with the intent to kill her. Killing her was not an after-thought to molesting her. Whoever the killer is knew exactly what he was doing. Those knots in the cord are like a signature to the crime. They have to tell us something about the killer."

"It doesn't make much sense with Art as the killer," Wendy agreed. "You should keep doing research into the murder of those two girls in Eagle Rock. They were Hillside Strangler victims, weren't they?"

"Yeah, But Leslie Barry wasn't found on a hillside." I said.

"You should do some more research on it anyway," Wendy replied, "if the mother came home and interrupted the murder, you don't know what the killer might have planned to do with the body." I couldn't argue with her logic.

Chapter 12

Jeanne Marek was one witness I was eager to talk to for a couple of reasons. Art told the police that while he was out cleaning up the area and talking with his friend, Tony Barrett, Jeanne Marek's brother had driven up in a white car and parked in the carport area of the 406 Monterey Road building. The police had not followed up on that statement, and there was no name or statement in any of the police reports from Jeanne Marek' brother. I wanted to talk to her brother and verify that he had come to the apartments that day to visit his sister.

Purely from the defense perspective, if Marek's brother was there at the time of the murder, it would be one more male at the apartment complex the police had not questioned before focusing in on Anzures. Evidence like that went to the credibility of the police investigation and could help to establish a reasonable doubt.

I also wanted to ask Marek about a peculiar statement she made to the police concerning a man who had knocked on her door the Friday before the murder. The man asked Ms. Marek how many single and married women lived in the apartment complex. She didn't open the door for the man and was unable to give a description of him, but she recalled that he said his name was Eddie. Another female tenant corroborated Marek's statement about

"Eddie," saying he had knocked on her door and asked the same question. Wisely, neither woman opened the door for him.

With nothing more to go on than a first name, I didn't have the slightest idea how I would go about finding a guy named Eddie. Just the same I wanted to verify that the two women had made the statement and it was accurate. I wasn't going to leave any stones unturned in my first murder investigation.

Marek lived in an upstairs apartment at the front of the complex in the 406 Monterey Road building. I knocked on the door and was surprised when a man answered the door. From descriptions other tenants gave me about Jeanne Marek, I had an image of her as a single woman without much of a love life. I introduced Mark and myself, and after telling him why we were there, he invited us in. Jeanne, he informed us was not home, but she would be home in the early evening.

The man said his name was Frank Hall, and that he was staying with Jeanne for an indefinite period. I asked him if he was at the apartment on November 20, between 4:30 and 5:30 PM. He said he was staying there at the time, but late in the afternoon he had gone to the gym to workout and then played handball. At the actual time of the murder he was not at the apartment.

I inquired whether he knew Jeanne's brother and if her brother had come by that day to visit with him. He said he knew her brother, and his name was William Asper. He had not seen Bill that day at all. Hall gave me Asper's address and phone number and I told him that we would be back later to talk to Ms. Marek.

When Mark and I were out of earshot of the apartment, I nudged Mark.

"That was interesting, huh? What do you think about that statement?" I asked. "We just found two more guys who were here at the time of the murder that the police reports didn't mention."

Mark just shrugged. Sometimes his lack of enthusiasm infuriated me, and this was one of those times. We had quickly gotten a piece of information we didn't have before, and it indicated either a mistaken identity by Art or that someone, either Anzures or Frank Hall, was lying. It was a big deal as far as I was concerned, but I also knew that Mark was a low energy, laidback kind of guy by nature so his lack of enthusiasm didn't really surprise me. It just pissed me off.

I knocked on a few more doors and Mark snooped around the outside area of the apartments. Not having much success at finding people home, I went looking for Mark. As I approached the stairwell located under Leslie's porch, Mark called to me.

"Look at this." Mark said, pointing to a red mark the size of a quarter on the wall of the stairwell.

I inspected the mark closely.

"Do you think its blood?" I asked.

"It sure looks like it to me." Mark said not showing the least bit of excitement in his voice.

"Look at the way it's going in downward streaks." Mark observed.

I nodded my head, then backed up the stairwell a ways so I could see where the spot was located in relationship to Leslie's front porch. The spot was in the opening of the stairwell where one would expect a jumper to land. The momentum of the jump would carry him into the north side of the wall with great force and it was a good bet that the spot was blood left behind by the killer. I made a note to call a forensic blood expert to find out the feasibility of testing for blood type. If we collected the blood for testing, we would need to follow the rules of evidence and maintain the chain of custody.

Mark and I continued our walk through the tunnel out to the carport area. At the end of the tunnel, after taking a quick look around, we made a right turn toward the alley. At the alley, we made another right and walked behind the apartment complex in the direction of the other apartment building. The killer, I noted, could've parked anywhere along the alley or in the carport and made a clean get away without anyone ever noticing his car. If Anzures was the killer then we were almost certainly walking his escape route. He would probably circle around behind the apartment complex and come up the tunnel from the 406 building, right into his apartment without anyone noticing him.

As we walked around the back of the apartments, I took in the sights and sounds of the alley. Across the alley from the apartment complex were railroad tracks. Beyond the railroad tracks was a pre-forties housing development. It was probably a solid middle class community at one time. Then the railroad tracks were laid and two or three times a day trains shook the plaster off the walls, blew whistles at three in the morning and the neighborhood went to hell. I had never seen or even heard of this section of town. I guessed it was a well-kept secret in the affluent, image conscious town of South Pasadena. These houses would've been a better fit located on the other side of the Pasadena freeway in the barrio of Eagle Rock.

We spent a couple of hours at the complex checking out the surrounding area. Again, I needed time to absorb what I'd seen and heard and contemplate how it all fit together.

That night Mitch phoned to see where I was in my investigation. I told him about Frank Hall being one of the males living at the apartments with Jeanne Marek. He was pleased and surprised that I had turned up a name that had not appeared anywhere in the police reports. I told him about the information Hall had given me concerning Jeanne Marek' brother and said I'd be following up on the information in the next week.

Mitch told me we had another problem concerning the jailhouse confession to George Winn. Mitch said another inmate had come forward saying he had overheard the conversation between Art and Winn. The inmates name was Art Aragon and apparently, he was Anzures' cellmate on the night Art was arrested. Mitch said he wanted me to do a thorough background on Aragon as well as Winn. He said he'd requested rap sheets on both of these guys, but he wanted me to find out if they had given snitch testimony before.

The next week Mark and I were at the apartment complex every day. We realized early on how difficult it would be conducting an investigation during Christmas time. People were trying to get into the holiday spirit and didn't want to think about the murder of their young neighbor. I sympathized with them, but I didn't have the luxury of time on my side. The State makes the arrest and the State sets the deadlines. Besides, I felt a sense of urgency about this case. If Art Anzures was innocent then he belonged at home with his family and not in the county jail. Furthermore, if he didn't do it then a very dangerous killer was still out there and the authorities needed to start looking for him.

Like the police, we failed to turn up an eyewitness to any part of the murder. In spite of all the activity and the number of people at home around the time of the murder, nobody saw anyone going into the victim's apartment; coming out of the apartment; walking down the sidewalk; or running down the alley. My hope of finding an eyewitness to the murder was a total bust.

Shawn Hagen was at the top of my list of people I wanted to speak with. After analyzing the facts, the escape, the murder weapon, and the time line of the murder, I was eager to ask him about the statement he made concerning knowing one of the Hillside Strangler victims. When I knocked on the door to his downstairs apartment in the 406 Monterey Road building his stepfather, answered the door.

I made the introductions and told him I wanted to ask Shawn a few questions about his statement to the police. It was early evening, just after the dinner hour, and Pollin told me Shawn was taking a nap and he didn't want to wake him up. I sensed from the tone of his voice that Pollin had an attitude and wasn't inclined to be cooperative with us. I persisted and asked him when a good time would be for us to return and speak to him. Pollin said he didn't want us bothering Shawn since the police had already questioned his stepson at length several times. He was afraid the kid would crack under the pressure. Shawn was a nervous wreck and his schoolwork was already suffering from the after effects of the murder.

I was a little peeved that we hadn't received any additional reports from the police detailing their interviews with Shawn Hagen.

"Well, let me ask you a few questions then." I said, "Who was the victim of the Hillside Strangler that Shawn knew?" I asked.

"He went to Stancliff School with Dolly Cepeda." Pollin responded. "Shawn, Leslie Barry, and Dolly Cepeda all attended Stancliff at the same time." He added. "I sometimes picked all three of the kids up at school and gave them a ride home."

I didn't want to push it by asking him any more questions. I might need to talk to him or Shawn later so there was no point in pissing him off. At any rate, I'd essentially gotten the information I wanted for the time being. Now I'd have to get more information at the library on the Dolly Cepeda murder before I could question them further about a possible connection between the two murders.

We had been on the case now for just over two weeks and I felt the investigation was going well. The evidence from the Sheriff's crime lab report was as disappointing as all the other reports. The lab identified all the fingerprints lifted from the crime scene, except for a partial thumbprint on the corner of the stereo cabinet against the south wall of the living room. None of the prints belonged to Anzures and the lab identified most of them as belonging either to Aina Barry, Leslie Barry, or the police and paramedics who responded to the scene.

The rape kit turned up no additional evidence that could shine light on the identity of the killer. No saliva or sperm was detected anywhere on the victim's body. The test results didn't necessarily mean those secretions weren't there. The killer could have been a non-secretor, a condition where the secretions and elements of the secretions are undetectable through the usual means of testing. The lack of tearing or trauma to the vagina and anus indicated the victim was not raped, and I considered the possibility that the killer either couldn't get it up or was so advanced in his psychosis that sexual gratification came from the violence and not the sexual act itself. Or, it could simply be that he didn't have time to complete the rape because of the mother coming home.

I began my research on the Hillside Strangler case at the Pasadena Library. Articles in the Los Angeles Times, revealed that Delores Cepeda and Sonja Johnson had disappeared on, Sunday, November 13, 1977, while on their way home from the Eagle Rock Shopping Plaza. Twelve-year old Delores Cepeda and fourteen-year old Sonja Johnson were the youngest victims of the Hillside Strangler. As I researched the articles, I remembered the incident from when it happened. I just hadn't been able to connect the names to the Hillside Strangler case from reading about it the year before. The articles jogged my memory, and I recalled that the disappearance had set off a massive manhunt, with hundreds of volunteers going door to door looking for the girls. I was reminded that their bodies had been found a week later in a ravine near the LAPD training academy in Elysian Park.

When a story on the Hillside Strangler case appeared, the Times would do a short biographical sketch of all the victims and include such information as when they disappeared, and when and where their bodies had been found. I noticed that another girl, Kristina Weckler, had also been found on November 20, 1977. Kristina Weckler lived in Glendale, and at the time of her murder, was attending the Art Center College of Design located in the hills of Pasadena.

I wasn't familiar with the locations where these girls either lived or were found, so when I returned to my office, I took out my Thomas Guide map book and looked up the sites. I noticed that Kristina Weckler had been found on Rawona Street just off Chevy Chase drive in Glendale. Both Sonja Johnson and Delores Cepeda lived a short distance from each other on streets that intersected with York Boulevard in Eagle Rock. Leslie Barry lived on Monterey Road on the border of South Pasadena and Eagle Rock, and all three of these main arteries intersected and formed a half moon shape from top to bottom.

To get from, say, the Art Center in the hills of Pasadena to Monterey Road in South Pasadena, a person could use Chevy Chase, York Boulevard and a short stint on Pasadena Avenue to Monterey Road. A killer, who might have lived in the hills above the Rose Bowl, could easily be familiar with these streets and the surrounding areas to know where the best spots to drop the bodies were.

The more I learned about the murders of Delores Cepeda, Sonja Johnson, and Leslie Barry the more I began to get nervous about the case. I felt I was getting in over my head. I didn't have the experience and financial resources to investigate a serial killer case.

While I didn't have access to the police and autopsy reports on the Cepeda/Johnson murders, I had become intimately familiar with the facts of the Barry case and felt that the date of Barry's murder, November 20, was more than a mere a coincidence. It was also the date the bodies of Dolly Cepeda and Sonja Johnson was found, and if I was correct in my conclusions that the guy who killed Leslie Barry had killed before, it was a safe bet that two of his earlier victim's would be Dolly Cepeda, Sonja Johnson, and a third might very well be Kristina Weckler.

The evidence and facts surrounding the Barry murder were leading me to the conclusion that to believe that Art Anzures killed Leslie Barry would require me to believe that Anzures was the Hillside Strangler. It would be hard for anyone to convince me that the frightened young man I met in Glendora a few weeks earlier was a clever and diabolical killer who had teased, taunted, and evaded one the largest and best equipped police departments in the world for nearly two years.

On January 2, 1979, Mark and I interviewed William Asper at his home in Pasadena. I had to rap hard on the door several times before anyone answered. After verifying that the person at the door was William Asper, I told him we were investigators for the defense of Art Anzures and that we would like to ask him a few questions. Like many fringe witnesses, Asper was less than thrilled about being involved in a murder investigation and he balked at the idea of answering questions. We stood on the porch and talked to him through the screen door.

Asper was a big man about 35 years of age, 6'2" in height, weighing 220 pounds. He had curly, brownish-red hair and the pale, freckled skin of a redhead. Asper looked about as Irish as an Irishman can look. I asked him if he was Jeanne Marek' brother and he replied that he was.

I told him that on the day of the murder, November 20, 1978, Art Anzures was standing in the alley behind his sisters apartment complex talking to a friend when he saw a man drive up in a white car and park in the carport area of Jeanne' building. Art identified the person driving the car as "Jeanne Marek's brother." I asked Asper if he had gone over to visit his sister that day. He said he had not gone to the apartment complex that day, and furthermore, he did not own a white car and had never owned a white car. He said he owned a red Porsche and that was the only car he owned and ever drove.

I didn't think Art was the kind of person who would point the finger at someone else, and he wasn't clever enough to give false statements to throw investigators off track. Kushner and Beck hadn't bothered to check out this part of Art's statement, and I didn't know if Asper was telling the truth or not. There were only two possibilities: either William Asper was lying about being there or it was a case of mistaken identity on Art's part. If he was lying, he had to have a good reason. He might be lying because he just didn't want to get involved in a murder investigation, or maybe he was lying because he was involved in the murder.

The other option was that maybe he was telling the truth about not being there. His denial about being at the apartment complex at the time of the murder gave me a strong inclination to alibi him. I asked him what he was doing on the day of the murder. Asper said he was a photographer and spent a lot of time in his darkroom. He said that as far as he could recall, he was working in his darkroom at that time. I thanked him for his cooperation and Mark and I left.

On the way back to the office, I discussed the interview with Mark and asked him what he thought of William Asper. As usual he was reserved and noncommittal. I told Mark I thought we might have our first real suspect in the case.

"After all," I said, "his alibi is weak. He was identified as one of the people at the apartments that day, and if he was the one who drove up in the white car, then he's lying about not being there. All we have to do is find out what kind of car he drives, and since he doesn't have a real alibi, we'll call him a good suspect."

"Yeah," Mark said, "if we can connect him to a white car, show he was at the apartment complex at the time of the murder, and then place him inside Leslie's apartment, we can call him a suspect.

Mark was always a spoiler.

If Asper didn't own, or have access, to a white car and didn't go to the apartments that day, then the unknown person that drove up in the white car might very well be the killer.

Chapter 13

The preliminary hearing for Art lasted for less than a week. Much of the time was spent in Law and Motions with only a short time used for taking court testimony. The prosecutor called Deputy Jerome Beck to lay the foundation that a crime had been committed. Most of Beck's testimony was hearsay, but hearsay evidence is admissible in a preliminary hearing.

After establishing the elements of the crime, the jailhouse duo of George Winn and Art Aragon took the stand to testify about the alleged jailhouse confession and make a case against Anzures for the murder. Winn testified about how, on the night Art was arrested, he helped Anzures get settled in his cell, and Art confessed to him that he "didn't mean to kill her." Art Aragon backed up Winn' testimony, but his sketchy statement about the confession needed a lot more credibility than Aragon could give it.

Other than the murder weapon, the only physical evidence found at the scene of the crime and on the body and blanket at the hospital was three strands of hair. The prosecutor called her hair expert from the Sheriff's Crime Lab to testify about his analysis of the hair. The expert testified that all he could really do to determine the source of the hair was to analyze the pattern of hairs. The expert testified that the hair booked into evidence was pubic hair and that the pattern of hair was consistent with the pubic hair samples supplied to the police by the defendant, Art Anzures.

Mitch had done his homework on hair analysis. On cross-examination, he got the expert to admit that he could not distinguish, by looking through a microscope, head hair from pubic hair. When Mitch asked him what the acceptable standards in the scientific community was on analyzing hair as credible court evidence, he reluctantly acknowledged that he needed at least twelve hair samples to determine the pattern of hair and the possible source of the hair. The hair expert admitted during cross that he couldn't testify with any degree of certainty as to the source of the hair. Nevertheless, scientific evidence, even if it's little more than voodoo science, plays well in court and to that extent the hair expert did his part. The prosecutor conspicuously failed to introduce the best evidence left behind by the killer—the murder weapon.

Mitch opted not to present any witnesses or other evidence on Art's behalf. He felt it would be better not to tip his hand concerning his strategy at the trial. Since a solid trial strategy had not yet been determined, I agreed that it was a good decision. On cross-examination, he had made short work of the convict's testimony about the alleged jailhouse confession. From the rap sheets we obtained through our discovery motion, we learned that both Winn and Aragon were career criminals dating back to their teenage years. We suspected that both were old hands at the snitching game, and Mitch was able to elicit statements from both Winn and Aragon that they had been offered help with their pending sentences in exchange for their testimony.

At the end of the preliminary hearing, Mitch moved to suppress the alleged confession because, he argued, Winn and Aragon were acting as agents of the police and therefore were required to read Art his Miranda rights before talking to him. The motion was mostly perfunctory. It's damn hard to prove a negative and since the defense was unable to present evidence to dispute the confession, or demonstrate that the alleged confession was anything but a voluntary utterance, none of us was surprised when the judge denied the motion. If the judge had thrown out the jailhouse confession, it would leave the State without a case, requiring a complete dismissal of the charges.

I could tell from the expression of distain on his face that Judge Franciscus was unimpressed with the prosecutor's case and the testimony of Winn and Aragon.Actually, the judge seemed bothered by the whole presentation, particularly since the prosecutor had failed to present solid evidence to support probable cause for the arrest itself. As he had promised at the arraignment, at the end of the preliminary hearing the Judge again entertained recommendations on bail.

The prosecutor reiterated her argument that by law no bail could be set for a defendant charged with capital murder and that the defendant should be remanded without bail. When prompted by the judge to cite a specific statute or case law in support of her position the prosecutor was unable to come up with any authority. The judge gave her a look as if to say, "There seems to be a lot you don't know about this case, lady."

Mitch made the same argument for bail as he made at the arraignment. Art was not a flight risk, nor a danger to himself or others; he had a long-standing connection to the community; he had not been convicted of the crime with which he was charged, etc.; therefore, Mitch asked that bail be set at $25,000. The judge prodded Porges to make a counter recommendation on bail. Stubbornly she stood by her argument of no bail for a defendant charged with capital murder.

I detected a flash of annoyance cross the Judge's face. It seemed to me that what he really wanted to do was throw the case out. However, It is difficult for a judge to dismiss a murder case, regardless of how weak the evidence is, because in doing so the judge is going against some powerful political forces. A judge is a sitting duck for attacks from political action groups, especially victim rights advocates. The risk of invoking the ire of these forces increases considerably when the case involves the murder of a child or a cop. Franciscus did the next best thing and chose to send Porges and the police a warning about the strength, or lack thereof, of their case. Noting that the prosecutor was unable to cite authority for her position on bail, but not wanting to give Mitch everything he asked for, Judge Franciscus set bail for Art at $50,000, but ruled that there was sufficient evidence to proceed to trial.

If you can find humor in a frame-up, the prosecutor's case against Art Anzures, in all its transparency, was becoming hilarious. Immediately after the preliminary hearing, the police showed that they had gotten the Judge's message about the weakness of their case. That very day another jailhouse confession surfaced. This time the snitch was an inmate named Steven Lyle Jackson. A trustee at the County Jail serving a sentence for armed robbery, Jackson claimed to have heard Anzures confess to the murder after one of his court appearances during the preliminary hearing.

According to Jackson's statement in a police report dated February 7, 1979, "He was assigned to module D-1 of the Men's Central Jail where he met, talked with, and played cards with Art Anzures. Jackson told investigators that on January 15, Art returned from court and appeared to be pissed off. Anzures said he had been run in and out of court all day long. My lawyer had got on my case cause when I was in the other modules I told a couple of Essey's about my case and how I strangled somebody. One Essey came to court and testified, and the other one is supposed to come tomorrow and testify against me. He got on the stand and told the court what I had told him. My lawyer told me I fucked up for talking in the module. I had no witnesses against me until these guys came. Nobody saw me at the scene of the crime, and nobody saw me leave the scene of the crime. I told the cops that I was at home with my kids who are 2, 5, and 7. The 7 year old believes in Santa Clause (spelling mistake is their's). My wife was at work and no neighbor was home."

The report goes on to say that, "Art told Mr. Jackson that he had paid his lawyer $17,000 and that he lived in South Pasadena or south of Pasadena. Mr. Jackson stated that he would testify. He did not ask for, nor was he offered, any consideration."

In Cross examining Winn and Aragon, Mitch did a good job of discrediting the alleged jailhouse confession by showing that the two snitches were offered help with their cases in exchange for their testimony, and the prosecutor didn't want to fall into that trap with Jackson. There was also the matter of timing of the statement. Did the police think we were so stupid as to believe that this confession was not a response to the Judge nearly throwing their case out of court? Maybe I was overestimating their intelligence, but I would've thought that Kushner and Beck would have had the good sense to wait for a few days before manufacturing more evidence.

This statement from Jackson further convinced me that the purpose of arresting Anzures was to cover up the truth behind the murder. It also demonstrated that they didn't know their suspect very well. For one thing, Art Anzures didn't talk that way. He didn't sound tough and never used the street lingo of Mexican gangsters. He was strictly middle class. That's the way he thought and talked. Furthermore, the details of his life, like how many kids he had, the ages of each one, and how much he paid his lawyer was out of context with the rest of the statement. Cops supplied these details to Jackson to bolster the credibility of his statement concerning this confession and not too far down the road, it became a curiosity to me how far they would go to keep the probability that Leslie Barry was a Hillside Strangler victim from becoming public.

Despite how obvious it was that these jailhouse confessions were phony, Mitch was clearly concerned about the statement from Jackson. We all want to believe in the honesty and integrity of our police officers, but what I was witnessing was a disgrace to law enforcement. These cops weren't the least bit interested in the truth. What worried me most was that the defense lawyer seemed to be buying into their bullshit.

"If Art didn't make that statement to Jackson, how did Jackson get the information about how many kids Art had and how much he paid me for representing him?" Mitch asked me in a phone conversation shortly after I had read the statement.

"Easy," I responded, "the cops supplied Jackson with the information about Art's kids and your retainer."

"Where would the cops get the information?" Mitch wanted to know.

"They could've gotten it by monitoring the jail phones during family visits." I responded. "They do that all the time."

"I talked to Art about it," Mitch said, "and he denies making the statement. He told me he had a witness who could verify that he didn't make the statement. The guy's name is Lorenz Karlic. Karlic was in the same cell as Art and this Lyle Jackson character. I want you to locate him and get a statement from him and find out if he would be willing to testify in court for Art."

This exchange with Mitch upset me. By phone I had been keeping Mitch informed of every step of my investigation including my analysis and conclusion that the Barry murder was most likely connected to some of the Hillside Strangler murders. It was early in the case, and I didn't have any good suspects in the murder. I had cleared William Asper by determining that he really did own a red Porsche, and that he was telling the truth about not being at the apartments that day. It seemed like the stronger my argument became, the more concerned Mitch was that he was representing the Hillside Strangler in Art Anzures.

After the preliminary hearing, the Anzures family raised the bond money to spring Art, and that evening Art spent the first night in six weeks at home with his wife and kids.

My spirits were buoyed by Judge Franciscus' decision to set bail in the case. I thought that, in spite of the dishonest conduct of the police, the system might work after all. For several weeks, I had been considering calling the Hillside Strangler Task Force to inform them of the facts surrounding the Barry murder. Now, I felt, was a good time to go for it.

I dialed the main number for the LAPD and asked for the Hillside Strangler Task Force. My call was immediately routed to the appropriate extension. After a few rings, a man with a deep, gruff voice came on the line and identified himself as Lieutenant Ed Henderson. Maybe it was just his rudeness, but he didn't sound like a man interested in getting tips from the public about the Hillside Strangler investigation. Henderson had all the subtlety of an earthmover, and I thought the LAPD would've been better served by assigning a more personable individual with a better understanding of public relations to answer the Hillside Strangler Task Force telephone.

I identified myself and told the grating voice on the other end of the line that I was a private investigator in Pasadena. I didn't want to stay on the phone too long with this guy, so I got right to the point. I had picked up a murder case that the Task Force might be interested in. Just as I started to run down a few facts on the Barry murder, the asshole interrupted me to inquire who the homicide cop assigned to the case was. When I replied that it was Sergeant Dave Kushner and Deputy Jerome Beck from the Sheriff's Homicide Bureau, Henderson told me that Dave Kushner had been on the task force and was privy to all the information on the Hillside Strangler case. Kushner, he said, would have informed them had there been any indication of a connection between the two cases.

The conversation, if you could call it that, had lasted for less than two minutes, and when I got off the phone, I felt embarrassed. Henderson' unwillingness to talk to me, or even listen to what I had to say, gave me an inkling of why the Hillside Strangler Task Force was unable to solve the case and catch this killer. Far from being discouraged, I would meet his stubbornness with my own. It made me more determined than ever to find more evidence to show a connection to the Delores Cepeda/Sonja Johnson/Kristina Weckler murders. "Fuck 'em, I thought, "I'll do it myslf."

I went back to work. From the beginning, I had approached the investigation from two different angles. As the defense investigator it was my responsibility to investigate facts and locate witnesses to discredit the prosecution's case and help the defense lawyer establish a reasonable doubt in the minds of the jury. To that end, I tracked down witnesses, took statements and served subpoenas to assure their appearance in court. It was a time consuming process but an extremely important job. While I was working on the Anzures case, I let my other work slide and incoming cases had slowed to a trickle.

This case, in sheer magnitude of what was at stake, was more important than any case I had ever worked on or would ever work on again. From an investigative standpoint, what made it such a valuable case was that in all the other Hillside Strangler murders, the police had not had a crime scene to work with. They had complained publicly about how the lack of a crime scene made it difficult to collect and piece together evidence. All they had to go on were sketchy statements from a few eyewitnesses and the bits and pieces of evidence left at drop sites. I was offering them a crime scene to investigate and they weren't interested in it. For some reason this murder had fallen on me to solve, and if I couldn't solve it, there might be a lot more Leslie Barrys.

I felt that the Hillside Strangler had tripped up big time on the Barry murder and this case deserved more attention than the police were willing to give it. Given the importance of the case, letting my work slide for the time being didn't bother me in the least. I couldn't afford to spread myself too thin and I figured that when this case was over I'd have more clients beating down my door than I could possibly handle.

Art's trial was six weeks away and if I was going to clear him of the Barry murder I needed to know more about what kind of person the Task Force was looking for in the Hillside Strangler case. I went back to the library to dig deeper into the background of the infamous serial murders that had Southern Californians gripped by fear.

My earlier research had turned up an interesting police profile of the killers. In analyzing what little evidence they managed to obtain, the Task Force profilers reached the conclusion that they were looking for two or more suspects. Heterosexual serial killers rarely murdered in pairs and profilers concluded that the killers were acting out a shared psychosis. The expert criminal behaviorists speculated that for two people to be acting out the same episodes at the same time probably meant that they were related by blood and raised together in the same environment. That they shared a common genetic pool and were raised with identical parental influences and parallel mental and emotional development was the only reasonable explanation for having multiple serial killers connected to the same murders.

In addition, the way some of the victims had been abducted indicated that one of the killers might be a police officer or at least someone extremely familiar with police procedure. The Task Force was keeping much of the vital information out of the press. At the time of my research, I couldn't find the evidence to support it, but the profilers seemed to believe that one of the killers might be a disgruntled cop, ex-cop, or someone who had been turned down for employment with the LAPD.

The more I learned about the Hillside Strangler case the more I wondered how the Leslie Barry murder fit into the scheme of things.

The facts of the Barry murder didn't jive with what I was learning about the Hillside Stranglers. Other than being a sexually motivated, ligature strangulation murder, there didn't seem be many similarities between Leslie Barry and the other victims. For one thing, the profile I developed from the facts of the Barry murder didn't match with the profile on the Hillside Stranglers.

Rather than a police officer, evidence in the Barry murder indicated that the killer was adept at tying knots and had a good working knowledge of anatomy. Those facts led me to the conclusion that in the Barry murder I was looking for a single perpetrator with a medical background. Yet, I was certain that because of the close connection between Dolly Cepeda and Leslie Barry the murders were somehow related.

It stood to reason that if the Task Force were looking for multiple killers, it would be a logical assumption that one of the killers might have a police background and the other one a medical background. It was also apparent from the facts that there was only one killer in the Barry murder and not two as was the consensus in the Hillside Strangler profile. If Barry was a Hillside Strangler victim, did that mean they were now killing separately? If so, had there been some kind of rift between the two killers? Had one of them moved to another location? The possibilities were overwhelming, and I needed to let it rest and get back to doing what I could for Art's defense.

I went to the LA County Jail to talk to Lorenz Karlic. I knew what Karlic would say even before I talked to him. There are inmates who snitch and there are those who don't. Snitches are the worst kinds of cowards. They do the crime but they don't want to do the time, and they always expect a get-out-jail-free card in exchange for helping the cops put someone else away.

Then there are convicts like Lorenz Karlic who know how to do hard time. It was a simple matter to locate Lorenz Karlic. He was up for second-degree murder and still in County Jail awaiting sentencing. At the men's central jail in downtown Los Angeles, the jailer wanted me to talk to Lorenz over the visitors phone, but I refused and told him I wanted an attorney conference room. He asked for my bar card and I told him I wasn't a lawyer but I worked for an attorney and what I had to say to Karlic was protected by the attorney/client privilege. After calling a supervisor, he relented and gave me an attorney room.

Lorenz Karlic was a convict who looked and acted the part. He did not disappoint me or waste my time with niceties. His statement was short and simple. He and Art usually played cards when Art got back from his court appearances, and Art never talked about his case or what went on in court when he returned to the cell. Lorenz said he would be more than happy to testify to that in court. I knew that by being a convict, his credibility, like that of Winn, Aragon, and Jackson, would be suspect. I asked him if anyone else was in the cell at the time the alleged confessions were made who could back him up. It was a four-man cell and Lorenz gave me the name of the other inmate who shared the cell at the time.

Besides researching the Hillside Strangler murders, my interview with Lorenz Karlic gave me another important task to do on the case. I needed to track down Armando Gonzales and take his statement. If Gonzales backed Karlic and was willing to testify, the statement from Lyle Jackson would be sufficiently discredited.

It was perplexing to me why the Task Force was not interested in the Barry murder. With the baffling rejection by Ed Henderson ringing in my ears, I went to work in earnest to learn everything I could about the Task Force and the Hillside Stranger investigation.

CRIME SCENE PHOTOGRAPHS

(Full color photographs can be viewed on author's Myspace page)

Figure 3

Open door to victim' apartment can be seen left of the stairs

Figure 2

Porch swing to the left of the apartment door partially blocks killer's
escape route see figure 3

Figure 3

Porch swing and stairwell leading to the carport area demonstrates the level of difficulty of the jump the killer made to escape the crime undetected

Figure 4

Mother's bedroom where victim spoke on the phone before the murder

Figure 5

Victim's bedroom poster lying on the floor adjacent
and the TV set facing the window and not the bed.

Figure 6

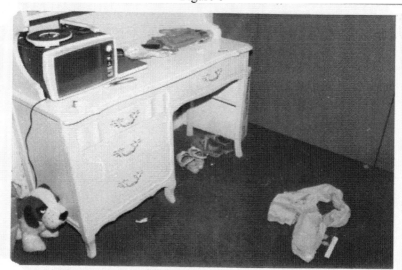

Victims pink pajama bottoms and pliers laying on the dresser
were used, without evidence, to convict Anzures.

Figure 7

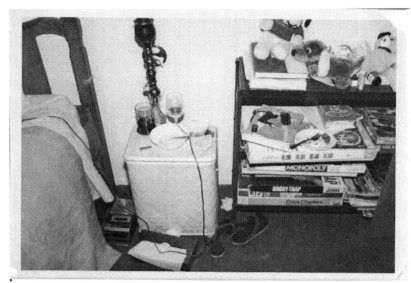

The murder weapon stretched across a cluttered hamper.
The cord on the bed was to a lamp paramedics brought from
another room.

Figure 8

The murder weapon with the bedroom door in view. The pliers are
visible in the lower right hand corner

Figure 9

Two views of the murder weapon.

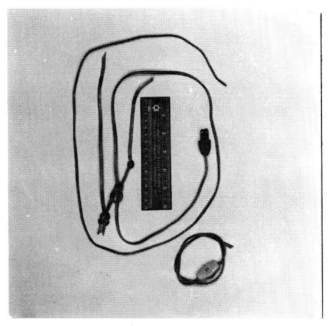

Figure 10

Figure 11

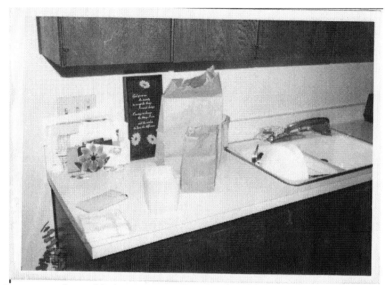

Grocery sacks on kitchen counter. Det. Beck said the sacks contained dairy products and were brought to the crime scene by South Pasadena police officers.

Figure 12

Cigarette butt in toilet tossed there by Det. Kushner

The Hillside Strangler

Chapter 14

The discovery of the body of twenty-six year old Laura Collins on September 9, 1977, near Forest Lawn Drive, passed without notice in the media. Between the gang bangers, stick up men, drug dealers, violent domestic squabbles, and a plentiful supply of garden-variety psychopaths, Los Angeles is never short on murder victims. In a city and county the size of Los Angeles, they are as common as lithe, suntanned beach bunnies. From 1974 to 1978, on average, there were seventeen strangulation murders of females in Los Angeles County.

On October 18, joggers found the body of Yolanda Washington in a wooded area near Griffith Park. Hardly a month went by without a prostitute being beaten, stabbed, shot, or strangled by her pimp. There was no apparent link between the murders of Collins and Washington, and the media afforded them the same consideration as most of the other eight hundred murders in Los Angeles that year. They ignored them. The press corps wasn't beating a path to the LAPD headquarters to demand that a task force be formed to find the killer of a Hollywood prostitute.

The discovery of the body of fifteen-year-old Judith Lynn Miller on October 31 in La Crescenta, ushered in the deadly month of

November, when the bodies of young girls and women began to turn up with a frightening regularity.

Nineteen-year-old Theresa Berry was found on November 4 in the city of Walnut. She was partially clothed, and the cause of death was strangulation. On November 6, a woman hiker discovered the body of twenty-one year old Elissa Teresa Kastin in a ravine near Chevy Chase Drive in the city of Glendale. She was nude and the cause of death was strangulation after molestation. On the same day as Ms. Kastin, seven-year-old Margaret Elizabeth Madrid turned up in a gutter in the City of Industry. The young girl was fully clothed and had been strangled.

On November 10, the body of eighteen-year-old Jill Barcomb was found on a road leading to the Franklin Canyon Reservoir in West Los Angeles. The cause of death was not immediately determined, but it appeared she died of blunt force trauma to the head. Later the coroner would confirm that Jill Barcomb died from a head injury.

On November 17, the body of seventeen-year-old Kathleen Kimberly Robinson was found in the Wilshire district. She was fully clothed, and sexual assault was not immediately determined.

Three bodies were found on Sunday, November 20, making it the deadliest day of the month. The nude body of a twenty year old art student from Glendale was discovered in the bushes along the side of Wawona Street in Highland Park. Kristina Weckler was abducted from her Glendale apartment the night before her body was found. The sheets on her bed were turned back, and her nightgown was found neatly folded and lying on the toilet seat.

On the afternoon of November 20, a neighborhood kid, playing in a ravine off Landa Street in Elysian Park, made the grisly discovery of the nude bodies of twelve-year-old Delores Cepeda and fourteen year old Sonja Johnson. The two girls were found a short distance from the LAPD police academy.

On November 23, the body of twenty-eight year old Evelyn Jane King was found near Griffith Park; and on November 29, the carnage of November ended with the murder of eighteen-year-old Lauren Rae Wagner. Her nude and strangled body was found on Mount Washington.

The press started to pick up the serial killer story in early November. The coverage escalated to an all out media blitz when Delores Cepeda and Sonja Johnson disappeared while returning home from a shopping trip to the Eagle Rock Plaza. The disappearance of the two girls touched off the largest manhunt in Los Angeles history. While hoping for the best, everyone feared that the girls had fallen victim to a fiend who was on the loose in the area. Hundreds of volunteers posted fliers and searched door to door for the girls. The story dominated the front-page news and was the lead on every TV news station in Los Angeles. These girls were not Hollywood hookers; they were not connected to the street scene at all.

Both girls came from solid, middle class families. Their parents cared about where they were and kept a close watch over them. Dollie Cepeda and Sonja Johnson were representative of every girl. If something like this could happen to good Catholic girls like Dollie and Sonja, it could happen to anyone. The press was all over the story and every decent person in LA was hoping and praying that the girls would be found alive and returned home safe.

A week after the disappearance a pall loomed over Los Angeles when the heartbreaking announcement was made that the nude and strangled bodies of the two girls were discovered in a ravine near the police academy. The media went nuts. They couldn't seem to find enough people to blame for the deaths. Mostly they focused their venom on the LAPD. The police had waited for forty-eight hours before taking a missing persons report on the girls, and the delay caused the trail to become cold. The press also took them to task for not committing enough officers to the search. The police, as saddened as everyone else by the grim discovery, were stung by the criticism from the media.

The LAPD responded to the attacks by putting together a thirteen-man task force. As time wore on without arrests being made, the discovery of each new victim brought more headlines and more pressure on the police to solve the murders. The police reacted to the intense public pressure by increasing the size of the task force. It went from thirteen detectives and officers to twenty-nine to forty and kept climbing with every Headline. Within a few months, the size of the task force reached a peak of more than two hundred detectives and police officers from three different jurisdictions.

The massive publicity brought out the worst in people and hampered the investigation more than it helped. Everyone wanted a piece of the action. Editors were playing up the murders to sell newspapers. Reporters were coming up with angles to please their editors, and some saw Pulitzer Prize written all over the story. Citizens were calling in with bogus leads in hopes of collecting reward money. Domestic disputes often ended with a wife or girlfriend accusing her husband or boyfriend of being the Hillside Strangler.

The police were not immune to the Hillside Strangler mania either. Getting credit for solving the case could produce huge rewards. It could bring promotions in rank, movie deals, and the love and gratitude of a thankful city. Rather than being an incentive for cooperation, with so many egos on the case, the potential for all the perks and benefits caused divisions in the ranks. Detectives were not eager to share information they collected with other detectives for fear that someone else would get the credit for their work. If that wasn't bad enough, they were presumably looking for a police officer--one of their own-which meant that members of the task force were suspect as well. The public wondered, with the spotlight of the investigation shining on a suspected cop, if the task force was putting their best efforts into capturing the killer.

They had to be careful to whom they gave access to inside information. If insider knowledge about the investigation leaked to the public, or fell into the hands of the killer, it could enable the killer to escape detection and hinder arrest and prosecution. Information in the wrong hands could make a phony confession look real.

Other police departments were looking for a piece of the action too. If a woman was found strangled in a jurisdiction other than the original jurisdictions involved in the case, a suburban department would report it to the task force, and the next day the murder ended up on the front page of the LA Times as the work of the Hillside Strangler.

When Pasadena Park rangers found the partially clothed body of Paula Gwen Ward, dumped under a tree in a secluded area of

Pasadena near the Rose Bowl, they quickly determined that the victim had been strangled. They contacted the task force and the next day it was reported in the LA Times that Ward was the twelfth victim of the Hillside Strangler. The Pasadena Police, not getting the kind of response they were hoping for from the Hillside Strangler task force, formed their own task force. A few days later, they had a suspect in custody, and Paula Ward was immediately dropped from the list of Hillside Strangler victims.

The December 1, 1977, Los Angeles Times headline read: <u>10 Murders Believed Linked;</u> and the sub-headline read: <u>More Officers Will Probe Strangling Of 13 Women.</u> Huh? It wasn't until the last two paragraphs that the article informed the reader that three of the victims, Laura Collins, Theresa Berry, and Margaret Madrid, were eliminated by the task force as victims of the Hillside Strangler. To the media, more is better. More cops plus more victims equals more newspapers sold and more people tuning into the local TV news. "If it bleeds it leads" goes the old journalism adage about headline stories. This one bled and led for a long time.

The relationship between the press and the task force was like a Ping-Pong volley. If a body turned up anywhere in the great outdoors the press reported it as a hillside strangling. Within a day or two, the task force would eliminate it regardless of similarities it might have to other murders. Another body would turn up and they would go through the same process. Back and forth, day in and day out, the press attributed murders to the Hillside Strangler, and the task force would inevitably deny that a connection existed. After a while, the public didn't know how many strangler victims there were and which ones were actually linked. So many victims were turning up that even the task force couldn't make connections with much certainty. The murders all began to look alike and yet different at the same time.

This saturation and exaggeration made the female population so frightened they were afraid to go out after dark even to haul the trash to the curb. Nothing described the mood of certain areas of Los Angeles as poignantly as an LA Times editorial written by a woman so scared she was afraid to use her own name on the opinion piece. Calling herself Deirdre Blackstone, the Eagle Rock resident wrote

"Whoever he is, he's out there, he is stalking us where we live. These young women whom he rapes and strangles, then dumps naked in the ivy by the sides of our quiet streets—they could be ourselves…Even if the criminal does not, we know he wields a perverted power over us—almost as perverted as his deeds. Our only hope is that he will not wield that power much longer, or panic as well as death will overwhelm this neighborhood, once so seemly and serene."

In this war between two separate but equally cynical forces--the police who solve crimes and the press who report them--truth was taking a beating. Frustrated by the fierce competition for scoops and their inability to get exclusive information from the task force, the press stopped reporting the news and began making the news. They became active participants in the story by conducting their own investigations and reaching their own conclusions about the Hillside Strangler and who his victims were.

The daily criticism by the press forced the cops into a defensive position. The public was shaken to its core with fear. The mass hysteria following in the wake of every grisly headline seemed to guide many of the Task Force decisions and actions. The public saw their attempts to solve the case as pathetic, and with the knowledge that a police officer was suspected of being the Hillside Strangler, the LAPD had no credibility. Public support for the police was paper-thin, and the public had lost all confidence in the cops ability or desire to solve the murders. Public safety, collateral to the Hillside Strangler case, became a major issue.

The sale of small caliber handguns to women increased significantly. There were reports that women were afraid to pull their cars to the side of the road when beckoned by the flashing lights of a patrol car. Officials felt that it was only a matter of time before a police officer and a frightened female citizen would get into a running gun battle ending in death or serious injury. Emotions ran high, and it was a dangerous and volatile time in Los Angeles.

Extraordinary circumstances call for extraordinary measures, and the press entered into an uncomfortable truce with the LAPD. Concessions were made, and the media stopped reporting every murder as a connection to the Hillside Strangler. They agreed to wait for the task force to make the call as to which murders were connected to the Hillside Strangler and which were not. Without the media running up the body count causing the public to panic, the task force was able to quell public hysteria by keeping the number of victims low. The Hillside Strangler was no longer getting credit for his murders when the Task Force settled on ten victims. The task force kept the count at ten victims simply by not looking at any other strangulation murders as a possible connection to the Hillside Strangler. However, they didn't keep the same ten victims from beginning to end. The task force sometimes substituted one victim out for another victim. The press stopped counting too, limiting their victim count to thirteen.

Although they had stopped attributing every strangulation murder to the Hillside Strangler, the media still kept the pressure on the task force to solve the murders. The press switched from the tactic of relying on public fear to apply pressure on the cops, to the less frightening, but still maddening issue of wasting the taxpayer's money on a huge, awkward task force that wasn't getting the job done. The already low morale in a police department under siege plummeted even further.

Within the first few weeks, the costs of the investigation escalated to half a million dollars. Still there were no suspects in the murders and investigators started to chase shadows. Two members of the task force were dispatched to England to investigate a lead so remote that the trip came under scrutiny by the media. It was easy to dismiss the excursion as a desperate attempt to turn up a lead in the case. With two investigators spending nearly 3 weeks in England, presumably investigating a lead, it looked like a fishing expedition at taxpayers' expense. There was some speculation that investigating a clue to the case was just a cover story, and that the real reason the Task Force sent investigators to England was to get advice and help from Scotland Yard.

If the behavior of mainstream society seemed bizarre, it was nothing compared to the reaction of the fringe crowd. The massive media attention brought out the loonies. To the many psychos and sociopaths of Los Angeles, the massive publicity suggested it was open season on women. Got a woman you'd like to see dead? Just strangle her and drop the body in the brush or on a hillside and you either get a free pass, or, if you get caught, a lot of notoriety as the

Hillside Strangler. Either would work for the true lunatic, but the proliferation of copycat murders was playing hell with the task force's ability to connect the dots.

The case was also a boon for the crazies who loved to confess to crimes they didn't commit to get publicity. Some phoned in their confessions, at least one wrote a letter, and still others showed up at the Parker Center in person. Most were easily eliminated as viable suspects by not possessing detailed knowledge of the murders. These confessors supported the legitimacy of their confessions with a few well-publicized facts that anyone could get from reading the newspaper.

If fake confessions weren't enough, overreactions by the police themselves exacerbated the problem. Police departments often sell their old cars to the public at auction. In one instance, a police captain was driving home in his car when he spotted what he thought was an unmarked police car. He waved at the fellow driving the car but the guy didn't wave back. Knowing that they were looking for a cop or a cop impersonator as the Hillside Strangler, the captain made a U-turn, pulled the guy over, and arrested him for impersonating a police officer. After hauling an innocent and bewildered citizen in for questioning they released him from custody after realizing he didn't have anything to do with the murders.

By December, the serial killer, who had become known worldwide as the Hillside Strangler, had either quenched his thirst for death, or the media and task force were successfully keeping the public from hearing about new victims. There was only one victim attributed to the killer in the last month of the year. On December 14' the body of seventeen-year-old Kimberly Diane Martin was found in the Silver Lake district of Los Angeles. Kimberly Martin was discovered just a few hours after she was sent on a business outing to an apartment on Tamarind Street in Hollywood. The attractive young victim was a nude model for the Climax Nude Modeling Service. Kimberly Martin was the last victim of 1977.

The New Year began with no new reports of strangled women. Then in February, the Hillside Strangler struck again.

On February 17, 1978, the nude and strangled body of Cindy Lee Hudspeth was found in the trunk of her car. The car was shoved off Angeles Crest highway and into a canyon in the hills above the affluent area of La Canada. The headlines and front-page stories started again. Just when things seemed to be getting back to normal, the news that the strangler had claimed another life renewed public awareness that the Hillside Strangler was still on the loose. Public pressure on the task force to solve the case and catch the killer was, to quote famed Yankee catcher, Yogi Berra, "déjà vu all over again."

The task force was working on the notion that Hollywood was the common thread providing the connection to the murders, but the connection to Hollywood and some of the victims, Kristina Weckler, Sonja Johnson, Delores Cepeda, Lauren Wagner, and Cindy Hudspeth was weaker than weak.

Police made an all out effort to tie every one of these women to Hollywood. The connections they found between some of the victims and Hollywood pushed the envelope on believability. At the height of public attention on the case, so-called witnesses would tell investigators anything about anyone in hopes of getting recognition for helping the police solve the case. Most of it was just rumors, gossip, lies, and speculation. The task force came up with things like Cindy Hudspeth loved to go out dancing and had once gone to a dance party at the Palladium on Hollywood Boulevard; or that Sonja Johnson was into the drug culture and would secretly catch the bus from Eagle Rock to the Sunset Strip to hang out. There were even reports that Sonja had gang ties and was heavy into drugs and prostitution. The task force felt certain that the connection between the killer and the two youngest victims originated with Sonja Johnson and not Dolly Cepeda.

Serial killers usually have a criteria for selecting their victims, and the task force did everything it could to establish a link between the prostitute victims and the other victims. Given the various ages, lifestyles and races of the victims, it was a confusing and daunting task.

Normally, if a serial killer is preying on prostitutes it is a part of their pathology and psychosis to kill prostitutes and they stick with killing prostitutes. A part of the general profile on serial killers is that they select their victims based upon a particular look. For example, all victims would be in the same age group and have long brown hair and large breasts. With pedophile serial killers, their victims would all be under the age of twelve or look like they were.

Black serial killers would always kill within their own race, while Caucasian Serial killers would usually have special criteria for victim selection.

Among the ten victims the task force determined were linked to the same killer, a selection criterion was not easy to find. A likeness between the victims didn't jump out at you. The victims ranged in age from twelve to twenty-eight; they wore different hairstyles; had different body types; and one, a black female named Yolanda Washington, was a different race than the others. Even Cepeda and Johnson were Hispanic.

The methods employed in abducting the victims weren't the same either. A hooker, by the nature of her work, is a vulnerable target. A prostitute will get into a car with anyone she perceives as a potential John and they don't object if a guy wants to take them to a secluded area for sex.

Dollie Cepeda and Sonja Johnson were abducted from the street without a struggle during daylight hours. Kristina Weckler was lured or abducted from her apartment while getting ready for bed. According to an eyewitness, two men in the dead of night forced Lauren Wagner into a car. Cindy Hudspeth was the only victim found stuffed in the trunk of her car. Her red Datzun was found in such a remote area that it would have been nearly impossible for the killer to walk back to civilization without being noticed. There must have been two killers.

The major variations in victim selection, method of abduction, and the psychological profile of the killer, indicated that more than one killer was committing the murders. Deputy Chief of Police, Daryl Gates, stated publicly that the task force believed there could be as many as five killers involved in the Hillside Strangler murders. Such public statements concerning the thoughts and mental processes of investigators upset members of the task force and inhibited private discussions about the case even within the secure walls of the Parker Center.

On January 19, 1978, a letter was sent to Mayor Tom Bradley. It was a bizarre document professing to be from the Hillside Strangler. When the letter arrived it sat on the Mayors desk, unopened, for a couple of weeks. Bradley came under intense criticism by assistant Chief of Police, Daryl Gates, for not arranging to have his official mail opened by a member of his staff or the deputy mayor while he was out of town. In the letter, the writer indicated he wanted to turn himself and a friend in, but he feared for his safety. He asked in the letter for the Mayor to respond publicly to the letter and give him assurances that he would be treated fairly if he turned himself in.

The writer requested publicity for the seven-page, hand written letter, and it was given front-page attention by the Los Angeles Times. The Times published the entire first page, which read:

"Dear Mr Mayor
PLEASE!!
Lisson to me. I am very
Sick. But I do not want
Go back to that place.
I hate that place. My mother
Told me to kill those bad and evil
Lady. Its not my fault. My
Mother makes my head hurt. That
Why I kill her but I can't
get her out of my head. She
keep coming back. I hate her.

Mayor Bradley did as the writer requested and gave his public assurances that, should the writer turn himself and his friend in, they would be treated fairly and not harmed in anyway. The Mayor also asked the writer to respond again and include the same information he had put in the letter.

Although the letter appeared on the front page of the LA Times, the media kept publicity at a minimum. After a week or so, without a response from the writer, it was dismissed as a grotesque prank from another loony and faded from the public consciousness.

In May, 1978, the task force saw some real promise for a solution to the case. A man named Richard Reynolds was lying in wait in the parking lot of Glendale Community Hospital for Roxanne Barnwell to come to her car. The task force would never get an opportunity to question Mr. Reynolds about other murders he might have been involved in.

Roxanne Barnwell, armed with a pistol, shot Reynolds once in the head and five times in the chest. Reynolds managed to get off a couple of shots, which struck Roxanne Barnwell, killing her. They both died in Barnwell's car and Glendale police called it a double murder.

Several things about the Barnwell incident interested the task force. Their investigation quickly turned up a criminal history on Reynolds for assault and rape. He was a registered sex offender. Besides that, Windsor Road, the location of the car where Reynolds and Barnwell were found, was only a block from Garfield Avenue where two of the Hillside Strangler victims, Kristina Weckler and Cindy Hudspeth, lived.

The task force got a search warrant for Reynolds' place on Foothill Boulevard in La Crescenta, and while they didn't find any evidence to link him to the Hillside Strangler case, they did note that he lived just two blocks from where the body of Judith Miller was found. A neighbor of Reynolds told reporters that he had found women's clothing in a trash bin and reported it to the police. It looked to the neighbor as if the clothing had bloodstains on it. The information slipped through the cracks of the bureaucracy and the police didn't investigate the lead.

Richard Reynolds, a respiratory technician in Altadena, was from a prominent family of doctors in Oxnard, an oceanside city about sixty miles north of Los Angeles. It didn't escape the discerning eyes of investigators that a respiratory technician might have special knowledge of strangulation techniques.

When word of the shooting reached the Oxnard and Port Hueneme Police Departments, they notified Los Angeles Police that Reynolds closely resembled a composite drawing of a man wanted for questioning in the strangulation deaths of three Oxnard prostitutes.

Kimberly Fritz was discovered in a motel room in Port Hueneme on May 29, 1977, and Velvet Sanchez was found strangled in an Oxnard motel room a few months later. A third Oxnard prostitute, Loraine Rodriquez, was strangled and her body unceremoniously dumped along the roadside in December. The similarities of these three murders left little doubt that they were connected to one another. Whether they were also connected to the Hillside Strangler case was not something the task force really wanted to consider. They had more than enough victims already and didn't need the additional pressure from the press.

The task force might have been more interested in Reynolds if he hadn't been dead and if they didn't already have a live suspect in custody at the time. George Shamshak, a petty and not very bright criminal doing time for armed robbery, escaped from a minimum-security prison in Massachusetts in October of 1977. After escaping from prison, he immediately hitchhiked to California.

Upon his arrival in California, Shamshak moved into an apartment with an acquaintance from Massachusetts named Peter Mark Jones. His brother, Sam Shamshak, a struggling actor, lived in the same building as Jones. Thinking that his brother George had been legally paroled from the Massachusetts prison, Sam recommended him for a job as the apartment manager of the apartment building where they lived. George Shamshak, fearing that the fingerprint check necessary to secure a bond for the job would reveal his escape from the Massachusetts prison, went on the lam again.

Shamshak was re-arrested in Massachusetts in February of 1978, as he got off the train in Boston. He was taken back to Walpole prison to finish serving his sentence for armed robbery. Shamshak had snitched on some inmates at Walpole and feared for his life. Two days after being locked up, he contacted a Massachusetts State Police Investigator and told him that he had knowledge about the Hillside Strangler case in Los Angeles.

Providing details about a couple of the murders attributed to the Hillside Strangler, he told the Massachusetts investigator that he was driving a blue van while the man he was with, a friend of his from Massachusetts now living in California, beat up a girl in the back of the van. Portraying himself as an innocent bystander, Shamshak told the investigator that he hadn't personally been involved in the murders. He said that he didn't know at the time he agreed to drive the van that Jones planned to kill the girls. His story sounded credible to the Massachusetts State Police and they contacted the Hillside Strangler Task Force.

Members of the task force were sent to Massachusetts to check out the lead. A number of things interested them about the Shamshak story. In a couple of the murders, witnesses had mentioned a dark colored van being in the area at the time of the abductions. Also, Shamshak seemed to know, like instant recall, that Jill Barcomb had been beaten to death rather than strangled. Being an escaped convict in Los Angeles during November, when most of the murders occurred, gave added credibility to his statements.

There was also the matter of his look. With his bushy hair and bad complexion, Shamshak had the general physical appearance the task force was looking for in one of the Hillside Stranglers. The cops believed he was telling the truth and had him brought back to Los Angeles for further questioning.

Shamshak' statements seemed credible to the task force, and Peter Mark Jones was arrested and booked on suspicion of murder on Thursday, March 30, 1978. The timing of the arrest gave the task force very little time to make a case against him or let him go.

If being arrested and fingered, as the Hillside Strangler wasn't bad enough, to add to his woes, the next day Jones was the front-page headline of the Los Angeles Times. The Times assigned several reporters to do background stories on Jones. After interviewing neighbors and coworkers, what they came away with was a profile, not of a dangerous serial killer, but of an honest, sincere, hard working, pleasant guy who was liked and respected by everyone who knew him.

On Monday, April 3, 1978, after spending his weekend in jail and being the lead story in the media around the world, Peter Mark Jones was released from custody. Daryl Gates made a very public apology to him but the damage had been done, not only to Jones's reputation, but the task force's credibility as well. Even though they still had George Shamshak in custody, the task force had egg on its face.

To insure that this sort of reckless accusation didn't happen again, District Attorney John Van De Kamp assigned a couple of his top prosecutors, Roger Kelley and James Heins, to oversee the Shamshak investigation.

Members of the task force, wanting desperately to avoid further embarrassment, were pushing hard for charges to be filed against George Shamshak in at least some of the murders. Roger Kelley was the one who would have to try the case and he wasn't eager to file murder charges without evidence to take to court.

As a result, of the continuing investigation into Shamshak, it was revealed publicly that one victim, Jill Barcomb, had teeth marks on her body. Kelley fought for weeks with Shamshak's Boston attorney,

Henry Wynn, to force Shamshak into allowing investigators to take plaster molds of his teeth. Finally, the suspect agreed and gave the teeth impressions voluntarily.

Dr. Gerald Vale, the forensic dentist for the Los Angeles County coroner's office, compared the plaster mold to the bite marks on Jill Barcomb and determined they didn't match. George Shamshak was a suspect for more than four months and during that time the task force was unable to find evidence to independently corroborate any part of his original confession. George Francis Shamshak was eventually returned to Massachusetts from the federal prison in San Diego where he had been held during much of the Hillside Strangler investigation. A short time later, he was released from the Massachusetts prison and disappeared. To this day some task force members still wonder how he came to know intimate details of a couple of the murders.

The release of Shamshak meant that the Hillside Strangler was still on the loose. The public was scared out its wits and in no mood to hear about other murders. They especially didn't want to hear about any more kids like Dolly Cepeda and Sonja Johnson being murdered. With the enormous political pressure bearing down on the police to solve the case, the Task Force was more than happy to oblige. They took a see-no-evil hear-no-evil attitude.

I wasn't aware of it at the time but that was the mindset of the Task Force when the Hillside Strangler struck again brutally murdering twelve-year old Leslie Fae Barry in her apartment in South Pasadena.

Chapter 15

I had asked Denise Anzures for the rental applications she had on file for the apartments early in my investigation. The applications contained vital information about the people who lived at the apartments or had applied to rent there, and I was surprised that the police had not taken the applications at the beginning of their own investigation. Without the information in those applications, the police didn't have a prayer of solving the Leslie Barry murder. Unlike the police, I hadn't jumped to any conclusions about the guilt or innocence of Art Anzures, and I wanted to do a thorough investigation. After analyzing the facts from police and autopsy reports and the crime scene photographs, conducting my own interviews and developing a specific profile of the killer based on evidence from the crime, I needed to learn all I could about the people who lived at the apartments and anyone who would be familiar with the layout of the complex.

For weeks, Mark Southerland and I had haunted the Court Clerks Office and the Hall of Records using the information from those applications to locate past tenants and applicants and develop background profiles on each one. Specifically, we were looking for anyone connected to the apartments who might have a record of child abuse or violent behavior against women and would fit the specific profile I had developed of the killer.

Since we were already there checking records on tenants, I thought I might as well pull the criminal court records on Armando Gonzales. Gonzales was the fourth man in the jail cell with Lorenz Karlic and Lyle Jackson when Art allegedly made the confession reported by Jackson. It didn't take me long to find his court file from the criminal index and locate Gonzales' probation officer.

Gonzales had been charged with rape but the charges had been dismissed because of a lack of evidence. Nevertheless, he was pressured to plead guilty to a lesser charge of breaking and entering and had received a suspended sentence with probation. As I suspected, the probation officer wasn't inclined to give out information on his probationer. Instead of getting information, I gave him information about contacting me and asked him to pass it along to Gonzales.

Art's trial date was creeping up on me and the closer it got the more pressure I felt from the constraints of time. While I waited for Gonzales to call, which I was certain he would do, I carefully reread all the reports, studied the photographs and reread the evidence and statements collected during my investigation.

After several months of talking to witnesses and analyzing the facts, I had come to believe completely in Art's innocence. He didn't fit the profile of the killer and from what I knew about the facts like the narrow timeline, the murder weapon, the route of escape and the statement from Shawn Hagen, I concluded that the Barry murder was undoubtedly linked to the infamous Hillside Strangler case. Still, a clear picture of the Leslie Barry murder had not yet emerged, and I was sure I had missed an important piece of information that could tie-up some loose ends and give me a better understanding of how the victim was murdered and who might have done it.

Browsing through the rental applications for the umpteenth time, I spotted something that I somehow had missed on previous readings. Well, maybe I hadn't missed it, but I hadn't connected the dots either.

Having just finished reading the statements given to the police from tenants, I was scanning the rental applications when I saw the name "Eddie" at the top of one of the applications. Seeing that name suddenly triggered the statement from Jeanne Marek about a guy named "Eddie" coming to her apartment and asking how many married and single women lived in the apartment complex. What caught my attention as much as anything was that he used the name "Eddie" and not Ed or Edward, and that told me he thought of himself as Eddie and would, out of pure habit, use Eddie when introducing himself to other people.

I sat there in stunned silence letting it sink in. Could this be the "Eddie" going around to apartments asking how many married and single women lived in the apartment complex? I hadn't come across the name Eddie Castillon in any of the statements from tenants and I wondered if the application might be a ruse of some sort to give him access to the apartment complex without raising suspicion. Maybe he never lived in the apartments or maybe he had moved out before the murder. I didn't know but I was going to find out.

I put the application down and called Denise.

"I've been going through these applications you gave to me," I said, "and I've come across one for Eddie Castillon. What can you tell me about him?" I asked.

"Well," Denise said after a short pause, "he moved into the apartment in the winter or fall of 1977 with his cousin, Tony. They were both students, and I think Eddie was going to dental school. Tony moved out in the summer and went back to Texas. I think he went there to become a police officer. I know they were both from Texas but I'm not sure where."

Denise continued her monologue and I was doing my best to contain my excitement over this new information. As I listened to Denise, I was mulling over in my mind the facts from my research on the Hillside Strangler case: They were related; one was a dental student and the other one was a police officer.

"After Tony moved out," Denise was saying, "a girl moved in with Eddie for about a week, then another friend of his named Dennis Cantu moved in with him. I think Dennis was a doctor or medical student or something like that."

Denise had no idea what she was telling me. Of course, there was no reason for her to know. She hadn't researched the Hillside

Strangler case and she hadn't read the reports or investigated the Barry murder.

"Dennis and Eddie moved out about a week or two before the murder," she added.

"Do you know what Tony was studying in college?" I asked.

"I think," Denise, responded a little uncertain about the accuracy of what she was saying, "that he was majoring in police science or criminal justice or something like that. I know it had something to do with law enforcement because he really wanted to be a police officer."

Denise had just given me information that fit with both my profile of the killer in the Barry murder and the profile developed by experts in the Hillside Strangler case. I told her I would call her back and hung up.

Eddie Castillon and Martin Anthony Smith had both filled out applications for renting the apartment, and I studied and compared the information on the applications about previous residences, landlords, and personal information like their names and dates of birth. I noticed that Eddie's middle name was Martin and Tony's full name was Martin Anthony Smith. It was an old custom to use the mother's maiden name for the son's first or middle names, and since they had different last names, I surmised that they were related on the maternal side of their family. They were also the same age and I wondered how I would ever find out if they were raised together.

Before moving to 400 Monterey Road, they listed their address as Crescent Street in Los Angeles. I was not familiar with that street, so I took out my Thomas Guide to find the exact location of Crescent Street. It was a short street just across the Pasadena freeway in Eagle Rock. The street was off York Boulevard not far from where Dolly Cepeda and Sonja Johnson had disappeared. It was less than a half mile from where both Dolly Cepeda and Leslie Barry lived.

Before moving to Crescent Street, they lived on Ontario Street in Pasadena. Again, I looked up the location for Ontario Street and saw it was located near the border of Glendale in the hills above the Rose Bowl. Ontario Street was not far from the Art Center College of Design where Kristina Weckler attended school. It was also near

Chevy Chase Drive, a major artery close to the street where Kristina Weckler's body had been found.

The rental applications gave me considerable personal information about the suspects to work with, and I wanted to start checking out these guys by talking to their previous landlords. They hadn't listed the landlord of the Crescent Street address but they did provide the name and phone number for the landlord of the Ontario Street address. I called the number for Nell Ritterrath.

When Mrs. Ritterrath answered the phone, I identified myself and told her I was investigating the murder of a twelve-year-old girl in South Pasadena and I was trying to locate all the former tenants of the apartment building where the young girl had been killed. I went on to tell her that I had gotten her name and phone number from a rental application filled out by Eddie Castillon and Martin Anthony Smith. I said I wanted to ask her a few questions about her former tenants. I was floored when she informed me that they were not former tenants but that Martin Smith was her son and Eddie was her nephew.

After learning of the close relationship between Ritterrath, Castillon, and Smith, I was not about to get overly personal with my questions to Mrs. Ritterrath. The conversation was sure to get back to Smith and Castillon and I didn't want them tipped off about becoming suspects in the murders. I asked her if she could provide me with a phone number for Eddie and Tony. She was more than happy to comply.

I was not in a big hurry to talk to Eddie after talking to Mrs. Ritterrath. I had learned about another murder, and I wanted to get some information on it before interviewing any of these three suspects.

From the County Hall of Records, I had obtained the death certificates on Cepeda, Johnson, Kristina Weckler, Kimberly Diane Martin, and the most recent victim, fifteen-year-old Elizabeth Cevallos. Of the four, Elizabeth Cevallos was not listed as a Hillside Strangler victim. I read about the Cevallos murder in the morning newspaper a day or two after it happened. The article said that the nude body of the young girl was found in the Rio Hondo wash in Pico Riviera on March 27, 1979. The Rio Hondo wash is a long drainage system that snakes across several cities and under major arteries of the Southeast section of Los Angeles County.

After coming up with their names, I quickly learned that when Cantu and Castillon moved from their Monterey Road apartment in South Pasadena, they moved to an apartment on Beverly Boulevard in Montebello. Beverly Boulevard is a major thoroughfare running east and west through Montebello and Pico Rivera. The address I had for the two men showed that they lived near the Rio Hondo Wash. The article had not stated the exact location where Elizabeth Cevallos was found, but I figured that if it was several miles from where Cantu and Castillon lived I could drop her from my list of victims.

The newspaper listed Sergeant Ray Verdugo of the Sheriff's Homicide Bureau as the investigating officer on the Cevallos murder. Always looking to save time and money, I tried to consolidate chores that were in the same area. I needed to go downtown to the Hall of Records and the Courthouse to do some marriage and divorce searches and decided to stop in and talk to Verdugo about the Cevallos murder.

Ray Verdugo and his partner were friendly and we had a pleasant exchange of information. After finishing my discourse on the facts of the Barry murder, about my suspicions of it being a Hillside Strangler murder and that my suspects lived on Beverly Boulevard in Montebello, they gave me some information on their Cevallos investigation.

Verdugo told me that Cevallos' body was found stuffed in a drainage filter where the Rio Hondo Wash intersected with Beverly Boulevard in Pico Rivera. He said he was initially investigating the case as a possible gang rape because her pants were pulled down around her ankles.

Detective Verdugo said she had not died of strangulation as reported in the newspaper. The coroner had determined that she had died of a brain hemorrhage from a severe blow on the head with a blunt instrument. Verdugo explained to me that at first he believed death was caused by strangulation because of a mark around her neck. There was also an electrical cord found at her feet. The rape kit came back negative for sperm and that eliminated the possibility of a gang rape. At the end of this informal meeting, Verdugo asked me if I wanted to speak with Sheriff Pitchess about the case. My investigation was still in the early stages and I felt it might be a little soon to take it to the big boys. I politely declined saying I wanted to do a little more work on it first. I told Verdugo I should get out of his hair. We got a good chuckle over the accidental pun when he ran his hand over his bald dome.

Hillside Strangler victim, Kimberly Diane Martin held an interest for me for no better reason than because her last name was Martin. I thought there might be a family connection between her and the cousins. At the Hall of Records, I did a complete records search on her as well as some of the other victims. According to her death certificate, Diane Martin was from Texas and her mother's maiden name was Smith. Her mom was also from Texas but I never determined where in Texas or what, if anything, a connection to Martin Anthony Smith might be. The death certificate on Elizabeth Cevallos listed San Antonio, Texas as the birthplace of her father, Benjamin Cevallos. The Cepeda's were also from that area and it seemed to me that Texas was becoming a common theme in some of the murders. I felt that the Kimberly Martin murder deserved a better investigation than I could afford to give it. I hoped that eventually I'd be able to get the Task Force to take a closer look at it regarding my suspects.

I wanted to get more information on the Cevallos murder and made an unannounced visit to the parents. The victim's mother, Irene Cevallos, told me that Elizabeth had ditched school on the Monday of her murder and her friends said they had seen her at the bowling alley on Beverly Boulevard and Howard Street. Mrs. Cevallos said she believed the friends because Elizabeth liked to ditch school and hang out at that bowling alley.

Getting a little more on point of my investigation, I asked her about any connection she might have to the USC/County Hospital or the USC Dental School. Mrs. Cevallos told me that she had gone to the dental school a few years back to have some work done and the student who did the work called her numerous times to come back in for a follow-up. I ran the names Dennis Cantu, Eddie Castillon and Martin Smith by her but they didn't spark any sign of recognition.

When I left the Cevallos residence, I decided to drive down Beverly Boulevard to see where the bowling alley was located in relationship to the site where the victim had been found and where my suspects lived. I was shocked to discover that the bowling alley was a short distance from the drop site and right across the street from the apartments where Cantu and Castillon lived. This was getting eerie and too bizarre to be a coincidence.

According to the media, the Task Force was hungry for leads and as far as I was concerned, Cantu, Castillon, and Smith were as good as leads ever get. If at the beginning of the case I felt like I was getting in over my head, it was nothing compared to the inadequacy I felt now. I needed to get rid of this case and turn it over to professionals with the resources and experience to do it right. I decided to try the Task Force again.

When I got the operator at the LAPD, I asked directly for Lieutenant Ed Henderson. The Lieutenant came on the line with the same gruff voice I had heard in the first phone call. It must've been an authority thing with him or maybe he was just an unhappy guy.

I reminded him that this was my second phone call to the Task Force and got right to the point of my call. I should've been suspicious when it didn't take much to get his interest this time. He took my phone number and address and said he'd have a couple of detectives contact me. I thanked him and hung up.

The next day I got a phone call from a Detective Mellecker of the Hillside Strangler Task Force. He and his partner wanted to meet with me at my office in Pasadena. I was delighted with this development. Finally, they were going to investigate this lead seriously and while I wanted to get back to work for my other clients, as long as Anzures was in the hot seat I couldn't abandon my investigation. In preparation for the meeting, I went through all the police reports and notes on my investigation and rehearsed my presentation. I was not taking this meeting lightly, and I hoped they weren't either.

When they arrived, I buzzed the two cops in and met them in the hallway outside my office door. Sergeant Mellecker introduced himself and his partner, Sergeant John Holder. I welcomed them to my office and directed them to take a seat in the two chairs in front of my desk. I hated talking to them with a desk between us but I needed somewhere to lay my notes and other materials.

Neither cop spoke much but when one did speak it was usually Mellecker. Holder didn't say anything during the meeting. I ran through the facts of the Barry murder starting with witness statements that established the time line of the murder. I told them about the mother's statement and how it indicated that the killer was inside the apartment when the mother got home from work and the daring escape over the wall and into the stairwell. I ended my synopsis of the Barry murder by showing them a picture of the knotted cord and explaining that according to the autopsy report two of the knots corresponded to pressure points on the neck.

I moved on to Shawn Hagen's statement about knowing one of the Hillside Strangler victims and explained how the three kids were connected by way of attending a small private school in South Pasadena at the same time. I covered Jeanne Marek's statement about "Eddie" coming by the apartment complex and asking how many single and married women lived in the complex and how that statement had been corroborated by another tenant.

I ended my presentation by telling them about how I came up with Castillon and Smith as suspects. I showed Mellecker a copy of the rental application and told him he was welcome to take a copy of it if he wanted it. He declined.

I told them how the suspects fit with the task force profile on the Hillside Strangler case. Smith was a police officer in Laredo and had been turned down for employment with the LAPD. He majored in police science at UCLA and was familiar with police procedure. Castillon and Smith were cousins.

The two suspects shared a house in the area where Cepeda and Johnson were abducted and would have been familiar with the area of the drop site of Kristina Weckler. To back up my statement with evidence I showed them a copy of my Thomas Guide in which I had marked the drop sites and the streets where victims Cepeda and Johnson lived as well as Castillon and Smith.

The meeting lasted for nearly an hour and I did most of the talking. I told them I felt that Cantu was involved someway, but I didn't have any idea how he figured into the murders. When I was finished with my presentation, Mellecker had one question for me, "What did the two suspects look like?" He asked.

I didn't have an eyewitness in the Barry murder so physical appearance was not important to me. Furthermore, I hadn't met either Smith or Castillon in person and didn't have the slightest idea what they looked like. The LA Times had published composite drawings of the Hillside Strangler suspects, and I had copies of those articles with the composites in my file. I answered Mellecker truthfully. I had never seen them and I didn't know what they looked like but if they had a physical description and were looking for someone with a specific look, they should go talk to the three suspects themselves.

As they were leaving, Mellecker's question weighed heavily on my mind. It was like nothing I said in the meeting was important to them unless I knew what the suspects looked like. As the two cops got up to leave, I told them that I felt that Cantu was involved in the murders in some way but I wasn't sure how he fit in.

"Maybe I'll see you out at Cantu's apartment." I said as they walked out the door.

I knew by the way they were acting that Mellecker and Holder were not going to investigate the case. For one thing, they weren't interested in taking any of the evidence or documents that I offered to copy for them. For another, they didn't ask any questions during the meeting. I was just a big pain in the ass to them and they only came out to my office to appease me and because a superior had told them to. If they thought they were through with me though, they were badly mistaken. I phoned Mellecker one more time about the Barry murder and his reaction to that phone call and my mounting frustration over their blasé attitude threw me into a blind rage.

A few months after the meeting at my office, Mellecker and I butted heads on another murder case unrelated to the Hillside Strangler case and if I didn't have any credibility with him on the Barry murder, he would soon find out that I could investigate a murder case as well, if not better, than anyone.

Chapter 16

Mellecker and Holder were not interested in my investigation of the Barry murder. In fact, they were not interested in anyone's investigation of the Barry murder. I was on my own. There would be no cavalry riding in to save the day for Art Anzures. I thought it was about time someone talked to Castillon and Smith and see what they had to say for themselves. If members of the Task Force wouldn't do it, I would. Mellecker wanted to know what the suspects looked like and I wanted to give him an answer. Besides, Art's trial was coming up and if was going to clear him of the Barry murder I needed to get busy. I phoned Eddie Castillon first.

My plan was to get background information on Smith by talking to Castillon and opening a line of communications with him. With limited financial resources and not having experience with an in-depth murder investigation, I was taking it slowly. Since Castillon lived locally, it would be easier and cheaper for me to check him out and get information on Smith from him. Ever since learning about Eddie's close residential proximity to the drop site and bowling alley where Elizabeth Cevallos was last seen alive, I was getting anxious about confronting him. Smith was not living in California at the time of either the Barry or the Cevallos murder and in my book, an alibi doesn't get much better than that. However, Smith was living with Eddie on Crescent Street in Eagle Rock shortly before the disappearance of Cepeda and Johnson and I suspected that he and Eddie had abducted and murdered the two girls.

Because of the geographical separation of the two men, my plan from the beginning was to play one against the other. I would ask Eddie questions about Smith and when I phoned Smith, I would ask him questions about Eddie. I decided to keep the conversational tone low key and objective. I didn't want him to know that he was a suspect in the murder. I planned to ask him general questions about the apartments and people he knew there and then get more detailed personal information about Smith later and see if there were other bits and pieces that fit with the Hillside Strangler profile.

Pretending he wasn't a suspect also quieted my jangling nerves. As I picked up the phone to dial Eddie's number, my palms were sweaty and I could feel my heart pounding inside my chest. I could've done with a strong shot of whiskey right about then. I needed to cover my nervousness or he would know I suspected him of something. I took a deep breath and dialed the number.

When Eddie answered the phone, he was friendly but cautious. When I introduced myself, he indicated that he knew who I was and I assumed he had heard about me from his aunt, Nell Ritterrath. He told me he knew about the Barry murder but he didn't say how, where, or what he'd heard about it. When I told him Art had been busted for the crime, he seemed genuinely surprised by that information. Eddie said he didn't know Art very well but he didn't think Art would commit murder.

I needed to get more personal with Eddie and he had already told me that he and Smith were cousins related on their Mothers' side of the family.

"Your mother's maiden name wouldn't happen to be Martin, would it?" I asked.

The question caught him off guard.

"Yeah, how did you know that?"

I debated with myself whether to keep him off guard or to clue him in that since both he and Smith had Martin in their names it was a good bet that Martin was a family name. I decided to keep him wondering.

"Well, Eddie," I replied, "I'm investigating a murder here. I find out a lot of things during the course of my work."

Eddie said he was a third year dental student at the USC School of Dentistry and that he moved out of the apartment on Monterey Road about a month before the murder. That period didn't jive with what Denise Anzures had told me and I wondered if he was trying to distance himself from the crime. Eddie told me that he lived at the Monterey Road apartments with Tony before Tony went back to Laredo to become a police officer. After Tony moved out, he lived with a girl for a brief time but that didn't work out and Dennis moved in. When Castillon said the name Dennis I didn't hear him correctly and I thought he said "dentist". We were going back and forth like an Abbott and Costello routine.

When I finally caught on to what he was saying, I asked him what Dennis did for a living. He said Dennis was a doctor doing his internship at USC Medical School. At that time, I wasn't that interested in Cantu so I let it drop.

I inquired as to why Tony hadn't joined a police department in California. Castillon replied that he had tried to get on with the LAPD but for some reason he was turned down.

I tried to pry a little deeper about Smith's police experience and aspirations but Eddie clammed up. I did get him to tell me that he and Smith were raised together in Laredo from the time Tony was about 12 until they graduated from high school; but when I asked him what circumstances caused that situation, he didn't want to discuss it. The little information I got from him was like pulling teeth and while I didn't voice it, I chuckled at myself for the pun.

I asked Eddie if he knew Leslie Barry or her mother, Aina. He said he had seen them around the apartment complex but couldn't say he really knew them.

I thanked him for his cooperation and he added that if there was anything he could do for me not to hesitate to call. That I would be contacting Eddie again was one thing in life he could count on.

By late April, I decided to crank up the investigation a notch and see if I could put some pressure on my suspects. I dialed the number

Ritterrath had given me for Tony Smith. When a woman answered the phone, I asked for Tony. It was one of my investigative techniques that when I didn't want to answer questions like "may I say who's calling?" or "may I ask what this is concerning" I always used the familiar name of the person I was phoning. You ask for Mr. Smith and it raises all kinds of questions about who you are and what you want. Use the familiar name and you're just an old friend calling up to shoot the shit.

I decided to use the bumbling private investigator ruse and play on his ego about how his superior knowledge and experience as a police officer could help me solve the case. Feeling like I was in over my head, I'm not sure the bumbling private eye routine was much of an act. Private Investigators often take on a disguise persona to get information. Some PI's even do it illegally. Personally, I never found it beneficial to impersonate a cop or an IRS agent as some PI's do. It's best to stick to the roles you know and when I start talking through my nose, I can sound like a country bumpkin who couldn't find the ass end of a mare if she was swatting me in the face with her tail.

I figured Smith to be the kind of person who prided himself on his adeptness at hiding the dark side of his personality behind a façade of respectability. In fact, I felt that was true of all three of these guys. After learning they were from Laredo, Texas, for weeks the lyrics to the song "Streets of Laredo" tumbled through my head. I hated that song. The song was about death and it was the most depressing song I ever had to learn. "I spied a young cowboy all dressed in white Linen." Who would make a kid learn a song like that, anyway?

Nevertheless, the song seemed appropriate in describing the aura surrounding these guys. They were quite successful at hiding their path of brutal murders behind the pearly white image of civic responsibility. 'Who could possibly think that a doctor, a dentist, and a cop were serial killers?' Later I found out where they had learned that way of life.

I wanted him to think I was buying into his civic persona. He might loosen up a bit and make a few blunders.

The first mistake he made came just a few questions after 'how are you doing'. He asked me when the actual incident took place. I replied November 20 of last year.

"November 20?" he asked rhetorically, "That's curious." He said more to himself than to me.

I instantly caught it. Why would the date be "curious" to him? Without being aware of the link between the Barry murder and the discovery of the bodies of Delores Cepeda and Sonja Johnson on the same day a year earlier, November 20 was just another date on the calendar. The date had triggered a memory of something significant to him and since I suspected him of murder, I assumed it had something to do with the discovery of the bodies of Cepeda and Johnson.

I didn't want Smith hanging up on me so I let it slide. I knew if I wanted to keep him on the phone, I couldn't challenge him on anything he said.

If I could get Smith talking about the people he personally knew at the apartment complex from the time he lived there, I might be able to get him talking about himself and Eddie as well. I could tell from the way he described the people he knew at the apartments that he was mentally going from apartment to apartment remembering little bits and pieces of information about them. He couldn't remember the names of most of the tenants but he could recall what they did for a living or maybe some other incidental bit of information about them.

"Let's see," he was recalling, "above him was the guy who worked down at the market on the corner."

"Steven Bialek?" I prompted.

"Right, and his girlfriend. Next to them was the CHP dispatcher and her boyfriend. Living below the dispatcher was a middle-aged couple. The man was engaged in some sort of professional work. That's more or less the extent of the people I knew around there. Like he talks—like Eddie knew Jeanne, He probably told you about her right?"

Bringing up Jeanne Marek's name in that context gave me an adrenalin rush. Eddie hadn't mentioned Jeanne Marek. With Smith bringing her up unprompted I was certain that Eddie was the one going around the apartment complex asking how many married and single women lived in the apartments. Why hadn't Jeanne told the police that she knew an Eddie who lived at the apartments? That oversight was a little strange. Maybe it didn't occur to her at the time she talked to the police or maybe there was some other reason.

When I first mentioned the possibility of a connection to the two girls murdered in Highland Park, Smith ignored the reference to the Hillside Strangler murders completely.

"Well, how strong is the evidence they have against Art? I mean what is the evidential link?" He asked in response to my statement about the Barry murder being connected to the Cepeda and Johnson murders.

"They didn't have any evidence at all against Art until they arrested him." I replied. "After they arrested him they planted snitches in with him. Now we have three inmates coming in testifying that Art confessed to them in jail."

"Well, I don't believe that of Art. I knew Art pretty well and as far as I think he had a pretty good character."

"We don't think he did it either. We think whoever did it has done it before." I responded. "It just doesn't make sense to me that Art would be doing his laundry in preparation to go out to dinner and decides to kill Leslie while the laundry dries. But he did see Leslie at the laundry room just before she was murdered." I added as an afterthought.

"Leslie was doing the laundry?" Smith inquired. "I thought her mother always did the laundry."

Again, my ears perked up. He had said earlier that he didn't know the victim and now he was saying that he knew enough about the victim to know that her mother did the laundry.

Then Smith brings up the Hillside Strangler case as if I hadn't mentioned it before.

"Yeah, I'm sure. Right there in the general vicinity over there in Highland Park they had those girls abducted. Do you recall? Before, like the Hillside Strangling deal." He seemed to be struggling to get it out and selecting his words carefully.

"So, I mean that area, especially being so close to the Highland Park area, you know, that girl used to play outside a lot—okay—so I mean you could take it for example that she would've been playing and somebody would have come along and she was very friendly. She used to play downstairs in the lower parking lot area which very few people come to. So the possibilities are really great."

He did it again. He showed more knowledge about the victim than he had initially indicated. How would he know she played down there frequently if he didn't watch her frequently? Had Smith been stalking her as a potential victim?

After that lengthy monologue, Smith changed the subject and started pumping me for information about what kind of evidence they found at the scene of the crime and information contained in the police reports. Smith wanted to know who was investigating the case for the South Pasadena Police Department.

I told him that agent Hatfield had investigated part of the case and asked him if he knew Hatfield.

"I think he's the guy with the mustache, isn't he?" Smith asked.

That described half the police officers in Los Angeles.

"Yes," I answered, "the skinny guy." Which, given the cops penchant for donuts, narrowed the field considerably.

"He's been there for a long time as I recall." Smith said. "You see I used to work with the South Pasadena Police many years back. I was a police explorer there."

After discussing the police officers on the case, Smith went back to pumping me for more information on the Barry murder. One of the benefits of playing the fool is that you can be evasive without seeming rude or abrupt. You just sound baffled, stupid, and ill informed. My natural ability for playing dumb was shining through.

I wanted to get him talking about his police experience but he was being evasive about it. Every time I tried to pry into that area, he would change the subject back to the case against Anzures.

"So you say they only have circumstantial evidence?" He asked.

"Yeah. They don't have anything really." I blurted out through my nose. "Just some cons coming in and telling lies about Art confessing."

"Okay," Smith said beginning to sound a little frustrated, "I don't know how they do their office reports but there was nothing listed under evidence?"

I knew what he was after. He wanted me to read him the list of items booked into evidence at the scene of the crime and I wasn't going to do that. I continued to play dumb like I didn't know what he was talking about.

"Yeah. What they got was some pubic hair, like four strands of pubic and head hair. That's all they got." I said.

"That's it?" Smith asked.

"That's it." I responded.

"And microscopically analyzed?" Smith inquired.

"Yeah. The Sheriff's Department criminologist testified at the preliminary hearing that, 'hey this isn't conclusive at all." I said.

"He said that? That it wasn't conclusive?" Smith asked a little too excitedly.

"Yeah." I replied

"Was there an outline of the circumstantial evidence then—or just the fact that he was there—well, you said they had prints, didn't ya?" Smith pushed.

He was getting clever now. I hadn't mentioned fingerprints and he was trying to do an end run around my evasiveness and play on my stupidity.

"No." I answered and then added, "Well they have prints that are unidentified."

"That is unidentified?" Smith asked with a bit of concern in his voice.

"Right. You know, they didn't belong to him." I responded.

"And you said she was killed with a telephone cord, right? Smith asked.

I hadn't said anything about a telephone cord or any murder weapon to Smith. I told Eddie that Leslie was strangled with a telephone cord because the newspaper had erroneously described a telephone cord as the murder weapon. Earlier in my conversation with Smith, I said she was strangled with a cord. It indicated to me that he and Eddie had discussed the details of my conversation with Eddie. No wonder he was trying to pump me for information. Maybe he wanted to see if what I told him was consistent with what I told Eddie. An inconsistency would tell him I considered both, or at least one of them, a suspect in the murder and I was trying to trip him up.

"Yeah." I answered to the telephone cord question.

"Were there any prints on the telephone?" Smith asked.

"No." I answered. "Just hers—the victim's."

During the conversation, Smith made a comment that I didn't catch until later when I was going through my notes on the conversation. The Task Force had made it clear in the media that they thought the Hillside Strangler was an excellent student of police procedures. The only evidence I had found in the newspapers that indicated a police officer was involved was in one or two instances when women told police investigators that a man, posing as a police officer, had tried to abduct them. Smith gave me something else to think about.

"How convinced are you of his innocence?" Smith asked.

"About ninety-five percent." I responded.

"Because the possibility is, and even though he is of good character and all, he had been out of work for such a long time," Smith went on. "and there is a lot of frustration involved with that. There is a slight possibility that he may have committed it."

"Well yeah," I said, "that's why I say I'm only ninety-five percent sure that he didn't. I could never be one hundred percent sure, don't think, you know, even if they arrested somebody else."

"But like I say," Smith said, "working on the case for so long with that kind of percentage I would say—you probably know more about it than the police as well."

"Yeah," I agreed, "because I've got all their information as well as the information I've collected myself."

"Yeah," he responded, "because they also have a very segmented investigation. While one guy does one thing, one guy does another thing."

Before Smith said it, I hadn't thought about how fragmented a police investigation was. The bodies of Hillside Strangler victims had been dropped in various jurisdictions. Furthermore, to calm the public as much as possible, the LAPD had let the Task Force grow into a monstrosity. At one point, there were over two hundred detectives and officers on the case. If the killer wanted to cause confusion and further fragment an already segmented investigation, he couldn't do it any better than by crossing jurisdictional lines and having two hundred cops taking statements, analyzing evidence, and trying to communicate with each other. By that statement, Smith had told me he knew how big city investigations worked.

As suspects in the Hillside Strangler case, Castillon and Smith were as good as it gets. In the Barry, Cepeda, and Johnson murders, I had at least three related murders involving multiple killers with different profiles and now I had suspects that fit both profiles. I was certain that Cantu fit into the equation somewhere but I wasn't sure how.

 It was of intense interest to me that when Cantu's name initially came up in my interview with Martin Smith, he tried to distance himself from Cantu by pretending not to know anything about him. Later in the conversation, Smith gave quite a few details on Cantu and admitted that the three of them had grown up together in Laredo. I had the distinct impression that Smith was afraid of Dennis Cantu.

He had every right to be afraid of Cantu. I was becoming frightened by all three of them. It scared the hell out of me for what they were capable of doing and for what I was convinced they had already done. These were three brutal killers. Three intelligent, experienced and sadistic serial killers clever enough to evade capture for as long as the justice system was willing to look the other way; and given the political nature of the case the justice system was willing to look the other way forever.

Chapter 17

Armando Gonzales called shortly after I spoke to his probation officer. His command of English was tolerable and I told him I wanted to talk to him in person about his stay at the Los Angeles County Jail. He worked odd hours bussing tables at a Mexican restaurant, but after a little discussion, we found a common time to meet.

Gonzales was nineteen years old and immigrated to the United States illegally when he was thirteen. He lived alone in a rented studio apartment in a rundown building in a depressed area of Valencia. He was still illegal and I appreciated his candor on his immigration status. Armando told me that when he first came to the United States he was taken in and supported by a Hollywood man who also took care of his schooling. He wasn't inclined to talk about the specifics of why his benefactor had been so generous, but I had the feeling it had something to do with obtaining sexual favors from the young boy. Whatever his situation with the Hollywood man, it wasn't important to my purpose for being there so I left it alone.

After eliciting a little background information from him, I got to the point of my visit. I told Gonzales about Jackson's statement concerning Art's confession in the jail cell. The young man had nothing to gain from talking to me, and considering his own problems with the judicial system and his illegal status here, I was concerned about whether he would cooperate with me. He didn't leave me in a quandary for long.

He told me he remembered Art and Lorenz Karlic, and that he had been approached by the cops himself to snitch on Anzures. They offered to help him out with his rape case if he would be their "ears" in the cell. He told the police that he hadn't raped anyone and that he would beat the rap and didn't need their help. Gonzales corroborated Karlic that Art had not said anything about his case while in the cell. He was a street- smart kid and while he beat the rape charge as he said he would, it still wasn't in his best interests to testify for Art. Nevertheless, he agreed to testify in court if I could provide him with transportation to Pasadena and then home again.

With Karlic's statement corroborated by Gonzales, I was satisfied that Art had not confessed in jail as Jackson claimed and as far as I was concerned it reinforced my notion that Anzures was being framed for the Barry murder. I wasn't sure about the motive for the frame up but he was being framed, that much I was certain of.

It felt like the case was turning inside out. It wasn't my job to solve the case, but if the cops weren't going to conduct a proper and thorough investigation then someone else had to do it. The effect a case like this can have on the lives of other people can be far-reaching and devastating. If the wrong man is convicted in one serial killer case, it can start a chain reaction whereby another wrong man is convicted and continue on and on until the real killer is caught. Maybe I was empathizing with too many sides for my own mental health, but that was how I felt. Being a father myself, I could imagine the pain of losing a child so suddenly and senselessly. Yet, seeing the look of confusion, devastation and betrayal on the faces of the Anzures family as Art's case wound it's way through the courts made the judicial system seem like a festering sore that I couldn't leave alone. I needed to keep picking at it until I made it bleed.

Like most people from the middle class, the Anzures family believed in the objectivity, honesty, and integrity of the judicial system and that it would work for them. Yet, it wasn't working for them and that disturbed me. As Art's trial date neared, my feelings of desperation to put a stop to these proceedings intensified. The total lack of credible evidence plus the emergence of another, more feasible suspect, made the idea of trying Anzures for the murder of Leslie Barry absurd.

A few weeks before the trial started, I called Denise Anzures to find out about the condition of the apartment when Cantu and Castillon moved out. Specifically I wanted to know if the suspects had left anything of an evidentiary nature behind and if she had, by any chance, held on to the stuff.

Denise told me that she and Art, and their friends, Donald and Peggy Woodbury cleaned out the apartment about a week before the murder. Denise said it was a filthy mess. They left trash bags full of crap strewn all over the floor. The carpet was soiled and stained throughout the apartment and there was an inch of dirt on everything. Denise listed specific items they found in the apartment. A pair of leather hiking boots found in a closet; an electrical extension cord with both ends cut off in a kitchen drawer; a PA system like the kind mounted on a police car; and numerous other items such as an old shirt and a pair of men's jeans left in a heap on the living room floor. It was interesting to me that a dental student and a medical intern could live in such squalor and unsanitary conditions as Denise described.

I asked Denise if she could make a list of the things she could remember that were left in the apartment. She said the only thing she saved was the pair of hiking boots and I was welcome to have them. I told her I would like to see the boots. I wanted to keep Denise in the dark about why I was so interested in these guys and she never asked me for an explanation. Given the response she and Art got from Kushner and Beck, I gathered she had learned her lesson about asking too many questions of detectives.

I thought about the condition of the apartment and the stuff left behind. That kind of disorganization and lack of cleanliness, if not psychotic, was damn close to it. It didn't fit with the image of who Cantu and Castillon wanted people to believe they were. These guys were from prominent families and I would guess that they weren't raised in a pigsty. Too, some of the items left behind were of particular interest to me. The electrical cord with the ends cut off and the car mounted PA system were odd items to keep around the house. For two guys under suspicion for strangulation murders by means of impersonating a police officer, I thought the electrical cord and the PA system would raise a few eyebrows. It certainly had me wondering. Was the electrical cord something they were planning to use in a future murder? Or, maybe it was a souvenir from a previous murder. Was the PA system used to further their ruse of being police officers to pull unsuspecting women over?

Since Mellecker and I had hit it off so well I knew he would love to hear from me and get this information. I called the Task Force again and asked for my friend K.R. Mellecker.

"Hey, Sergeant Mellecker." I said in an upbeat voice when he came on the phone. "I was talking to my client's wife the other day, and she gave me a list of items that were left behind in the apartment when Cantu and Castillon moved out. I thought you might be interested in the list."

I guess I was becoming a royal pain in the ass to the task force because my friend Mellecker was not as happy to hear from me as I thought he'd be.

"What do you expect to get out of this?" He snapped without commenting on the information I was calling about.

Being questioned about my motives irritated the hell out of me. Actually, irritated might be an understatement. It infuriated me. Beyond doing a good job for my client, I really hadn't thought much about what I might get out of the case.

"Look." I said trying hard to control my anger, "I have a client about to stand trial over here in Pasadena for a murder he didn't commit. All I'm looking for is a little justice for my client."

"Well, I'm not going to investigate the Barry murder as a connection to the Hillside Strangler case." Mellecker stated flatly in an arrogant tone of finality.

"Well, you just investigate these guys on the Hillside Strangler side of the case and I'll make the connection to the Barry murder." I responded unable to contain my anger and frustration.

I failed to see any humor in this conversation, but Mellecker started to laugh. It was a mocking laugh. This idiot couldn't solve the case and he was making fun of me for trying to help him.

"Maybe Mrs. Cepeda and Mr. Johnson would like to know what you find so funny about the deaths of their daughters." I yelled and slammed down the phone.

It was the last contact I had with detectives from the Task Force until I joined the defense for Angelo Buono. Later that year Sergeant Mellecker was the arresting officer on another murder I investigated for the defense. Though he did a fair job of investigating the case, I didn't get a warm fuzzy feeling that he was all that as a detective. Certainly not to the extent of cockiness that he displayed when I contacted him about the Barry murder. The defendant in that case was not completely innocent but Mellecker's investigation and analysis of the crime put the murder weapon in the wrong hands and the defendant charged with first degree murder, skated with a measly five years for manslaughter.

Art's trial got under way and except for testimony from inmate Steven Lyle Jackson and a few other minor witnesses the prosecutor's case was a replay of the preliminary hearing in municipal court. At trial, they called the mother, Aina Barry, to establish that a crime had been committed and to testify about how she had come home and discovered her daughter's still warm body on the bedroom floor; how she cut the cord from her daughter's neck, performed CPR, and called the paramedics.

Beck testified about his investigation and how much overtime he put in while investigating the case. He and Kushner must have spent a lot of time at Winchell's Donuts because I hadn't seen any evidence that the time was used wisely to conduct a murder investigation.

The prosecutor called the hair expert who gave an encore performance to the one in Municipal court. The trial was delayed for a day because neither the police nor the hair expert could find the actual hair samples booked into evidence at the time of the murder. For a while, it looked like they might have to forego the hair testimony all together. Overnight they found the hair, or at least they produced some hair, and it was presented in court the next day.

Defense strategy meetings turned into daily arguments between Mitch and me about what witnesses he should call. Over a period of three or four months leading up to the trial, I watched Mitch closely for signs that he might be folding under the pressure. The defense lawyer was feeling the crunch and after one strategy meeting I wasn't certain if he would make it through the entire trial. Mark, John Neece and I were sitting in Mitch's office discussing the upcoming trial when Mitch took a phone call from a man who had been arrested for masturbating in the lingerie department at a major department store. It was obvious that the man was threatening to commit suicide and Mitch was trying to talk him down. When he got off the phone, he was shaking so badly he had to take a break from the meeting.

Mitch didn't see much evidence against Art that needed to be attacked and he wasn't inclined to call many witnesses for the defense. I agreed with him that the prosecutor's case was almost nonexistent. However, I feared that Mitch was underestimating the power of the victim in this case. When the victim is a child or a police officer, they can arise from the grave and bite you in the ass. If the prosecutor had one thing going for her, it was the sympathy factor inherent in the tender age of the victim.

I argued for a more aggressive defense. I wanted to subpoena Shawn Hagen to testify about knowing Hillside Strangler victim, Delores Cepeda. For some reason Mitch wasn't inclined to bring up the Hillside Strangler case. While he didn't say so, I assumed his hesitation to introduce that evidence was because he didn't want the jury to think Art was the Hillside Strangler, or at the very least a competent and dangerous killer. I didn't immediately consider the possibility that maybe it wasn't the opinion of the jury he was worried about as much as the opinion of victim Sonia Johnson' father, Tony Johnson.

Along with emphasizing the time line of the murder and the knotted cord, Shawn Hagen's testimony would establish a reasonable doubt by showing the competent nature of the crime and the probable connection between the Leslie Barry murder and the Hillside Strangler case. I argued that the jury might believe that Barry was a Hillside Strangler victim, but there was no way they would believe that Art Anzures was the Hillside Strangler.

I took my argument one step further. I might have been over reaching a bit at the time, but I pleaded nightly with him to make a case against Eddie Castillon as the killer. While Mitch admitted my argument was convincing he wasn't going to give the jury a straw man. I responded that he might be giving the jury the worst possible straw man—his client.

I did talk him into calling Lisa Ballatore's baby-sitter to help establish a time line of the murder. However, without demonstrating to the jury the significance of the time line, that ploy may have backfired in making Art appear to be an able killer.

The biggest nail in our trial strategy coffin was the pair of pliers found on the dresser in Leslie's bedroom. Essentially the pliers were inadmissible. There was no evidence linking the pliers to Art or showing it was used in the commission of the crime. The crime lab analyzed microscopic material removed from the jaws of the pliers and determined it was inconsistent with having come from either the TV set or the murder weapon. There was no evidence linking the pliers to the murder.

Realizing how weak her case was, Prosecutor Marilyn Porges decided she had one chance to get around the admissibility problem with the pliers. To be successful she needed a stipulation from Mitch to the effect that the police had searched Art's tool closet for a pair of pliers and was unable to find one. She caught Mitch off guard one day and Mitch agreed to the stipulation. When he realized his mistake, he beat himself up pretty bad over it. While the pliers weren't admissible as evidence, the stipulation was. He gave the prosecutor the gift of being able to use the stipulation to place Art inside the apartment with the implication that the pliers belonged to him and that Art had left them there after murdering the victim. It was weak but with the lack of a cohesive and aggressive defense, the stipulation was enough to give the case to the prosecutor.

Mitch called Lorenz Karlic to the stand to counter the snitch testimony of Steven Lyle Jackson. Karlic made a good witness for the defense but during his testimony he was asked if there was anyone besides Art Anzures, Lyle Jackson, and himself in the cell at the time the alleged confession was made. He answered truthfully and gave the jury the name of the other man in the cell.

After Karlic testified, I told Mitch I would call Armando Gonzales, to come to court and corroborate Karlic' testimony. That evening I called Gonzales at his place of employment and told him we needed him to testify for the defense the next day and that I would be out to pick him up. The next morning when I arrived at his apartment in Valencia, he asked me if I could get his cleaning out of hock at the dry cleaners. I figured that was the least we could do for him. There was no way they could view paying a dry cleaning bill as consideration for testifying. He was just a bus boy making minimum wage and he needed clean clothes to wear to court. Besides, he had already given me a statement favorable to the defense without promise of payment or other benefits.

When I arrived at the courthouse with the witness, I met Mitch in the hallway. In retrospect, I probably shouldn't have said anything but I told Mitch about paying for the dry cleaning and I wanted reimbursed for the expense. By this time, money was a big issue with me. I felt the case had cost me enough already. It wasn't like I was asking for gas money or additional pay for the time it took to pick him up.

Without explanation, Mitch told me he wasn't going to call Gonzales to the stand. I nearly hit the roof. It was one thing not to present evidence of the Hillside Strangler connection. I could understand a defense lawyer, without prosecutorial experience, not wanting to pin a murder rap on someone else; but not to call a defense witness who's name had already come up in court and who was sticking his neck out by testifying for us was inexcusable. Worse still, since his name had been brought up in court, Mitch knew that the jury would think we were hiding something if we didn't call Gonzales to the stand. I thought it was his second big mistake and it just added to my frustration. I was getting a major depression on about the whole process.

I drove the young man back to his apartment and apologized profusely for taking up his time. I can't remember a thing about my drive back to Pasadena from Valencia. I was in a daze. This incident along with my experiences with the Hillside Strangler Task Force had driven me into a deep funk and for the next few days, I laid low and didn't do anything on the case.

Besides all the rejection I was getting from the Anzures case, It didn't help my emotional stability that while in the middle of the most important case of my life my wife was planning to take an editorship in either Chicago or New York, depending upon which job offer seemed the most promising for her career.

Wendy's anchor client in our public relations business was as editor of a computer magazine called Small Systems World. The publisher had sold the magazine to Hunter Publications in Chicago and since Wendy had done such a great job in building the magazine, Hunter Publishing wanted her to stay on as the managing editor. The salary and benefits package was an attractive offer, and Wendy was getting tired of being self-employed. The worry of not knowing if there would be enough money to pay the bills was taking it's toll on her as well as causing stress in our marriage. Earlier in the year, Hunter Publishing had arranged for both of us to fly to Chicago to look things over and see if we could live in Chicago.

Then another computer magazine, Datamation, made Wendy an offer comparable in salary and benefits to the offer on the table with Hunter Publications. Datamation was a larger and more prestigious magazine than Small Systems World. At one time, Datamation, located in Culver City, was considered the Bible of the computer industry.

The magazine had decided to move their offices from Culver City to New York and the position they were offering was as articles editor. Wendy and Datamation were not strangers. Wendy went to work for Datamation right out of college and worked her way up to articles editor in a very short time. The company was starting a new magazine and tossed in an additional incentive that Wendy would be named managing editor of the new magazine.

Still, it was a toss-up whether we wanted to live in New York or Chicago. Finally, Wendy decided that New York, being the capitol of the publishing world, would be the best move and we began looking for a house in New York.

Wendy and I discussed what I was going to do about my business and I told her there was no way I could abandon the Anzures case right now. I still had unfinished work on the case and believed that if I stayed alert and pushed on in my efforts to get evidence against my suspects that the system would work to correct it's mistake. We decided that I would stay in Pasadena and take care of closing the sell of the house and other personal business and work toward getting some kind of favorable resolution on the Anzures case. After finishing my investigation, I would join the family in New York and maybe start another detective agency back there.

Art's trial lasted for less than two weeks. I was really discouraged by the legal system thwarting my every effort on the case. It was my first real foray into the criminal courts and nobody seemed to be as interested in the truth and the facts as they were in the process itself. In his closing arguments at the trial, Mitch contended that Porges, even with the pliers and snitches, hadn't shouldered the burden of proof.

I wasn't worried so much about the evidence as I was the sympathy factor. Had this been any other case besides the murder of a child, Mitch would've been right in his assessment of the case. As I expected, Porges played the sympathy card to the max. The mother's testimony had an emotional impact, but it was nothing compared to the school pictures. Showing the jury school pictures of a pretty, little, blond girl after showing them autopsy photographs of the same little girl had been devastating to the defense. Mitch had tried to keep the photographs out by objecting that the pictures were prejudicial to the defendant. Judge Fletcher overruled the objection and allowed the jury to see the pictures.

Mitch tried to have the school pictures suppressed by arguing that they were irrelevant to the murder and would be inflammatory to the jury. Porges argued that by entering the apartment without permission to take the pictures, Art and Denise had displayed a consciousness of guilt, which made the school pictures relevant to the case. The judge ruled in favor of the prosecutor and the pictures were admitted.

Art's jury deliberated for three weeks. Most lawyers would agree that it was judicial error to allow the jury to stay out for that long after such a short trial. By allowing such a lengthy deliberation, the judge was telling the jury that the court would not accept anything less than a final and complete verdict in the case.

When the jury came back, I was sitting in the courtroom next to a reporter from the Pasadena Star News. I had become friendly with Ann Sutherland during my involvement in the case and I was fond of her. She was one of the few reporters who knew about my investigation of the case. As they filed back into the jury box from the deliberation room, I noticed that many of the jurors were crying. A few were sobbing loud enough to be heard by the spectators in the courtroom. When I saw the tears, I knew this was not going to be good news for the Anzures family. I grabbed Ann's hand and leaned over and whispered to her, "They've convicted him."

My mind shut down and I just heard parts of the decision.

"Has the jury…verdict…would the defendant please rise…"

"We the jury… entitled action… find the defendant…guilty of murder in the first degree…special circumstances…child molestation."

The Anzures family occupied the front row as they had at the Municipal Court preliminary hearing and throughout the trial. Some of the members of the family burst into tears while others sat in stunned silence. Art reacted to the jury's verdict with an outburst.

"I didn't do it!" he screamed.

He turned to his wife sobbing and gave her a hug until the bailiff separated them.

"I'm sorry." He said.

It was hard to believe the drama I was witnessing. It was like something out of a movie. These people were in pain and with good reason. Their son, their husband, their brother was now a convicted murderer and nothing would ever be the same for them again. Even if he were later cleared of the charges and set free, Art and his whole family would carry the stigma of his conviction like a scarlet letter. They would never be able to trust the system again nor would people completely trust them. Every time they saw a police car in their rear view mirror, they would wonder if they were about to be pulled over and begin another nightmare like the one they just went through with Art. For Art there would be the dehumanizing experience of prison life, exiled from society and forced to live in a maximum-security cage shared by gangbangers, rapists, murderers, and all types of sociopaths and career criminals. It was not a pleasant sight watching an innocent man take a fall for first-degree murder.

By the time, I got back to my office I was boiling inside. I stuck my arm out and sweeping it across my desk knocked everything to the floor. Papers, in and out baskets, pens, paperweights, file folders and my phone went flying all over the office. Picking up my phone and spitting out a string of profanities, I slung it against the wall.

I paced back and forth cussing like a mad man and trying to blow off steam. I picked up my phone and checked to see if it was still working. It still had a dial tone so I dialed Mitch's office.

"You fucked up royally." I screamed into the mouthpiece when he answered.

"The only way I fucked up was by hiring you." Mitch snapped back. "I want to see you in my office right now." He added still angry at my outburst.

"I'll be right over." I said and hung up the phone.

My emotions had turned icy cold by the time I reached Mitch's office in Highland Park. I could've easily gunned down a lawyer, any lawyer, and not felt one ounce of remorse for it. When I arrived, Mitch was clearly upset. He sat across the desk from me and spoke in a tone that alternated between anger and contrition. His contrition wasn't because his client had just been convicted of murder on evidence so flimsy it bordered on whimsical, as much as for himself. I got the distinct impression that Mitch saw his bar card going down the shitter, and he really wanted to patch things up with me if he could. I sat quietly during most of this passive/aggressive confrontation not wanting to speak for fear of what I might say. Every time I tried to speak Mitch interrupted me with a lecture about how he had done the best job he could possibly do. I knew that wasn't true but what's more I knew he knew that wasn't true. He had a lawyerly explanation for everything.

Apparently, I had a smug look on my face, and Mitch could see I wasn't buying any of his bullshit.

"Wipe that smirk off your face." He said.

I was tired of listening to his excuses for not giving his client the best defense.

"I'm not smirking." I replied as I got up and stomped out of his office slamming the door behind me.

Chapter 18

I'm somewhat of a backyard mechanic. At times, I've dug deep into my car's engine to replace leaky gaskets, fix a busted piston ring or change a clutch. Inevitably, after putting it all back together, I'd still have parts left over that I didn't know what to do with. Usually the left over parts didn't amount to more than a bolt or two or a bracket that came off and fell into a hard to see crevice of the engine compartment. If the car would start and run smoothly, I'd toss the extra parts into the trunk and hope the engine didn't fall out while driving down the freeway. If the car didn't run right, it was a pain in the ass, but I'd have to take everything apart and find out where they belonged. Or, if I wanted to spend some money, I could call a real mechanic to fix it.

The Anzures trial bore remarkable similarities to my mechanical work on cars. I had many left over parts I didn't know what to do with, but some of the parts left out of the Anzures trial were more like motor mounts than minor bolts and brackets. My car couldn't run without those vital parts any more than the judicial system could function properly without the facts.

The mechanics of a good defense for Art Anzures was presenting and emphasizing the simple and easily verifiable facts about the murder itself. Facts like the date of the murder; the timeline; the daring and undetected escape by the killer; and the lamp cord, fashioned into a murder weapon with a complex system of knots that corresponded to pressure points on the neck. These facts could've been elicited from police detectives on cross-examination and they would've shown the jury what a competent and able murderer they were dealing with.

Then the defense could call Shawn Hagen to the stand. Shawn would testify that he knew Leslie Barry and that he knew one of the Hillside Strangler victims, Dolly Cepeda. He would testify that Dolly Cepeda and Leslie Barry knew each other. The defense could call to the stand a member of the Hillside Strangler Task Force to establish the facts of the Dolly Cepeda and Sonja Johnson murders.

If the defense went no further than that and the judge allowed the trial to continue, Shawn Hagen's testimony along with the other facts, would've opened the door for a powerful closing argument by the defense.

The defense lawyer could argue that the adeptness with which Leslie Barry was murdered was consistent with the belief that the killer has killed before, and if he's killed before, who would've been his most likely victims? Shawn Hagen testified that Leslie Barry knew another murder victim. Her name was Delores Cepeda. Both of these girls were 12 years of age at the time of their deaths. Both girls were murdered by ligature strangulation. Sexual gratification was the motive in both murders. The body of Delores Cepeda was found on November 20, 1977, and Leslie Barry was murdered on November 20, 1978. These two girls attended the same small private school and the fact that these two girls had crossed paths with each other makes it an almost certainty that their paths crossed with the same killer.

If Art Anzures was guilty of the murder of Leslie Barry then why wasn't he charged with the murders of Delores Cepeda and Sonja Johnson? To believe that Art Anzures killed Leslie Barry, you would have to be convinced beyond a reasonable doubt that the defendant is the Hillside Strangler. The prosecutor doesn't think he's the Hillside Strangler or she would've charged him with more murders. The defendant in this case, Arthur Anzures, is being used as a patsy to cover-up the fact that the Hillside Strangler is still out there, still killing and Leslie Barry is his most recent victim.

A closing argument like that would end up as headlines in the newspaper the next day and cause some problems for Mitch. For one thing, he might have to convince Tony Johnson that Anzures hadn't killed his daughter. For another, he might end up having to defend Anzures in the court of public opinion and none of us were experienced at handling the mass media. The idea of having 30 microphones shoved in our faces scared the hell out us. It was a difficult position to be in, but that's one of the risks when you take on a murder case.

What I argued about nightly with Mitch was taking the defense to the forefront of the truth. That was just about where my investigation was at trial time—on the brink. So close I could almost say I knew who the killer was even if I didn't have the kind of conclusive evidence I needed to prove it. Alone, Jeanne Marek's statement about a man named "Eddie" going from apartment to apartment asking how many married and single women lived in the apartment complex was not a particularly damning piece of evidence. Yet, if the defense presented other circumstantial evidence like the victim leaving her apartment earlier in the day to go to the store, along with Jeanne Marek's statement, it could raise the whole issue of whether the murder was a random act or committed by someone the victim knew and trusted. Without giving the jury further information, "Eddie" would appear as a phantom killer that the police had failed to locate.

This isn't merely second-guessing the defense lawyer. It was my job to get the facts and it was his job to make it all work. I did my job and I expected him to do his; but even if Art Anzures had been acquitted of the Barry murder, I still would not have been satisfied. To me the case wasn't merely about an innocent man being charged with murder. The police are human and they sometimes make honest mistakes, but this was no honest mistake. The more important issue for me was the motive behind the charges against Anzures. That the police could take one of our citizens and charge him with murder just to cover-up their own incompetence was disturbing. I had read about such things, but I never thought I'd witness a cover-up let alone have one of my investigations be the subject of one.

As Wendy prepared for her move to New York, the Hillside Strangler case was heating up. The Bellingham, Washington Police Department had arrested Kenneth Bianchi in January of 1979 for the murders of Karen Mandic and Diane Wilder, and Bianchi was ratting out his cousin, Angelo Buono claiming that Buono was his accomplice and masterminded the murders. If they arrested Angelo Buono or tried anyone for the murders, it would give me another opportunity to air all the left over facts from the Anzures case.

As a bonus an arrest would provide an opportunity to study more evidence collected by police during their marathon search for the Hillside Stranglers. I couldn't imagine what kind of evidence I'd find in the many clues that the Task Force received from the immense publicity surrounding the Hillside Strangler murders. Someone had to know something and there was no way I was going to walk out in the middle of this. I had paid the price of admission and I wanted to be there for the ending.

When the Anzures verdict came in, Wendy was already working out of New York. I told her about Anzures being convicted and knowing the commitment and hard work I had put into the case, she sent me a sweet note of condolences. I appreciated the sentiment. We had sold our house on El Molino and gotten a good price for it. Wendy returned home from New York just long enough to oversee the packing and loading of the moving van and then she was gone. After Wendy and the family left, I rattled around in the big empty house for about thirty days while the sell went through escrow. Having become accustomed to many people and activity around the house, it didn't take long before the feeling of loneliness overcame me.

I spent a lot of time at the office thinking about the Barry murder while trying to get my business back on track. My work was important to me, and I stewed about how things had gone so bad in such a short time. The rejection of my investigation by both the defense lawyer and the Hillside Strangler Task Force caused my morale and self-esteem to plummet. Many of my clients were angry for the long period of neglect I'd shown them during the Anzures trial, and many of them had found other investigators to handle their caseload for them.

I made a few drinking buddies at the John Bull Pub and sucked them into my cause. Knowing a private investigator fascinated them, and I seemed to have found an attentive audience for my PI stories. My new friends considerately allowed me to wallow in self-pity. In fact, they encouraged it. Not to imply that I lied or embellished stories, but I could always count on my swashbuckling PI tales being worth a few free beers at the bar.

When escrow closed on the house, I sent all the money to Wendy to put down on the house we had bought in New York. I deluded myself into thinking this case was nearing a conclusion, and I wasn't going to be in Pasadena long enough to bother about renting an apartment. I decided that the only economical answer to my housing problem was to camp out on the floor of my office.

The front of my office was completely windows, and after a fitful first night sleeping on an air mattress on the floor, I awakened to the sounds of two elderly women from Pasadena giggling. I cracked my eyelids open just wide enough to see through the hazy blur of a bad hangover. One of the blue hairs was bending over in the hallway outside my office window pointing her finger at me while saying something to her friend that caused them both to giggle. That afternoon I went to Pier1 Imports and picked up some bamboo curtains to give me a little privacy.

A month or so after Art's trial I decided it was about time I confronted Eddie Castillon about my suspicions. I phoned him and told him about Art being convicted and that I was continuing my investigation. Eddie didn't seem anymore pleased to hear from me than detective Mellecker had been. I told him that I would like to meet with him in person at the USC Dental School. He reluctantly agreed to the meeting and we set up a time.

I don't know if Mark Southerland thought I was a certifiable lunatic or not, but when I told him about setting up the meeting with Castillon, he was not amused. Mark said he wouldn't go inside with me but he would accompany me down to the dental school to ensure that if I got myself killed he could at least be a witness to the murder.

I couldn't decide if I wanted to surreptitiously tape the conversation or not but just in case, I packed a tape recorder in the side pocket of my soft leather briefcase. At the dental school I told Mark to hang around outside and I'd be back in a few minutes.

There weren't many students inside the classroom so it wasn't hard to find Castillon. The classroom was a dental lab with dental chairs, spiral type mouth washers and all the paraphernalia one might find in any dental office. We introduced ourselves and Eddie directed me to sit down in his dental chair. He was visibly nervous and I was trying to hide my own nervousness behind a false display of self-confidence. The conversation went downhill fast.

"How can I help you?" Eddie asked in a voice that sounded like he would rather be pulling teeth than waiting for my answer to that question.

I wasn't there to get answers as much as to gauge reactions.

"Well, Eddie," I began slowly, "I think you killed Leslie Barry." I said bluntly.

I don't know what kind of a reaction I expected to get from the accusation. I didn't think Eddie would break down and start confessing, but maybe if he didn't do it he would say something like "this conversation is over, asshole. Get the hell out of my face." I thought he could've at least recoiled from the directness of the statement or acted surprised. He did neither. He just sat there expressionless.

"Well, it wasn't me." Eddie responded confidently without a trace of anger or fear.

"Well Eddie," I said feeling the anger well up inside of me for what I considered an inappropriate reaction to my accusation,

"there's only one of two people who could've killed Leslie Barry. It was either you or your roommate, Dennis Cantu."

"Why do you think that?" Eddie asked.

"Because of the knots." I said, more to myself than Eddie and letting my voice trail off.

"Were they surgical knots?" Eddie wanted to know.

"I believe they were, Eddie." I responded in a friendlier tone.

"Well, it wasn't me." Eddie denied again. "If you think it was Dennis you should probably talk to Dennis." He added.

"Oh, believe me, I will talk to Dennis." I said without hesitation.

At that point, Eddie looked down at my brief case and saw the tape recorder in the side pocket.

"I hope you're not recording this," he said, showing the first sign of emotion since the exchange began.

"I'm not recording it, Eddie." I responded truthfully. "I just brought my recorder in the off chance that you might allow me to record our meeting. I take it you don't want me to record it then?" I asked taking the recorder out of my bag and showing him it was not turned on.

He didn't respond.

"Well, Eddie. Here's the thing." I began with sarcasm dripping off my chin like gravy, "I know where you and your cousin, Martin, have lived in the past few years, and it just seems to me that every where you've lived the bodies of young women drop out of the sky. You lived on Crescent Street in Highland Park and that was near the point where Delores Cepeda and Sonja Johnson disappeared. Before that you lived up on Ontario Street in Pasadena and that's close to drop site where the body of Kristina Weckler was found. You lived at the apartment complex where Leslie Barry was murdered and now you and Dennis live in Montebello and low and behold, the body of Elizabeth Cevallos turns up in the Rio Hondo wash just blocks from where you live. What am I supposed to think, Eddie?"

This statement of facts clearly made him nervous.

"This is like a movie." Eddie responded.

He was right too. Everything about this case was like a drama out of a movie, but Eddie didn't know half the story. If he wanted drama, he should've been in the courtroom when the jury came back with their decision in the Anzures case. He was responding only to my accusations concerning him and his friends being serial killers. His comment of this being like a movie intrigued me and I wondered what part he thought he was playing in the drama. Was he the wrongly accused man or was he the killer about to be brought down, not by the cops he had evaded for so long, but by a private investigator without jurisdictional boundaries or interdepartmental and bureaucratic politics thwarting his investigation?

Thanking Eddie for his time, I told him I would probably be seeing him again after I had spoken with his pal, Dennis.

All I could think about on my way back to Pasadena was how much I needed a drink. I had no idea what I'd gained by confronting Eddie like that but it sure felt good. I thought it might at least put him on notice that someone was on to him and his friends and maybe they'd stop killing for a while just out of pure paranoia that I might be watching them. In fact, I did start watching them. I staked out their apartment and tailed them every chance I got. I also made certain that I knew where they lived at any given time.

It wasn't long after the Elizabeth Cevallos murder that Cantu and Castillon moved from Beverly Boulevard in Montebello to the East Los Angeles community of El Sereno. Like Highland Park, El Sereno is a barrio that borders on the southwest edge of South Pasadena. It struck me as almost metaphysically weird that Cantu and Castillon moved into a house overlooking the Anzures family residence. It was almost like they were God watching over the Anzures family from above.

There was only one road leading up to their rented Hilltop house and one day I staked out a street corner with my high powered, 400 millimeter, telephoto lens and took a picture of Dennis Cantu in his white car on his way home from the hospital where he was doing his internship rotation.

I studied the picture and thought about the statement Anzures had made about seeing Jeanne Marek' brother drive up in a white car and park in the 406 Monterey Road carport area.

Art only knew Marek's brother by having seen him a few times when he visited his sister at the apartments. There was a slight physical similarity between William Asper and Dennis Cantu. They were about the same size and both had curly hair, although with a different tint to it. While up close they didn't look much alike, I could see where Art could've mistakenly identified William Asper as the man in the white car actually being driven by Dennis Cantu. After all, Anzures had already misidentified the person he saw sitting in a dark car in front of the apartments on the evening of the murder as a man when it was a woman.

When Art saw the man drive up and park, he was engaged in conversation with Tony Barrett and not paying close attention. His mind was more likely to see someone connected to the apartment building than a former tenant or someone who didn't belong there. I had confirmed through the DMV records that Asper drove a red Porsche and didn't own a white car so I knew for certain that he was not the person Art saw drive through the alley and park in the carport that day. Cantu was a suspect in the murder and he drove a white car. The photograph of Cantu was evidence to prove it. With the photograph of Cantu as the centerpiece of my investigation, I felt that it was time to do a detailed report on the results of my findings in the Leslie Barry murder.

Ferndale is a beautiful, quiet, little village located at the mouth of the Eel River in Northern California. My son was in California for the Christmas holidays and Wendy wanted me to drive him up to Ferndale to spend the holidays with is Grandparents. Ever since the arrest of Kenneth Bianchi and Angelo Buono in the Hillside Strangler case, I was becoming increasingly concerned that the Task Force was going after the wrong men and the real killers were going to escape justice. Eager to put my investigation in writing and see how it looked on paper, Ferndale provided me with the perfect setting to do that.

I was no longer working for a lawyer and beyond wanting to see for myself how it all looked on paper, I had no idea who I was doing the report for. I would figure that out when the report was completed.

Chapter 19

When the hoopla over George Shamshak subsided in June of 1978, the press and the task force took a break. The task force was licking their wounds from having accused an innocent man, Peter Mark Jones, of the murders and from having to make an embarrassing public apology. Their inability to find any substantial evidence in which to base charges against Shamshak made things worse. The Task Force was skittish about making any more arrests and the DA's office was cautious about filing charges on any suspects the task force might bring to them.

While it's hard to find an upside to murder, in January of 1979, the Hillside Strangler Task Force got what they considered to be a big break in the case. The nude and strangled bodies of two female students, Karen Mandic and Diane Wilder, were discovered stuffed in the trunk of a car parked at the end of a cul-de-sac in Bellingham, Washington. The cause of death was asphyxiation by strangulation and it didn't take long for the trail to lead Bellingham detectives to the front door of Kenneth Allesio Bianchi.

The Chief of Police in Bellingham, Terry Mangan, a former police officer in the Los Angeles area, was keeping up with events in the Hillside Strangler investigation. After learning about Bianchi's close ties to the Glendale and Hollywood areas of Los Angeles County, Mangan called the Task Force to inform them of Bianchi's arrest in the murders of Mandic and Wilder. By then my attention to the case had piqued to more than a casual interest.

My investigation of the Barry murder had barely gotten started and while I didn't have any suspects in the case, the statement from Shawn Hagen and my analysis of the murder was down right scary. I had initially informed the Task Force about the possible connection of the Barry murder to the Hillside Strangler case a few weeks before the arrest of Bianchi, and I mistakenly thought the cops would be interested in having this information.

The arrest of Kenneth Bianchi didn't shake my confidence in my theory about the Barry murder in the least. I was convinced that Leslie Barry was a Hillside Strangler victim, but I didn't like Bianchi for the Barry murder and never considered him a suspect in the case. He didn't fit the profile. He didn't possess the intelligence, athleticism, or the medical background, and he didn't have a familiarity with the apartment complex, all of which were important elements of the facts I used in my analysis of the Barry murder.

I was looking for a very specific type of killer. There were not many people in the world that would or could, commit a murder the way Leslie Barry was murdered. The facts, plus a little common sense and deductive reasoning eliminated the majority of usual suspects. Kenneth Bianchi may have been a serial killer but he wasn't the killer I was looking for. The killer of Leslie Barry knew the apartment complex and Bianchi had no connection to the apartments in South Pasadena. Furthermore, Bianchi would have tripped over his feet trying to make that jump into the stairwell. If I was right in my analysis of the case, and Leslie Barry was another Hillside Strangler victim, the task force was headed down the wrong path with Bianchi and I feared for future victims.

My investigation was only a few weeks old and with the arrest of Bianchi, it had begun to run parallel with the Hillside Strangler investigation. By then, I was convinced that Art hadn't killed anyone, but I wanted to be certain of it by investigating my client carefully. If Art Anzures were guilty of the Barry murder, it would mean that he was one of the Hillside Stranglers. It struck me as comically absurd when I tried to imagine my frightened young client as the infamous serial killer who had for two years, evaded capture and stumped the largest, best equipped and best trained police department in the world.

It was clear that a thorough investigation of the Barry murder was pivotal to preventing a whole string of injustices from wrongly accused defendants to finding the bodies of more murder victims. If I couldn't solve the case, I could do the next best thing by amassing enough evidence on behalf of the defendant to devastate the prosecutor's case and assure an acquittal for Art Anzures. If I could do that, I would at least prevent one injustice.

The District Attorney was coming under enormous pressure to bring charges against Bianchi in all ten of the murders linked to the Hillside Strangler. The press, once the bitter nemesis of the Task Force, was now touting Bianchi as the Hillside Strangler, and applauding the Task Force for finally solving the case. The DA had charged Bianchi with only five of the ten murders attributed to the Hillside Strangler and for whatever reason he seemed to be dragging his feet when it came to bringing more charges against the Task Force's suspect of the day.

Every morning I anxiously opened my newspaper to see if more charges had been filed in the case. As time passed, I was encouraged by the DA's reluctance to charge Bianchi in the murders of Dolly Cepeda, Sonja Johnson, and Kristina Weckler. It gave me hope that someone close to the case didn't think Bianchi had murdered the younger victims. At the very least, the DA didn't feel he had the evidence to continue against Bianchi. Either way, it was all the same to me. Lack of evidence was sometimes an indication of a smart, slippery, killer but at other times, the lack of evidence was reason to believe that the police had the wrong man. As far as Bianchi was concerned, I was betting they had the wrong man.

Though I was focusing my investigation primarily on Cepeda and Johnson, it was a let-down when the DA caved to the pressure and decided to file charges against Bianchi for the Cepeda, Johnson, Weckler, Wagner and Hudspeth murders. I knew very little about the Weckler and Hudspeth cases and even less about the Wagner murder, but from what I did know, those particular homicides didn't make sense when grouped together with the other victims.

For one thing, these girls weren't hookers or connected to the street scene, and I felt that the killer of these girls would have a different pathology than one involving the murder of prostitutes or runaway street urchins. I didn't think that Cepeda, Johnson, Weckler, Wagner, and Hudspeth were random victims. The killer knew them, if not personally, then at least insofar as he researched and stalked them before abducting and murdering them. From the few facts I did have on those murders, I sensed that the killer or killers of these girls was an organized serial killer. Later, when I got the opportunity to study the police and autopsy reports on some of these Hillside Strangler murders, I would become certain of it. Equally strong were my feelings that the prostitutes and runaways were the random victims of a disorganized serial killer.

Shawn Hagen's statement provided me with a solid connection between Leslie Barry and Dolly Cepeda, but I still wanted to find a connection to another victim. Any kind of link, no matter how remote, between Kristina Weckler and Cepeda, Johnson, or Barry would do. Show me a cousin who dated the brother of a victim, or, a common friend like Shawn Hagen was with Leslie Barry and Dolly Cepeda. Give me two victims who went to the same doctor or medical facility, ate at the same fast food place, or attended the same church. I would accept anything that would show a crossing of paths where the victims could have met their common killer.

Wearing a hole in the sole of my shoes looking for that elusive connection made me feel like a real gumshoe but it was still a frustrating act of futility. I didn't have enough detailed information about the Hillside Strangler victims to thoroughly analyze the facts. I needed to know more about the victims, their families, and the crimes if I were to determine what, if any, similarities or connections existed between the various murders. Without having access to the police reports on the Hillside Strangler, I was analyzing in a vacuum of information.

I felt there were more victims linked to the same killer or killers than the task force had attributed to the Hillside Strangler. Besides Cepeda, Johnson, and Weckler, I was also interested in some of the victims the task force had either eliminated from their list of victims or ones that had never made it to their list. I was particularly interested in Margaret Madrid, the seven year old who had been found in the gutter in the City of Industry.

The murder of Margaret Madrid had similarities to the Cepeda and Johnson murders, and later in 1979, the Elizabeth Cevallos murder. Her age, Hispanic ancestry, and the degrading way her body was left in the gutter were consistent with those other murders. Cevallos was found in the drainage filter in the Rio Hondo wash and Cepeda and Johnson were found among the discarded broken bottles, beer cans, condom wrappers, and old mattresses in the ravine off Landa Street near the LAPD Police Academy.

From what little I knew about the Margaret Madrid murder, I noted a few dissimilarities. Besides her tender age, the primary inconsistency between Madrid and the other victims was that, other than Elizabeth Cevallos, Madrid lived and her body was found beyond the five-mile radius of the homes or drop sites of the other Hillside Strangler victims. Madrid's age and the area where she was found were the only dissimilarities I could find to justify the task force eliminating her from the list of victims. Yet, the similarities showing a possible link between Madrid, Cevallos, Cepeda, and Johnson to a single killer or killers far out-weighed the dissimilarities.

Conversely, other than being murdered by ligature strangulation, those victims had nothing in common with Yolanda Washington, who was a black prostitute, and other than age, they had little in common with Judith Miller, a fifteen-year old runaway. The state of Texas was the only common denominator I could fine between Cepeda and Kimberly Martin, the pretty, young woman who worked for an outcall massage service in Hollywood. Texas covers a wide area and I couldn't assume a crossing of paths just because a couple of victims happened to be from there. I understood that the Task Force was attempting to use the Hollywood area as a focal point of the killings, but the five-mile radius was a flimsy and arbitrary factor for linking or eliminating victims.

In all of this, the thing that caused me the most anxiety was the press coverage. At the time of Bianchi's arrest, the media didn't know about my investigation of the Barry murder, and they were following blindly in step with the Task Force's investigation of Kenneth Bianchi and a short time later, his cousin, Angelo Buono. I knew that once the press labeled Bianchi as the Hillside Strangler I'd have a hell of time getting anyone to look at the case from a different angle. If they did reverse direction, it would be another George Shamshak debacle. Not the press, not the Task Force, and certainly not the politically vulnerable District Attorney's office wanted another Shamshak mess.

As far as my investigation was concerned, an upside to the arrest of Kenneth Bianchi was that once he had been charged with the murders it would open up access to police reports, autopsy reports, photographs, and the thousands of clues that flooded the Task Force headquarters at the peak of public attention over the case.

In California, the law of discovery requires that all information gathered by the police during an investigation of a crime be made available to defense counsel. I needed that inside, detailed data to do a proper analysis and investigation of all the murders I was interested in. While Bianchi had a private attorney representing him in Bellingham, he was stuck with the public defender to represent him in the Hillside Strangler murders. I tried several times to get a phone call through to the public defender's office but never got further than speaking with a secretary or a minor functionary.

Members of the Task Force were in Bellingham, Washington for weeks interrogating Kenneth Bianchi before they ever got a confession out of him. When they did get him to talk, his half-baked confession implicated his cousin, Angelo Buono, in ten of the Hillside Strangler murders. Bianchi's confession was suspect to me. For one thing, he only confessed to the murders the Task Force attributed to him. In the majority of serial killer cases, after an arrest has been made and the confessions start to flow, the killer will inevitably confess to other unknown murders. Bianchi's confession didn't include victims not known to the Task Force or victims initially thought to be connected to the Hillside Strangler and later dismissed by the Task Force. In other words, it was a forced confession and not a free-wheeling you-guys-don't-know-the half-it type confession.

During his confession to the murders, Bianchi stated to the Task Force that he and Buono had killed all the victims in Buono's upholstery shop in Glendale. The Task Force, after Sheriff Peter Pitchess alerted the media, conducted a very public search of Buono's upholstery shop and living quarters. They covered every inch of the shop and house, photographing, dusting for fingerprints, and vacuuming up the carpet looking for trace evidence. They cleaned the premises so thoroughly it would make the most dedicated maid-service look sloppy.

Again, the Task Force came under fire from the media. Inviting the press to observe the search smacked of politics and the media didn't like the Task Force manipulating them to further their own political agenda. It was apparent to some reporters and observers that the LAPD intended to try the case in the media before it ever reached the courts. The Task Force was certain that the search would produce some damaging evidence against Buono and they wanted the press to be there to observe it. However, it was a big gamble considering the embarrassment caused by the Shamshak investigation a few months earlier.

The explanation the Task Force gave for notifying the media about the search was that the media would have found out about it anyway, so why not extend an invitation to them to stand outside the residence and report the search as it happened. The LA Times was concerned about how the police would be able to make it right by Buono if he turned out to be innocent of all the accusations. The new LAPD Police Chief, Daryl Gates, responded to that question by telling the Times that even if Buono was innocent of the murders he (Gates) would have trouble mustering up sympathy for him based upon what he now knew about his prime suspect. The reference was apparently about the Task Force learning that Buono, a local upholsterer, had been doing some pimping on the side.

The search of Buono's upholstery shop and residence didn't produce the kind of evidence the Task Force hoped to find. They found an address book belonging to Buono containing the address and phone number of Yolanda Washington and a few carpet fibers in the trunk of his car. The search was more significant for what it didn't find. Much to the chagrin and embarrassment of the Task

Force, the search failed to produce any conclusive or substantial evidence to corroborate Bianchi's confession about him and Buono murdering the girls in Buono's upholstery shop. They didn't find one fingerprint, strand of hair, spot of blood, article of clothing, jewelry, or any other trace evidence that could be linked to any of the victims. Except for finding Yolanda Washington's name and phone number in Buono's address book, the search was a total bust.

The Task Force was not inclined to let the matter drop there. They put Buono under surveillance twenty-four/seven and dogged him everywhere he went.

Buono was smart enough to recognize plainclothes cops on a stakeout, and, upset at what they were doing to his life, began playing pranks on them. To see if he could shake the shadow he would drive onto a freeway and take the first exit he came to, turn around and get back on the freeway at the first on ramp going in the opposite direction. Then he would get off again and go back the other way. He did the same thing over and over leading the cops around in circles. The tail would follow him into fast food drive-up windows and Buono would order food for them and take off without paying. Below the surface of these fun and games was an anger and fear that the cops had ruined his life based solely on the say-so of his crazy cousin, Kenneth Bianchi. When his upholstery business dropped off to nothing Buono had had enough.

The first thing Buono did when he became a suspect in the murders was to contact his lawyer, Ron Bain. Bain was a general practitioner leaning more toward civil law than criminal cases and he wasn't that certain about how best to serve his client's needs. Despite Buono's persistence that Bain do something to protect his rights against the intense police harassment and public humiliation, Bain was hesitant to file a harassment lawsuit against the city and county of Los Angeles and bring more unwanted attention to his client. He also felt that the DA would consider the filing of a lawsuit a challenge to his authority and might respond by having Buono arrested for murder. The DA might think that if he had to go to court anyway, he might as well go to the criminal court as the plaintiff rather than to civil court as the defendant and he would have Buono's sorry butt arrested.

What Bain really wanted to do was ride out the storm. He figured attention would soon dissipate and no one would remember the name Angelo Buono. As the police investigation and media attention intensified, Buono became more desperate for some relief. He wanted to at least threaten a lawsuit against the local government and force the cops to cease and desist their physical surveillance and wiretaps. He also wanted his lawyer to demand a public apology from the police and be cleared as a suspect in the Hillside Strangler murders.

The police and DA refused to give the apology and when Bain filed the lawsuit, they arrested Angelo Buono for murder. The DA filed various charges against him including procurement for prostitution, pimping and pandering, and ten counts of first-degree murder.

Within a week or two of Buono's arrest, I contacted Ron Bain to see if he had received any of the discovery documents from the police. Bain told me he had referred the case to an Orange County law office that specialized in Criminal cases. The media started to report that Orange County criminal lawyers, Terry Giles and John Barnett were representing Buono on the case. Terry Giles seemed to be getting most of the press coverage and I mistakenly thought that his law firm was the chief legal counsel for Angelo Buono. I called Giles' office and spoke with John Barnett. After introducing myself and giving him a synopsis of the Barry case, I asked Barnett if he would allow me to come down to his office and review whatever information he had on the Dolly Cepeda and Sonja Johnson murders.

Barnett was polite and seemed almost glad to hear from me. Death threats against defendants and their lawyers are a very common occurrence in high profile murder cases and I guess anyone that wasn't phoning to say, "I'm gonna blow your ass up" was a welcome caller. Barnett said he would be more than happy to have me come down and review the police reports and photographs of any of the Hillside Strangler murders I was interested in. I arranged a specific time to meet with him.

I arrived at his Orange County law office at the appointed time and met one of the men defending the most famous murder defendant in the world, John Barnett. Barnett was a man of average height and he appeared to be in great physical shape. He wore heavy, dark rimmed glasses that added a look of intelligence to his powerful athletic build. It may have been the dark rimmed glasses he wore, but for whatever reason, his physical appearance reminded me of George Reeves, the actor who played Superman in the TV series. He greeted me with a warm smile as we shook hands.

Without much chatter, Barnett led me into a room that appeared to be a combination supply and copy room. Scattered on the floor throughout the small room were several cardboard file boxes. Barnett picked one up and indicated that I should get another one. We carried the boxes into a vacant office and he told me I could use the office for as long as I needed it. I'm sure he sensed my eagerness to get to work and telling me if I needed anything to just give him a buzz, he turned and left the room.

The boxes were disorganized and in going though the files, I found several copies of every report. After spreading the reports out on the desk, I took a quick inventory to see what reports and photographs were there and I found the initial police report on the Delores Cepeda and Sonja Johnson murders. As I picked it up and started to read, Barnett stuck his head in the room and told me that he didn't have all the reports. He said many of the reports and crime photographs were scattered around Orange County at other law offices and their private investigators offices. I was happy to get what I had right now and I would worry about the other reports later.

My earlier research at the library had familiarized me with the facts of the Cepeda/Johnson disappearance but the report I was now holding contained details I had been waiting to get my hands on for months.

According to the report, Cepeda and Johnson left Johnson's house on Avenue 46 at 1:00 P.M. to go shopping at the Eagle Rock Shopping Plaza. Sonja called home at about 4:00 P.M. and spoke with her mother about the price of drapes. The girls were supposed to be home by 6:00 P.M. but they didn't arrive at the bus stop on the corner of Colorado Boulevard and Sierra Villa until that time (6:00 P.M.).

The girls followed five teenage and preteen boys from the Mall to the bus stop: Louis, Anthony, and Douglas Landinguin, Louie

Chavez, and Richie Powell. While waiting for the bus, they were joined by another teenage boy, Tony Rosa. Rosa knew Sonja Johnson and the two struck up a conversation while waiting for the bus, and Sonja gave him a small, thin, white metal ring with a star on it. Rosa said he saw several similar rings in a paper bag carried by Sonja Johnson. Sonja told him she had earrings worth $100.00 in the bag and that she had stolen the jewelry while in the mall. Rosa also told Task Force members that Dollie Cepeda mentioned to him her plan to spend the night with a friend and he assumed the friend she was talking about was Sonja Johnson.

All the kids boarded RTD bus number 7, which took them down Colorado Boulevard to Eagle Rock Boulevard and a right on Eagle Rock Boulevard to York Boulevard where they caught another bus running east on York Boulevard to their bus stop on Avenue 46. It was just a short walk from there to Sonja Johnson's house, but the two girls would never make it to the safety of the Johnson house.

When the bus stopped at York Boulevard and Avenue 46, Cepeda and Johnson got off and crossed York Boulevard at the crosswalk. The bus was stopped for several minutes waiting for the stoplight to change so it could continue down York Boulevard. While the bus was stopped, Louis Landinguin, sitting on the street side of the bus, watched the girls cross York Boulevard. As they started to walk up Avenue 46 toward Sonja's house, Landinguin saw a car, which was also headed east on York Boulevard, make a left turn on Avenue 46 and pull up to the curb alongside the girls. One of the girls approached the car on the passenger side and talked with the occupants. When the traffic light turned green, the bus pulled out from the curb and continued down York Boulevard and Louis Landinguin lost sight of the girls. They were half a block from the Johnson residence and the two girls would never be seen alive again.

The report went on to say that the massive media coverage caused the formation of the Hillside Strangler Task Force, and that during the week between Sunday, November 13, when the girls disappeared, and Sunday, November 20, when the bodies of the girls were discovered, the Task Force had received numerous calls from the public reporting sightings of the girls. All but one reported contact had been eliminated as misidentifications.

It was an important statement and I will quote word for word from the police report dated December 18, 1977:

"Carlos DeLaTorre, age 14, told investigators that he met Sonja Johnson at the beginning of the summer in 1977. Sonja liked Carlos and would call him every day on the telephone. Carlos had not seen Sonja for several weeks and on Tuesday, November 15, 1977, at approximately 1530 hours; he received a telephone call from Sonja. Carlos recognized Sonja's voice, after the girl identified herself as Sonja Johnson.

He states that she began the conversation by talking to him in what he refers to as a code, or "Chinese talk." He asked her how she learned to talk like that and she told him that she learned it in school. She was giggling with another girl as she talked to him on the telephone and her voice sounded hollow as if she were talking in a room without furniture.

After exchanging greetings with him in her normal tone of voice, she told Carlos that she was staying with a roommate a few blocks away from her mother's house in Eagle Rock. She refused to give him her address. When asked who was with her, she told Carlos that Dolly was her roommate. Sonja then asked Carlos to do her a favor and call "P." Carlos agreed to do so and questioned her about who "P" was by naming several people whose names begin with the letter "P." She refused to explain whom she was referring to, stating that he would have to think about it.

The conversation concluded when Carlos heard a loud banging at the door and a man's voice demanding entrance in a loud manner. Sonja told him that she had to go as her mother was at the door. Carlos states that he was unaware that the girls were missing at the time of the telephone call, and found out about it from friends later. Investigators interviewed Paul Flores and Ruben Alamillo, friends of Carlos', who documented his statement.

The statement of Carlos DeLaTorre was of intense interest to me. I wasn't sure if Barnett would make copies of the reports for me or allow me to take the reports home so I made copious and detailed notes of all the statements. This statement was so important I copied it verbatim. Not only did it tell me the girls were alive for at least two days after they disappeared, but it also indicated they were held captive in the area for a short time.

The report raised questions for which I needed to get answers. Why would the killers allow the girls access to a telephone? Who was "P" that Sonja Johnson wanted Carlos to call? Could it have been the police? Her parents? Why was Sonja talking in code when she was apparently in the room with Dolly Cepeda? Did the fact that she didn't seem all that alarmed mean that she or Dolly knew the killers? The question that stopped me cold was: why did the room sound empty?

From the reports on the Cepeda/Johnson murders, I could see a pattern emerging. Eddie Castillon and Dennis Cantu had moved out of the Monterey Road apartment complex a week to ten days before Leslie was murdered. According to Denise Anzures, neither one had turned in a key to the apartment when they moved out. Furthermore, the men had left numerous things in the apartment and Denise delayed cleaning the apartment because she thought they would return to get It. Wasn't it logical that Cantu would have thought, when he returned to murder Leslie Barry, that if he was caught or spotted going into the apartment he would have a good excuse for being there?

Eddie Castillon and Martin Smith had previously lived on Crescent Street, east of Avenue 46, a short distance from York Boulevard and the spot where Sonja Johnson and Dolly Cepeda lived and were last seen alive. According to Louis Landinguin's statement the car he saw turn left onto Avenue 46 had also been traveling east on York Boulevard. Had the men in the car followed the girls from the Eagle Rock Plaza? The car was headed in the direction in which Castillon and Smith lived. Perhaps they were headed home when by chance they spotted the girls get off the bus and recognized one of them.

They had moved out of the house and into the Monterey Road apartments approximately two weeks before Dolly Cepeda and Sonja Johnson disappeared. If Castillon and Smith had kept a key to the house on Crescent Street like they did when they moved out of the Monterey Road complex, and used the house to imprison Cepeda and Johnson it would explain why the room sounded empty when

Sonja called Carlos DeLaTorre. Having put in a telephone disconnect with the phone company the two killers probably thought the phone service had been disconnected which would explain why Sonja had access to a telephone. It was speculation and conjecture but it was a damn good scenario with a lot of promise. All I had to do was find a way to eat, keep a roof over my head, and gas in my car while I proved it.

I'm a slow writer and by the time I'd finished taking notes on the initial police report of the Dolly Cepeda and Sonja Johnson murders, Barnett came into the room and told me they were locking up and going home. I asked him if I could come down the next day and finish reading the reports and looking at some crime scene photographs. Barnett said it was no problem and we left the boxes and information in the vacant office.

The next day I went down to Barnett's office in Orange County to finish my research. While I didn't find any reports on Hudspeth or Wagner, I did find a few reports on Kristina Weckler. Again, I was looking for anything that might show a link to the Barry murder; maybe a partial M.O. that would fit; like knots in a cord or anything that might indicate the killer had knowledge of the anatomy or some connection to the medical field. There were a couple of interesting bits of information from the Kristina Weckler files.

Interviews and statements taken by her friends said that she was extremely careful about her safety, particularly with the Hillside Strangler on the loose in the area. Yet, she had disappeared without leaving any evidence of a struggle. The top sheet and blanket on her bed were turned back as if she was about to get into bed and her nightgown was folded neatly and lying on the toilet seat. Her apartment looked clean and neat and nothing appeared to be out of place.

The description of Weckler's apartment reminded me of Leslie Barry's bedroom. I tried to imagine what the Barry apartment might have looked like had Aina Barry not arrived home when she did. Did Barry's killer intend to remove her body from the apartment? Remove Leslie's body from the floor of her bedroom and the two apartments would be described in a very similar way.

The autopsy on Kristina Weckler held a big surprise. The coroner had found a needle mark on Kristina Weckler's arm. Her friends had told police that she was a strong and outspoken opponent of drug abuse and refused to attend parties where drugs would be used. She was fervently anti-drug. This particular autopsy report was a preliminary report and didn't contain a toxicological screen. As a result, there was no report on what, if any, substance or substances were found in her system.

Learning about the needle mark on Weckler's arm was the kind of information I was looking for. Among other things, it was a possible medical connection. Doctors, nurses and other medical personnel had more access to drugs and syringes than even the most avid, everyday recreational junkie. The needle mark was also significant for another reason. It could indicate that Kristina Weckler knew her killer or killers and that they knew her well enough to know about her strong opposition to drugs.

Later, when I was formally on the defense team for Angelo Buono and had more time, access to reports, and others to discuss the case with, I learned that the substance found in her system was battery acid. It was another way of humiliating the victim in death through her strongly held beliefs and good character.

After reading the reports, I came away from Barnett's office more convinced than ever that the Barry, Cepeda, Johnson, and Weckler murders were committed by the same killer or killers. I never had contact with the Giles/Barnett Law office again, but a few months later, I would be offered the chance to join the defense for Angelo Buono.

Chapter 20

Ethel was a twenty-five pound, fifteenyear old guard cat that protected Wendy when she lived in the Pasadena Ghetto. When she moved east she left the cat in my care until I could deliver her to New York. I made a plane reservation to deliver the feline a week before I phoned Detective Kushner to talk about the case. Although Art's trial was over and he was headed to San Quentin, a place the jury said he should call home for the rest of his natural life, I was not giving up my efforts to clear him of the Barry murder.

Before the penalty phase of the trial began, Molino approached Detective Kushner about testifying on behalf of Anzures. Even when their client is innocent, some defense lawyers seem to think that winning a death penalty case means keeping your client from being juiced. Kushner agreed to testify that he didn't think Art was a danger to others nor did he think Art would ever kill again even if he were one day freed. While Mitch was thrilled about getting the detective to testify on behalf of Anzures, it really wasn't much of a concession for Kushner because he knew that Barry was a Hillside Strangler victim and that Art was not the Hillside Strangler. Somewhere in that conversation with Kushner, Molino told him to "remember the name Eddie Castillon."

During my phone conversation with him, the detective told me that he had alibied Castillon for the Barry murder. Given their total lack of interest in my suspects this information was a surprising revelation. Kushner told me that one of Eddie's professors at the USC School of Dentistry said he could state without reservation that Castillon was in class on the evening of the Barry murder.

Until Kushner told me about the alibi, I was convinced that Eddie had killed Leslie Barry. However, my analysis of the murder indicated that the killer had a good working knowledge of anatomy and was adept at tying knots so I also kept an open mind that as a medical intern, Dennis Cantu fit the profile as well. Also, as boyhood friends from Laredo, Texas, Cantu was linked to my two main suspects, and he actually fit the medical profile in the Barry murder better than Castillon. What I couldn't figure out was his involvement in the Hillside Strangler murders.

Interviewing neighbors at the South Pasadena apartments who knew the 3 suspects turned up what I considered some good stuff. Convinced that Eddie Castillon was the "Eddie" going around knocking on apartment doors a week before the murder, I went back and re-interviewed tenants to try to put together some background on the three young men from Laredo, Texas.

While asking questions around the apartment complex, I heard a couple of stories that were of great interest to me.

A young, shapely, female tenant who lived at the apartments told me that she was walking through the tunnel toward the carport area one evening, and suddenly got an eerie feeling that someone was following close behind her. She stopped dead in her tracts, turned around, and there, standing inches from her was Dennis Cantu. She let out a bloodurdling scream and ran to her car as fast as she could, got in, and locked the door. She said having her space invaded like that in a dimly lit tunnel, by a stranger, was the scariest thing that had ever happened to her. She thought it was very weird that Cantu was following so close behind her.

Another tenant told me a story about being at the pool one day while Martin Smith was walking around the pool deck with a lizard attached to a string like a puppy on a leash. Suddenly, he stomped down hard on the lizard with his boot and sprayed blood and guts all over the pool deck.

When put in the context of general profiles on serial killers, these statements were of great interest to me. Add to them the timeline of the Barry murder; the solid link between Barry and Cepeda; the statements by Jeanne Marek and Helen Marie Mahboub about a man named "Eddie" knocking on their door and it was all mounting evidence in support of Cantu, Castillon and Smith being connected to the Hillside Strangler murders.

One afternoon during cocktail hour at the John Bull Pub, I met a young woman who was a nurse at the USC Medical Center. The conversation came around to what I did for a living and that always led to me telling about the murder case from Hell. After telling her about my investigation of the Hillside Strangler murders, I told her that one of my prime suspects in the case was an intern at the USC Medical Center. She wanted a name. When told it was Dennis Cantu, she said she knew him and that he was one of the most arrogant doctors she had ever met. He always seemed angry and he never asked a nurse to do something for him; rather, he always commanded it like he was God or some omnipotent creature the nurses were to personally serve. Beyond taking Psyche 101 in college, I didn't know much about the world of bondage and dominance or sadomasochism; but, statements like these were encouraging and motivated me to keep searching for evidence and talking about the case.

In the conversation I had with Castillon at the USC School of Dentistry, he urged me to call Cantu and his statement that I should talk to Cantu was a constant tape playing in my head. I tried to get Cantu on the phone several times to talk to him about the Barry murder. He didn't have an answering machine at his home and no one ever answered the phone. I left messages for him at the medical school but he never returned my phone calls. I had the feeling that Dr. Cantu was avoiding me. I didn't pursue him as aggressively as the police might because, without the powers of arrest, short of shooting the bastard, I couldn't take any immediate action to subdue him. He could confess to killing thirty women and I'd have to tell him, 'well let me get back to you on that. In the mean time don't kill any more women, okay?' His avoidance of me didn't exactly point to his innocence.

When Kushner told me he had taken the initiative to alibi Castillon, I didn't have any trouble believing the alibi to be true. Had Deputy Beck conveyed that information to me it would've been a different story. Beck had lost all credibility with me early in my investigation when he told me that the police had brought the sack of groceries to the crime scene. It took about 2 seconds for my mind to process that as a bald-faced lie. That's how long it took to run through every possible scenario where a cop would stop and do his grocery shopping on the way to a crime scene and then, rather than leave his purchases in the patrol car, he brings them into the crime scene and sits them on the kitchen counter to be photographed.

After hanging up, it occurred to me that Kushner had done me a big favor and cleared one of my two suspects. I immediately called him back and said, "Hey, if it wasn't Castillon it had to be Cantu."

Kushner asked me what I wanted to do next and I told him I was on my way to New York and I'd give him a call when I returned from my trip. My hesitation to instantly move on the case seemed to dampen Kushner's enthusiasm, and I thought maybe he didn't think I was taking this case as seriously as I should if I really believed Cantu was a dangerous serial killer. Kushner' reaction caused me some guilt about going to New York; but he had all the information I had and all he had to do was connect the dots and conduct an honest investigation.

I'm not much of a cat person, but it was my responsibility to deliver the cat to Wendy still breathing. My trip to New York with Ethel was anything but smooth. The flight was okay, but when I retrieved Ethel from the baggage carousel at Kennedy International Airport, she wasn't moving inside her carry case. I had gone to the trouble of buying a top of the line leather carrying case to make the cat comfortable during the flight.

I shook the case violently and she didn't make a peep. She was dead weight and I thought she was dead, period. I stuck my finger through the air holes and wiggled it while cooing at her trying to get some indication of life. I thought she might paw at my finger in a playful way but when I didn't get a reaction from her, I thought the worst. She was either dead or very pissed off about her flight accommodations. After a few minutes of shaking the carry case, wiggling my finger in the air hole, and cooing at her I got nothing from inside the cat luggage. Not a whimper, not a meow.

I didn't want to open the case in the airport. If she escaped, I might never be able to catch her and get her back inside the carryall. On the other hand, I was becoming extremely concerned about her health. I didn't want to wait until I got her home to open up the pet traveler and discover a dead cat. It would freak Wendy out and put her in a funk that I didn't want to deal with on this trip. The oblong carry case had two flaps at the top on both sides and the air holes matched up when the flaps were closed. I carefully pealed one flap back and tried to wedge my hand between the other flap and the wall of the case to see if I could poke her with my fingertips. I got my fingers inside the case far enough to feel the fur but I couldn't really poke her. There was still no sign of life coming from inside the case.

My curiosity was getting the best of me and I had to find out if Ethel was alive. I slowly opened the other flap so I could see inside. When the flap was about three-fourths of the way opened she suddenly lunged at the opening. Though the attack took me by surprise and caused me to jerk my head back, my reflexes were fast. I grabbed her by the tail just as she cleared the wall of the carry case. When I grabbed her tail, she let out with a loud, primal, scream and curled into a ball clawing at my hand. My free hand moved quickly to her throat and letting go of her tail I managed to get her by the scruff of the neck and forced the struggling feline back into the carrying case. When I looked up people were walking by shaking their heads as if to say 'what part of Iowa did this rube come from?'

With Ethel safely back in the bag I boarded the bus for White Plains and settled into a seat at the back of the bus. After the long flight and my bout with the cat, I was tired and in dire need of a nap when the bus driver came up to me and said, I'd have to get off the bus. An old New Jersey blue hair had complained to the driver that she was allergic to cats. They threw me off the bus and told me to catch the next one. The next bus would be by in twenty minutes, they assured me. Six hours later, I was still sitting on the cat carrying case in the airport terminal waiting for the next bus. It was raining and accidents on the freeway delayed the limos, was the only explanation I was given for the long delay.

The trouble with the cat at the airport was just a harbinger of the week to come and by the time it was over, I couldn't wait to get back to California. It would be far more relaxing to investigate a murder case.

After getting Ethel to her new home, Wendy set her free and she climbed up a tree and didn't come down for two weeks. For all the trouble in getting her to New York, she died within a year. She was a California cat and just couldn't handle the cold weather.

When I returned from New York, I immediately tried to reach Detective Kushner, but I was never able to talk to him again. He started avoiding me as much as Cantu and pawning me off on his partner in crime, Jerry Beck. Beck didn't know a damn thing about the facts of the case and wasn't able to discuss it intelligently. Contrary to all the evidence, Beck was a true believer that Anzures killed Leslie Barry and his tunnel vision about the case was a source of great frustration to me.

In the fall of 1979, Mark Southerland rented an office down the hallway from Crisp and Marley and started his first law practice. He had taken up residence in a small cottage in the Arroyo Seco area of Pasadena, subletting it from a friend. The Arroyo was one of the most desirable residential areas in Pasadena. The streets were wide and tree-lined with lush green, manicured lawns decorating the front of large old mansions. Many of the homes in that area are listed on the historical registry and were built by the famed architects, Green and Green.

Still sleeping on the floor of my office, I began to realize that because of the refusal of the cops to look at the facts of the Barry murder, and the political nature of the Hillside Strangler case, straightening out this mess would be a longer project than I ever had anticipated. She hadn't said so, but Wendy was leaning toward not having me come back there to live. She wanted to get on with her life and on to her next husband, lover or whatever. Mark was looking for new digs and asked me if I wanted to take over his Sub-lease on the cottage. It was a cute little one-bedroom bungalow situated on a private cul-de-sac with five or six other cottages lining both sides of the driveway. The cottages were close together and each cottage had a small fenced-in back yard with a patio. It was private, quiet, and completely furnished, and it beat the hell out of sleeping on the office floor. I told Mark I'd love to take over the sublet for him.

My rent at the Green Hotel didn't amount to much, but I still couldn't afford to keep up rent on both an office and an apartment. I wasn't ready, though, to give up my funky office at the Green Hotel. That building, the Green Hotel, had hard–bitten-street-smart-private eye written all over it. Having an office there was good for my image and I wanted to hang on to it for as long asI could. Until the Barry murder came along and drained my resources, I had been a good tenant paying my rent on time and not bothering the senior citizens who called the Green Hotel home. The leasing manager liked me and some months she'd let me slide on the rent when my cash flow was down.

I was becoming anxious about my future and the future of Crisp and Marley. I had lost all interest in investigating personal injury and product liability cases, doing service of process, and skip tracing witnesses and defendants to civil lawsuits. Cases wholly about money didn't seem important to me compared to the high stakes of criminal cases. I knew, though, that even as criminal cases go, this one was special. The stakes were unimaginably high. Not only was one innocent man in prison and two more on their way, but also the cost in human life and misery was overwhelming.

I needed to find some way to enhance my credibility and gain more experience in criminal investigations. Doing a little networking with a friend and well-known Pasadena banking lawyer, I met a former Pasadena Municipal Court Judge, named Warren Ettinger. I liked Warren from the first time I spoke with him on the phone. Warren was a partner and chief litigator in the Los Angeles law firm of Beardsley, Hufstedler, and Kimble. I was awed by Warren's breadth of knowledge, not only about the law, but also about the court system and the people who ran it. I was far more impressed with Warren Ettinger than he was with me.

I knew and had worked with many fine lawyers in Los Angeles but I'd never met one who made the law come to life like Warren did. He was a walking, talking, law library. When I met him in person, my first impression was that he looked to conservative to be a Southern California Democrat. His subdued suits and crew cut hair reminded me of an ex-marine. With his intelligence and conservative appearance, I would've thought he was a nerd who had lived most of his life with his nose stuck in a book. To Warren the law wasn't just theory; it was the rules by which we lived and settled disputes, and Warren was as street smart as he was book smart.

He had a quick wit and a wry sense of humor that kept me in stitches for most of the time I worked with him. I don't know what impressed him about me but it certainly wasn't my fragmented recitation of the facts of the Barry murder. Maybe it was my single-minded determination to clear Art Anzures of the murder, or maybe it was just because I was a friend of the banking lawyer. Whatever it was, Warren had me appointed to a murder case he was handling pro bono and I immediately knew that he wanted to see if I was a raving maniac that saw a conspiracy in every arrest the cops made, or if I really knew how to analyze facts and connect the dots.

The case involved a petty drug dealer charged with two murders. It wasn't a double homicide, as neither of the victims, nor the circumstances of the murders, were related to each other. There was no question about guilt. The defendant confessed that he committed the murders so his only goal on the case was to avoid the death penalty.

The Defendant had the dubious ambitions of becoming a big drug dealer and wanted to live out his fantasy of being a hit man. The first murder he was charged with involved a heroin addict named Sammy Moreno, who had ripped him off for thirteen hundred bucks in drugs, and he wanted to make an example of him. The plan called for Williams and an accomplice to lure Moreno to an isolated area of the San Fernando Valley by dangling drugs in his face and then put a bullet in his head. Everything was going as planned. The San Fernando Valley has a number of secluded spots and the two would-be hit men drove their target around until they were a mile-and-a-half from nowhere. It was there that Williams gave him a sample of some high-grade China White heroin. Moreno kneeling by the open door cooking the heroin by the light from the door panel would've been the ideal time to put a slug in the back of his head, but these wannabe assassins became afraid of the dark and chickened out. Driving their mark back to civilization, they chose a well-lit area in the parking lot of an apartment building to do the job.

It was around 10:00 PM and all the tenants in the apartment were still awake. The two inept killers parked the car about twelve feet from a bedroom window and thirty feet from a living room picture window. As amazing as it may sound, it seemed as if they took comfort from the knowledge that if things went poorly during the shooting they'd get help from the tenants at the apartment building. When they started the shooting, it was apparent that these two idiots could've used some practice at the shooting range before they tried to execute this job. They opened fire on the victim and continued to shoot him nineteen times.

They shot him from through the car and they shot him from over the top of the car. When the victim fell to the ground still moaning, they shot him from under the car. They shot at him from the front of the car and they shot at him from the rear of the car. It's a wonder they didn't shoot each other in the crossfire. The coroner noted that the victim had thirty-three entry and exit wounds in his torso and the bullets formed a crisscross pattern through his body. Naturally, in that area and with that kind of firepower, there were witnesses to the murder. It was also apparent that the defendant and his accomplice had no aptitude as hit men.

The second murder Williams was charged with was even dumber. A pimp walking down Hollywood Boulevard had the misfortune of reaching the intersection of La Palma Street and Hollywood Boulevard at the same time as Williams. When the pimp crossed the street in front of his car, Williams, having such a well-rounded personality and a refined sense of humor, thought it would be hilarious to bump the pimp with the fender of his car. The pimp didn't find as much hilarity in William's foolhardy prank as William's did. He came around to the driver side window and started swearing and threatening the defendant.

Williams, who was with his girlfriend at the time, felt that the pimp should've taken the bump with a bit more levity. He began to feel less than a man himself for taking all this abuse from a black man in front of his woman. The straw that broke the camel's back, so to speak, came when the pimp, referring to Williams' girlfriend, told him he should take that "ho" out and sell her.

Williams reached under his seat, pulled out a .357 Magnum and shot the pimp once in the shoulder. After his arrest, Williams told the cops, and later his defense lawyer, that he had just intended to wing the guy and didn't mean to kill him. He just wanted to put a little hurt on him for disrespecting his girlfriend. His explanation made sense. The problem was that the bullet entered the victim's shoulder at a perpendicular angle and ricocheted inside his body damaging vital organs before departing out his lower back.

After analyzing the police and autopsy reports and doing a lot of legwork on the case, I wrote what I considered an excellent report. Warren was trying to reach a plea bargain with the DA assigned to the case to achieve his client's goal of avoiding the death penalty, but the Assistant DA was jerking him around. Warren felt that the DA should be more than happy to negotiate since the state's case involved two murder victims with a sympathy level lower than guards at a Nazi concentration camp. The jury was just as likely to give Williams a good citizenship award for exterminating vermin from society as to convict him of first-degree murder.

The defense also knew it was just a matter of blind luck that the Hollywood victim turned out to be a pimp because standing in society was not a factor in Williams' victim selection process. The pimp he gunned down on Hollywood Boulevard could just as easily have been a model citizen.

This was one of the few instances where a plea bargain achieved a defendant's goal while working to the benefit of the community. The plea bargain Warren hammered out with the DA was something akin to poetic justice. The defendant agreed to turn states evidence against his drug supplier in exchange for two life sentences for murder. The state got two for the price of one and it gave the criminal element an opportunity to police and punish each other. It was my sincere hope that Williams would get himself shanked in prison for being a snitch.

My report was irrelevant to the outcome of the case but I think I demonstrated to Warren that I knew how to connect the dots in a murder case and that all my investigations weren't without end like my investigation of the Barry murder seemed to be. Working with a lawyer of Warren's caliber challenged me mentally and lifted my quality of work. I had to stay on my toes to keep up with him.

A few weeks later Warren was contacted by the Public Defenders office to take over the defense for a man they thought might be wrongly charged with murder. Again, Warren requested that I be appointed by the court to investigate the case.

This second murder case was less cut and dried than the first case. The defendant was charged with the murder of a seventeen-year old donut shop employee during a robbery at a Beverly Hills donut shop. It was a five-year old murder case and witnesses were not easy to find, and when found, their memories of events that night were dulled by the passage of time. The defendant denied committing the murder and claimed to have an alibi. He asserted that he was in the army at the time of the robbery but his alibi didn't hold up.

He had been booted out of the army before the murder occurred, and the prosecutor had some damaging evidence. A partial thumbprint lifted from the counter of the donut shop matched his thumb.

Although there were three eyewitnesses to the robbery, the police only talked to two of them. In a photo show-up, one witness picked the defendant, the third person in the photo, and the other witness picked contestant number six. The third witness was not shown the photo lineup by the police and he was the one I wanted to talk to first.

This eyewitness was a lawyer and I tracked him down to an older office building in downtown Los Angeles. He was an entrepreneur lawyer employed in the importing and exporting of expensive jewelry. His office had security cameras and his receptionist was protected by a bulletproof glass window with a round pattern of speaker holes at face level. It looked like a fortress, and if this witness didn't want to talk to me, I'd have a hell of a time getting to him.

After explaining to his secretary who I was and what I was doing there, he agreed to see me. She buzzed me through the security door, and when I got inside the reason for such heavy security was not readily apparent. The office was small, cluttered and furnished with a filing cabinet against one wall and an old desk that wasn't worth stealing. Except for the Rolex watch on his left wrist, there wasn't a piece of jewelry in sight. It occurred to me that since he was a lawyer he might've needed to take these heavy security measures to hide from his clients or bill collectors.

After exchanging amenities with him, I got to the point of my visit. I opened the murder book to the photo show-up, laid the book down on his desk in front of him and told him to pick me a winner. Without any prompting from me or hesitation from him, he picked number six. He had not selected the defendant but he chose the same person from the photo as one of the other witnesses to the murder.

This case was turning out to be more interesting than I would've imagined. On the prosecution side of the case was a thumbprint taken from the counter matched to a defendant who probably wouldn't regularly patronize a Beverly Hills donut shop and a witness who picked the defendant out of a photo lineup. On the other side of the case, we had two eyewitnesses who not only picked the wrong man, but they picked the same wrong man. They both said that the person they saw shoot the kid was much bigger than the defendant. Eyewitness identifications are notoriously unreliable, and with the passage of time, they become even more fickle. Was it possible that all three eyewitnesses were wrong?

There was no doubt that the thumbprint placed the defendant in the donut shop at some point before the murder. One of the witnesses that picked the number six man in the photograph told me that the one outstanding physical characteristic of the person he remembered as being in the donut shop that night was that the guy waddled like a duck when he walked.

I told Warren that I didn't think our client was the shooter, but the thumbprint was compelling evidence that he was somehow involved in the murder. Talking to the defendant at the county jail one day, he let it be known that his nickname in the hood was "The Duck". I asked him how he got that nickname and he said it was given to him because of the way he walked. While proclaiming his innocence, The Duck told me a story about a wild ride he took through the streets of Beverly Hills one night. He went into considerable detail about hitting dips at intersections and taking corners at high speeds. He didn't say it, but the story sounded remarkably like a speedy getaway.

Politically the felony murder rule looks good on paper, and the more politicians can impute criminal liability to third parties the more support they gain from the law and order lobby. The felony murder rule says that anyone involved in a felony, which results in the death of another human, is guilty of the crime of murder, regardless of who caused the death. Defendants don't understand how they can be held accountable for something they didn't do and never intended to do, and jurors don't particularly like holding people responsible for the murderous acts of others.

When trial time came, Warren handed me a bunch of subpoenas to serve. The lawyer/jeweler was an important witness for the defense and, when I went back to his office to serve the paper, his secretary told me, very unconvincingly, that he wasn't in. His office was the only address I had, and if he were going to start avoiding service of process I'd have to find another place to lay the subpoena on him. I tried his office several more times, and his secretary, tired of my persistence, told me he was out of the country. I didn't believe her.

The home address I got from the police report was five-years old and he was no longer living at that Malibu house. None of my usual sources turned up an address on him and with time running out, Ettinger was pressuring me to find the witness and serve him. Warren knew how to push my buttons and motivate me. He told me over the phone that if I didn't find this witness there would be a miscarriage of justice in the case and he wanted him served and put on standby for the following Monday.

That weekend I got my ass in gear. The witness struck me as a hip, yuppie kind of guy who would live in Malibu until he was carried out in a wooden box or a brass urn. I drove down to Malibu not knowing what I was going to do to find him. I stopped at a real estate office on Pacific Coast Highway and asked the realtor if he knew the witness. He didn't. I asked if he had a reverse telephone directory thinking I could look up the old number and maybe find a new address with the old number. The realtor didn't have a reverse phone directory either. Some kind of real estate office, I thought.

Pissed and frustrated, I got in my car and gunned it out of the parking lot leaving a trail of dust in my wake. I was in a quandary about what to do next. It was a beautiful Southern California day so I just drove around Malibu enjoying the ocean views, the sunshine, and the bikini clad women. I turned onto a side street from Pacific Coast Highway and drove through a hilly neighborhood just east of the highway. I spotted a guy in his driveway washing his car and pulled up to the curb. I told him a lawyer friend of mine used to live in his neighborhood but had moved since the last time I saw him. I asked the man if he knew him and if he knew where my friend lived now.

I firmly believe that God blesses those who seek justice. The man knew him and told me exactly where he lived and gave me directions on how to get there. My witness wasn't home so the next day, Sunday, I drove to Malibu and staked out his house.

A stakeout is a boring job. You can sit in your car for hours wondering if you're wasting your time or if it will pay off. In this case, I only had to wait for about 3 hours before the witness showed up. It was after dark before he pulled into his driveway and got out of his jeep with a very large, mean looking dog. I approached the man cautiously. Paranoia runs rampant in Los Angeles and I already knew how security conscious this guy was. I didn't want him to mistake me for a mugger and shoot me and I didn't want to become Alpo for Rover. Besides, after the incident with Ethel, I didn't think I was in good standing with the domestic animal world. He was already on the porch fumbling with his door key when I reached him. It was too dark to see his face enough to recognize him so I called his name as a question. When he answered to his name, I handed the subpoena to him.

After I served the paper on him, he was polite and invited me in for a drink. With our drinks in hand we settled into some soft furniture and he told me I had used the right amount of caution in approaching him because he had just spent four thousand dollars to have his dog attack trained. I thought, "Damn I have good instincts!"

I told him he was on standby and didn't have to appear in court until either I, or Warren, called him to testify.

I finished my report to Warren before the trial started. I concluded in my final report on this case that the defendant was the driver of the getaway car. No other theory or analysis of the crime was more consistent with the facts. Warren added to my scenario that the defendant must have gone into the donut shop to case the joint, which is how his thumbprint happened to be on the counter. The eyewitnesses saw two different guys come into the donut shop. That explained why their photo show-up selections were inconsistent. The defendant then left and his accomplice, a man known only by his hood name of "Big Man" came in and committed the robbery and murder. A couple of years after the robbery, "Big Man" was gunned down on a street corner in Watts by a jealous girlfriend. It's funny how justice sometimes works out in spite of what we do.

The prosecutor handling the case didn't have the benefit of this analysis because his investigators hadn't done a complete job. He was trying to put the murder weapon in the hand of the defendant and some of the jurors didn't buy it. After a remarkable job of trial work by Warren Ettinger, the jury came back deadlocked seven to five for conviction. Rather than retry the case, the lawyers worked out a plea bargain for manslaughter.

The arresting officer on that case was Bob Mellecker, the member of the Hillside Strangler Task Force who had taken my report on the Barry murder. Mellecker had done a good job on the case, but I didn't feel that entitled him to be so cocky with me over the lead I tried to give him in the Hillside Strangler case. A short time after that case, I thought about Mellecker and his parting question to me when he came to my office and interviewed me concerning my findings in the Hillside Strangler case. "What do these guys look like?" He wanted to know.

I was sitting in my little cottage in Pasadena watching the news one evening when they brought Kenneth Bianchi back to Los Angeles. The TV cameras showed him at the airport walking from the plane and surrounded by members of the task force. There seemed to be something strangely familiar about the accused

Hillside Strangler. He might have seemed familiar because of the many news reports since his arrest in Bellingham. But my recognition of him seemed to be closer than a news source.

I had the file of the Leslie Barry murder in my briefcase and I took it out and searched through it for the picture of Dennis Cantu. I stared at the picture for what seemed like a long time. I seldom talk out loud when I'm alone but when I compared the photo of Cantu with the image on the screen I let out with, "Jesus fucking Christ". Cantu was a mirror image of Kenneth Bianchi. Dennis Cantu and Kenneth Bianchi were dead ringers. They had the same curly hair, the same prominent jaw line, skin texture, eyebrows, mouth everything matched. To an eyewitness the two men would appear indistinguishable from each other. Anyone who fingered Bianchi would also have to identify Cantu or suffer a blow to the credibility of his or her identification.

In the first week of January 1980, I got everything together and hand delivered a twenty-eight-page report I had written in Ferndale to the District attorneys office. I attached a photograph of Dennis Cantu to the report along with a copy of the rental applications for Eddie Castillon and Martin (Tony) Smith and a copy of the map page I used in plotting the drop sites of victims in relationship to the locations where Smith and Castillon had lived during the period of the Hillside Strangler slayings. Kelley never responded to the report.

A few months after delivering the report to Kelley, I was in the John Bull Pub knocking back a few beers when Mark Sutherland came into the Pub and told me I had a phone call from one of Angelo Buono's private investigators. I hurried over to the office to take the call from Chuck Boswell.

Chuck said he worked for the lawyers representing Angelo Buono and he wanted to talk to me about my investigation of the Leslie Barry murder. He said he had read the statement I gave to the police and he thought I was right about the connection between the murder of Leslie Barry and the murders of Delores Cepeda and Sonja Johnson.

Chapter 21

After feeling the sting of rejection from the cops and the defense lawyer for Anzures, I was delighted when the defense for Buono phoned to say that they thought I was right about the connection between the Barry murder and the Dolly Cepeda and Sonja Johnson murders.

Chuck Boswell told me that he and his partner, Joe Carroll, worked for a lawyer in Orange County named Jim Brustman.

"Jim Brustman is the chief defense counsel for Angelo," Boswell explained.

"I was just reading this police report of the interview you gave to the task force in 1979," Boswell said, "and I think your conclusions are right. I think the Barry murder was connected to the Cepeda and Johnson murders. My partner and I would like to talk to you about your investigation."

In truth, I had never heard of Jim Brustman. Terry Giles had been getting most of the press since Buono' arrest and I was under the impression that he was the lawyer representing the accused Hillside Strangler. Trying to follow this case from lawyer to lawyer was giving me a headache. I didn't think it mattered what lawyer represented Buono. I just wished they'd pick one and stick with him.

A short time later, when Gerald Chaleff was appointed by the court to represent Buono, I would reverse my position on that one.

My investigation was beneficial to the defense because it exonerated Buono of the murders. I wasn't concerned about the pimping and pandering allegations; those were a totally different issue, but I wanted the case to settle down with one lawyer. I needed to get to know the defense lawyer in order to develop a working relationship with him, and I had enough on my mind without trying to figure out who was representing Angelo Buono on any given day.

"I'd like to see that report." I said. "I never heard back from the Task Force after they came out to my office and I've been wondering for a long time how they treated the lead I gave them."

When would be a good time for me to come down to your office and look at what you have?" I asked.

"Why don't you come down tomorrow and we'll buy you lunch." Boswell offered.

The expectation of seeing the report on my interview with the Task Force and a free lunch lifted my spirits. Rejection was taking a toll on my morale and it was encouraging to hear from someone who agreed with me. This case had been an emotional roller coaster for me. Every time I discovered a new fact or piece of evidence, it gave me hope, but my elation would come crashing down with the rejection of the new evidence and the knowledge that very few people really gave a shit. The call from Boswell renewed my hope that I would find someone that cared about the truth.

Even Mark Southerland, my partner and fellow investigator on the Barry case, didn't know what to make of my conclusions that Leslie Barry was a Hillside Strangler victim. I knew he thought Art Anzures was innocent. He was there as I fumbled and stumbled my way through the investigation and, to paraphrase Charles Dickens, forge the case together link by link and yard by yard. I recall having a frank discussion with him about the case and I asked him directly if he thought I was right in my conclusions or if he thought I needed a tinfoil beanie cap to keep away the aliens.

The best I could ever get out of him was that I had been right before without reason so maybe I was right again. Without reason wasn't exactly a ringing endorsement from my closest associate who, during my investigation, had followed me down a dozen dead end roads before I finally came up with a couple of good suspects. I could tell by the tone and tenor of his answer that he was thinking about the missing horse case. He never quite understood my method of locating the horse.

The next day I drove to Orange County and met Chuck Boswell and Joe Carroll. Chuck was a man of about forty-five, balding, and sporting a mustache. He was five feet ten inches tall and wore a light colored, plaid sports coat with a crimson colored tie draped over a substantial potbelly. He looked like he might be of Hispanic heritage, but with a last name like Boswell, unless he was adopted and changed his name, he was more than likely Irish or Gaelic. My first impression of Chuck was of a nice enough; an easy-going guy, but not too bright. I liked Chuck and he told me his nickname was "Tracker." In all the time I worked with Chuck I never heard anyone call him that. I guess no one could remember his nickname.

Joe Carroll was shorter than Boswell and had a stocky build. He wore horn-rimmed glasses and his wavy black hair contrasted the redness of his face. He spoke in a loud, raspy voice and it was immediately apparent to me that the tangerine color of his skin wasn't from spending too much time in the California sun. It was only 11:30 in the morning and I could already smell alcohol on his breath. He seemed stressed out from carrying the weight of the world on his shoulders, and I figured that part of the red hue to his skin was from high blood pressure. Listening to Carroll rant and rave about this and that gave me the impression that he was a man with a serious persecution complex. His high blood pressure undoubtedly came from obsessing about all the slights he'd had in life.

Carroll's voice was rough and hoarse and it grated on me like fingernails scraping across a blackboard. Emotionally, he was wound tighter than a rattlesnake ready to strike. I thought he was about a heartbeat away from scaling the walls of the ARCO towers with a sack lunch and a high-powered rifle. The police referred to guys like Joe Carroll as fifty-one fifty, which was code for someone mentally over the top. I wondered how Carroll and Boswell ever got together. I might have asked one of them, but I really didn't care.

Chuck showed me around the office, which took all of five minutes. It was an oblong, two-room office with a long linoleum covered counter running along one wall of the reception room. It looked like it might have been a radio or TV repair shop at one time before private eyes moved in and ruined the neighborhood. A microfiche reader and a police scanner sat on the counter along with various papers, reports, and notebooks. I was impressed with some of the resources they had at their fingertips. They had microfiche indexes of county and state records such as marriages, deaths, civil plaintiff and defendant indexes, divorces and a whole set of reverse phone directories.

This was before personal computers took over the world, and these tools were the essentials for tracking down witnesses, credit scofflaws, missing people and anyone else a private investigator might want to find. When I tracked people, I had to use the County Hall of Records for my indexing and research. Because of a lack of workable microfiche readers and so many amateur sleuths using the few that did, indexing usually took longer than the actual research. Having these resources right in the office was a major convenience, and I could tell that Boswell was very proud of his office resources.

After introductions and the office tour, I was eager to get down to business. I told Chuck I wanted to see the report the Task Force had filed on their interview with me. He thumbed through a notebook until he found what he was looking for and handed me a one-page document. I stared at it in disbelief. It was only about three or four paragraphs in length. At first, I thought Chuck had handed me just the first page of my statement and I turned the page over to see if the report was continued on the backside.

"Where's the rest of it?" I asked Chuck.

"That's it." Chuck replied.

Looking at the bottom of the page, I noticed that Mellecker and Holder had signed off on it. I didn't think a forty-five minute statement could be adequately covered in half a page. They tape-recorded the entire interview so they couldn't blame the lack of details on poor note taking.

As I read the report, I could feel my face flush and the hair on the back of my neck bristle. Joe Carroll was pacing around the room muttering to himself and I tried to tune him out and concentrate on the report, but I was intermittently distracted by his running dialog and my shock that so much had been left out of the report. The more I read the more I begin to see why Carroll was talking to himself. This report made me feel like a fool. Worse still, it made me look like one.

Mellecker had left out everything of importance. There was nothing about Shawn Hagen's statement that he knew both Dolly Cepeda and Leslie Barry and had attended the same small, private school with the two victims. There was nothing in the report about two twelve-year old girls, living less than a mile apart, both rape victims, murdered by strangulation, and discovered on the very same day a year apart. These facts alone were compelling reasons to believe that a link existed between the two murders. Shawn Hagen's statement alone should've been enough to cause an eyelid to twitch. That statement forever linked the two victims in death and removed all doubt about whether the other facts were merely unexplainable coincidence or circumstantial evidence connecting the murders. Mellecker' report smacked of a cover-up and that caused me distress.

If leaving out the easily verifiable facts were not bad enough, they also omitted any mention of the profile I developed on the Barry murder that led me to Cantu, Castillon, and Smith in the first place. I had explained to Mellecker and Holder that the timeline of the murder was between ten to fifteen minutes in duration from the time the victim was last known to be alive until her mother came home and discovered the still warm body of her daughter lying on the floor. I had offered him the names, addresses, and phone numbers of the witnesses who gave statements establishing the timeline of the murder. I had explained how the knots in the cord corresponded to pressure points on the victim's neck which led me to believe the killer was knowledgeable about anatomy.

The report Mellecker wrote gave the impression that my conclusions were groundless speculation based solely upon the fact that the murders occurred on the same day of the year. Before seeing the report, I was suspicious that the Task Force was covering-up the Barry murder and others as well. Now I was certain that they were covering up the Barry murder. The report made me look like an idiot with nothing of substance to contribute. If this report was all anyone knew about me they would think I was just another crazy from the public wanting to get involved in a high profile murder case. I felt stifled on the one hand and slandered on the other. I could see that my investigation had been buried alive before anyone bothered to check for vital signs.

"This is bullshit!" I yelled, applying a lesson taken from Joe Carroll's course on anger management.

I opened my briefcase and took out a copy of the twenty-eight-page report I wrote and delivered to the District Attorney. The report had a picture of Cantu paper clipped to it, and I handed it to Chuck Boswell.

"This is what I told the Task Force." I said angrily. "You can keep it and add it to your files on the case."

Chuck took the report I handed him and without as much as a glance put it into the file he was holding. It didn't occur to me until much later that they probably already had a copy of my report to the District Attorney. Roger Kelley would've been required to hand it over to the defense as part of the pretrial discovery. If anything can be considered instant grounds for reversal on appeal, the DA withholding exculpatory evidence from the defense is it. Besides, Roger Kelley wasn't that kind of lawyer. From everything, I had heard about him he was an experienced, tough, but as honest and fair-minded a prosecutor as worked in the DA's office.

As a Deputy DA, Kelley had prosecuted over two hundred murder cases and maintained a high conviction rate for the District Attorney. A high profile case can be a political boon or a political disaster for an elected official, and District Attorney John Van De Kamp would never have assigned Roger Kelley to prosecute the case if he didn't have complete confidence in his ability to get the job done. However, getting the job done didn't include helping the cops' cover-up evidence or suborn perjury to frame an innocent man for murder.

When I finished the report I handed it back to Chuck and asked him if he would make me a copy of it. The one thing they didn't have in their well-equipped office was a copy machine. He said that

Jim Brustman wanted to meet me for lunch and we could make a copy of it at his office after lunch. While Joe Carroll continued mumbling to himself, Boswell called Brustman and told him we were headed for lunch. Brustman said he'd meet us down at the restaurant in fifteen minutes.

We got there first but we didn't wait long for defense counsel to show up at the coffee shop on Seventeenth Street in Costa Mesa. I learned that Brustman's office was located across the street from the Orange County Criminal Court building and he had walked the few blocks from his office to the restaurant. Jim Brustman looked to be in his late forties or early fifties. He was tall and lanky with a jutting chin and deep-set eyes. He introduced himself with a friendly and firm handshake and a smoky, baritone voice. His furrowed brow and the wrinkled lines running the length of his jaw gave the appearance of someone who had been around the block a few times. He seemed like a nice guy. He was down to earth, polite, and respectful but I could see a fierce competitiveness in his eyes that said, 'I'll crush you if you fuck with me, boy.'

We were seated immediately and the server gave us the VIP treatment while kidding around with Brustman and his investigators. It was apparent that the host knew Brustman and the rest of the gang and I surmised that they were part of the regular lunch crowd.

During the forty-five minute hamburger fest, I pushed the Mellecker report to the back of my mind and got acquainted with the defense lawyer. Listening to the rich, deep, texture, and resonance of his voice, I guessed Brustman to be an excellent orator. I certainly liked listening to him. I could imagine him giving a dramatic, Clarence Darrow type, closing argument to a jury. I liked him immediately and I didn't think my first impression of him was colored by the fact that he was buying me lunch.

I wanted to know how Brustman came to represent the infamous Angelo Buono when almost every defense lawyer in Los Angeles wanted the case. Brustman told me that he was, and always had been, the chief defense lawyer for Angelo Buono. He was a friend of Buono's civil lawyer, Ron Bain, and when Buono was arrested, Bain, who didn't handle criminal cases, referred his famous client to

Brustman. He told me that Terry Giles was no longer on the case. There had been a rift between the two lawyers but I really didn't

family was afraid of the system; and after what had happened to Art, they had every right to be. In a list of the pros and cons of joining Buono' defense, I put this one at the top of my list in the con column. My client, the Anzures family, did not want their son associated with the Hillside Strangler case.

By establishing that Leslie Barry was a Hillside Strangler victim, that my suspects were not connected in any way to Angelo Buono, Kenneth Bianchi, or Art Anzures, my investigation discredited Bianchi on the most important part of his confession--his statement that he was at the scene and involved in the murders of Dolly Cepeda and Sonja Johnson. There are many ways to discredit a witness and discrediting Bianchi by itself did not clear Angelo Buono and Art Anzures of the murders. Bianchi was already self-destructing by changing his story on a daily basis before I ever joined the defense.

Besides the objections of the Anzures family, there was something else nagging at me about joining the Buono defense team. It was a feeling and therefore hard to get to, and I wasn't sure if it was real or the result of my own paranoia. It was the fear of the possibility that I was wrong about Cantu, Castillon, and Smith. What if I had missed something important? What if there was a connection between Leslie Barry and Bianchi or Buono and one of them really had murdered Leslie Barry? Not everyone was familiar with my investigation or the report I did for Roger Kelley. My report to Kelley brought the whole identity question of who the Hillside Stranglers were into doubt. The picture of Dennis Cantu was a serious blow to the credibility of the prosecutors star witness, but did that knife cut both ways? After all, I still wanted the Hillside Stranglers brought to justice.

I was afraid someone might suggest that my motive for being on the case was to sandbag Angelo Buono by contributing another murder to him. Something like that could have a devastating affect want to pry into the details.

Knowing the egos of trial lawyers I assumed that the split between Giles and Brustman had something to do with Giles being a publicity hound who was stealing Brustman' thunder. Later I learned the whole story and it was a little more complex than that. The real reason for the animosity had something to do with a Las Vegas moneyman that Giles had brought on board who was going to finance the Buono defense in exchange for literary and movie rights to the story. The financier wanted a say in how the defense was run and apparently backed out when Brustman balked at giving up control over how the case was handled.

I felt an allegiance to Giles and Barnett for their kindness in first allowing me access to the police reports and crime scene photographs on the Hillside Strangler victims. I didn't want to get into the whole sordid mess but I did learn later that Jim Brustman was not the kind of person who needed to stand front and center in the spotlight to validate his worth as a lawyer. That he didn't cave into the money interests was a big point in his favor. With everyone wanting to get a piece of Buono' notoriety, Brustman was being careful to maintain his autonomy from all interests accept the ones that were to the benefit of his client. Another point in his favor was that he didn't appear to be politically ambitious. On the contrary, I could tell by his attitude that he liked being a criminal defense lawyer and that role suited him to a tee.

During lunch, Brustman told me he was associating another trial lawyer on the case by the name of Jim Wilcox. He spoke highly of the new lawyer saying that this guy was so good that he (Brustman) wasn't worthy to carry his briefcase. I thought the hyperbole might be a little over the top, but nevertheless, I was glad to hear a lawyer speak so glowingly of a colleague.

After lunch Joe Carroll, Chuck Boswell, and I walked with Jim Brustman down to his office to make a copy of the report. It was a hot Southern California day and the starched shirt collar was so tight around my neck that I couldn't get enough air circulating to my torso to stay dry. Before I had gotten very far down the road, my coat was off and slung over my shoulder with the necktie wadded up and stuffed in one of the coat pockets. If I was ever going to impress them with my suit, I had to have already done that so I opened my shirt down to the third button and made myself a little cooler.

As I walked beside Jim Brustman, he gave me an update on the Hillside Strangler case and where the defense stood up to that point. He said that he had many volunteers working for the defense and everything was a little disorganized for the time being. Without explaining in detail, Brustman said that when he was able to get some money out of the state of California for Buono's defense he would be able to get things in shipshape condition quickly. At the office Chuck made a copy of Mellecker's report and I said my goodbyes. Of course there was the obligatory, "we'll stay in touch" but I really didn't think they would.

To my complete and utter surprise, the next day Chuck Boswell called me to ask if I wanted to join the defense team. I had a few reservations about it and I told Chuck I'd get back to him the following day. Because of the results of my investigation, I felt they were asking me to join the defense for a very specific reason--to continue my investigation of Cantu, Castillon, and Smith, and to clear Angelo Buono of the murders. Looking at the best possible scenario of being a part of the Defense for Angelo Buono, I needed time to consider all the possibilities and consequences of getting involved with the defense.

The newly acquired knowledge that the Task Force was actively covering up my investigation was both infuriating and encouraging at the same time. Covering-up the investigation meant that they took me more seriously than I had imagined. While it angered me, it also told me I was being effective. Joining the defense for Angelo Buono might be the opportunity I needed to expose the cover-up.

One concern was my own autonomy. In speaking to the Anzures family about my investigation, I knew that they did not want to have Art's case associated in any way with Angelo Buono or the Hillside Strangler case; but they never quite grasped what was going on, and why Art had been arrested and tried for murder to begin with. It was beyond their experience and inconsistent with their belief in the fairness of the system for them to understand how Art was being used as a stooge to cover up what the police knew was another Hillside Strangler murder. Besides, by then I felt that the Anzures on Jim Brustman and his defense team. I didn't want to create problems for the defense, but I needed more evidence, and the only way to get it would be to have access to the detailed information on the Hillside Strangler case.

There were at least ten dead women and young girls and someone had to pay for those murders. The media and the public wouldn't accept anything less. What would happen if the prosecution changed direction and prosecuted Cantu, Castillon, and Smith for the murders? Would the defense for the three new defendants throw Kenneth Bianchi and Angelo Buono back at them? This case had become a convoluted mess.

The Hillside Strangler Task Force had applied relentless pressure on the DA to prosecute the case against Buono. Once I joined the defense, because of being a threat to their case, I'd be making myself a target for God knows what. They'd have to deal with me some way, and I was curious what they would do to counter my investigation and advance their cover-up.

I didn't know how far the Task Force would go to get a conviction against Buono. It occurred to me that by joining Buono's defense I would be declaring war on the LAPD. It would be a war like in the movie the Mouse That Roared where a little country on the brink of bankruptcy declares war on the United States for the purpose of losing the war and getting financial aid. I was the roaring mouse and I knew how far I would go to destroy their case against Buono. If I had to haul Cantu into court to show the jury the likeness in appearance between him and Bianchi, I would do that. I was determined to chip away at their case until there was nothing left but lies and political posturing.

I decided that the pros outweighed the cons and it was well worth the risk to join the defense. I also decided I would make an extra effort to keep the defense team apprised of everything I did or said concerning the case. I called Chuck Boswell the next day, and without mentioning my reservations, told him I wanted to work with the defense of Angelo Buono.

Jim Brustman called me back a little later and welcomed me to the team. He told me they were having a strategy meeting at his house on Sunday and wanted me to come down to Orange County so I could meet the rest of the defense team and the new lawyer on the case, Jim Wilcox. I had already met Chuck Boswell, Joe Carroll, and

Jim Brustman and, besides Wilcox, I wondered how many other people were working for Angelo Buono. I knew Brustman had to have a paper man lurking somewhere in the background. The law and motion department of the Los Angeles Criminal Court Division would be kept busy with a case like this. There would be motions and rulings, and appeals of the motions, and rulings and more rulings and appeals before the case ever made it to trial. They would have to cut down a forest to supply the Buono trial with paper. Then of course, someone had to shuffle all this paper and that would require additional secretarial staff to handle the typing and filing. I had the feeling from the way Brustman had said, "The rest of the defense team" that there was an army working for the accused serial killer.

Jim Brustman owned a two-story frame house in an upper middle class neighborhood in the southern part of Orange County. It was a nice house but not a mansion by any stretch of the imagination. Although I arrived a little early, there were quite a few cars parked on the street around the Brustman house, so I found a small piece of curb down the street to park my Datzun 260Z sports car, which I had already begun hiding from the repo man.

When I entered the house, my first thought was that Jim Brustman really knew how to throw a strategy meeting. There were about thirty people either sitting on sofas and chairs or standing around chatting like old friends. Everyone was holding a cocktail or a beer and the noise level was something akin to a rock concert. I headed straight to the wet bar where Jim Brustman seemed to be enjoying himself playing bartender. We shook hands and he asked me what I wanted to drink. Having been on a beer budget for so long, I was glad to have something hard to drink. I sat down on a bar stool and ordered a Bourbon and coke.

By this time, the case had been going on for over a year, and between fulfilling his duties as bartender and host, Brustman and I chatted about the case. When someone would come up to get a drink Jim would introduce me and tell me a little about the person and what they were doing on the defense. He introduced me to David Haight, his motions and appeals man. Besides being the brains on the team, Haight was also his law partner and Jim spoke highly of his prowess at motions and appeals.

Over in one corner of the room I could hear the unmistakably loud, grating voice of Joe Carroll ranting and raving about something the cops had done that he felt was a gross injustice. Brustman noticed that I was distracted by Carroll's behavior and told me that Joe Carroll was married to his sister. Brustman leaned over closer to me and confided that he was eventually going to find a tactful way to get rid of his loud mouth brother-in-law. He said that Joe and another investigator, who was no longer on the team, had caused many problems for the defense. They had gone down to the LAPD Headquarters at the Parker Center to research clues on the LAPD computer and were asked to leave because of the disturbance their obnoxious behavior had caused. Brustman said that because of the ruckus we could no longer search for clues at the Parker Center on our own. We were required to call the Task Force and request a specific document or article of evidence.

I was disappointed to hear that. It sounded to me like the police were just looking for any reason to exert control over the flow of information to the defense. The defense had a right to all the information they had on the case and using their computers was more than an accommodation to the Task Force. From what Brustman was telling me, in typical government fashion, they considered giving the defense access to all the reports and evidence on the case a privilege and not a right. I wondered how that would work since we couldn't request documents, clues, or evidence if we didn't know about them before hand. If any exculpatory evidence for Buono existed in the thousands of clues on the computer the police sure as hell wouldn't give it to us.

I was certain that there were raw clues in the computer that would benefit my investigation of Cantu, Castillon and Smith and it pissed me off that Joe Carroll had given them a reason to bar us from having direct access to that information and resource. Still, barring the defense access to potentially exculpatory evidence, and maybe even a smoking gun, because a couple of people made a disturbance was a piss poor excuse for violating Buono' right to pretrial discovery.

This setup worked against the defense in another way too. By having to request clues through whichever member of the Task

Force happened to answer the phone, we tipped them off as to what types of information we were interested in. This could hamper our strategy and give them the opportunity to react to areas we were investigating. It also denied us the opportunity to control our own work product. Since work product was an integral part of the attorney/client privilege, this request-a-clue policy in my opinion, breached the privilege. If they could keep us from information, it would make framing Buono and fostering the cover-up much easier. I wondered what kind of judge would let this go on.

I was on my third bourbon and coke and beginning to feel the buzz when Brustman came out from behind the bar and called the meeting to order. Everyone got quiet except for Joe Carroll who continued ranting until someone told him to shut up. Jim Wilcox was sitting on the sofa with his wife Susan, and Brustman motioned for him to come up and stand beside him. He introduced Wilcox to the rest of the team and asked him to say a few words.

What struck me immediately about Jim Wilcox were the physical similarities he had to Jim Brustman. He was tall and lanky and spoke with the same smoke filled, baritone voice. Wilcox had a more chiseled look than Brustman, with a narrow jaw line, high cheekbones and a leathery, weather beaten face. His face was etched in character. Deep crevices, the road map of hard times and lots of experience, ran nearly from his jaw to his ears. His sandy colored hair had probably been parted and combed over before he left home, but it had gone its own way long before he stood up to be introduced. The strands of thin hair hanging down to one side of his forehead reminded me of the way Will Rogers looked in photographs I had seen. I thought Jim Wilcox was a man of experience and character and I wanted to get to know him.

After Wilcox said a few words about how good it was to be joining the defense team and how much he looked forward to getting to know us and work with us, he sat down and Brustman introduced me to the room. I continued to sit on my barstool and he told the team that I was a private investigator from Pasadena. Without going into any detail, he said that I had investigated another murder case in Pasadena and was continuing that investigation now with the Buono defense. I waved at the audience like I was the Goddamn Rose

Parade Queen or something. Thank God, he didn't ask me to speak because when I get nervous I get tongue-tied and with a few drinks in me my personality changes from being friendly and outgoing to being shy, withdrawn, and way too philosophical. I didn't want to start blubbering in front of this crowd.

With the introductions over, Brustman said that he had received the videotaped confessions of Kenneth Bianchi on Friday and he wanted to play the tape for us. Everyone in the room moved closer to the TV set to get a good position to watch the tape. With a fresh drink, I moved my barstool a few feet closer to the screen making sure I didn't block anyone's view. He motioned for a woman standing near the television to turn on the TV and start the tape.

Joe Carroll came out of his corner and took a seat on the edge of the sofa next to Susan Wilcox. As the tape started to run so did Carroll's mouth. He decided to play Harry Carey and do a running commentary on the confession. Turning even redder in the face than normal, he made loud comments about how phony Bianchi's confession came across. When Bianchi came on the screen, presumably under hypnosis and in the personality of his alter ego I thought Carroll's head was going to explode.

"That son-of-a-bitch is faking it." Carroll shouted taking a big gulp of liquor and moving toward the bar to refill his glass. As he moved toward the bar, his commentary didn't stop for a second.

"Can you believe that shit?" He said looking at me. "Have you ever seen anything so pitiful in your life? Bianchi's lying his ass off."

I shrugged my shoulders and tried to focus on the tape. I agreed with Carroll that Bianchi was faking it. Much of what Bianchi said sounded as if it came right out of a police report. His statement sounded rehearsed and he was obviously telling the cops what they wanted to hear. The only problem was he seemed to be short on intimate details about the crimes. What pissed me off, besides Carroll's insufferable running off at the mouth, was that Carroll felt a need to say what the rest of us could clearly understand on our own. I knew he was struggling for attention, and under different circumstances I might have felt sorry for him. When I caught myself thinking about feeling sorry for him I grimaced. Pity was not a good thing to feel about the chief investigator for the defense of the highest profile murder case of the time.

His loud and obnoxious behavior was wearing thin with me. If the Hillside Strangler Task Force wanted to plant an undercover cop to disrupt the operations of the defense they couldn't have found a better mole. Not that I thought Carroll was a plant. He clearly wasn't sane enough for that job and he certainly wasn't clever enough to carry on a lunatic act forever.

When the tape got to a part where Bianchi was talking about Delores Cepeda giving him oral sex and he said the young girl really knew what she was doing the whole room groaned. If it didn't irk the cops that Bianchi was maligning one of the victims it sure irked the defense.

Dolly Cepeda was a twelve-year old virgin and it's doubtful that she had ever been kissed let alone exposed to oral sex. How the Task Force could take Bianchi's confession seriously after that statement indicated how badly they wanted to believe he was guilty. Before Bianchi surfaced, they had wanted to prosecute George Shamshak for the murders but they were never able to resolve inconsistencies between George Shamshak and certain evidence they had on the Hillside Strangler. Now they had an even better pigeon and along with Angelo Buono, they could resolve many of the conflicts they couldn't resolve with Shamshak.

Joe Carroll continued to rant and rave throughout the Bianchi show and I lost interest in watching any more of the tape so I turned my attention to drinking and wondering why someone didn't show Joe Carroll the door. After the tape ended, I dismounted my barstool and circulated a bit. I wanted to personally meet Jim Wilcox and get acquainted with him. I went up and introduced myself and we shook hands.

Jim and I, being the outsiders, found common ground in the fact that we were both new on the case and needed to get caught up to speed. Furthermore, we were the only ones from Los Angeles on the defense. I liked Jim and Susan Wilcox immediately and Jim gave me an open invitation to work on the case out of his office in Van Nuys. After a short visit with Wilcox, Jim Brustman joined us and asked me what I wanted to do regarding my investigation of Cantu. I told

Brustman that I had a number of witnesses I wanted to talk to but I had a big problem--I didn't have the money to put gas in my car to get out and interview the witnesses. Brustman took out his wallet and handed me a gasoline credit card. The gesture damn near made my eyes tear. I had finally found someone who wanted me to investigate the Hillside Strangler case.

Chapter 22

To avoid duplication of effort and bring a little order to the Buono defense, Brustman divided the investigative workload by assigning investigators to certain victims. It was like the Hillside Strangler Task Force had been organized. He assigned Chuck Boswell to work with me on the Cepeda/Johnson murders and I made a list of the witnesses I wanted to interview. At the top of my list was Louis Landinguin.

Landinguin was the young boy on the city bus with Cepeda and Johnson and the last known person to see the two girls alive. When Cepeda and Johnson got off the bus and crossed York Boulevard, Landinguin saw a car make a sudden left turn and stop at the corner. Cepeda and Johnson approached the car on the passenger side and talked to the occupants. Under hypnosis, the young boy gave the Task Force several descriptions of the vehicle he saw, and at least two of the descriptions fit with the cars owned by Eddie Castillon and Dennis Cantu. I wanted to verify his statement and ask him a few more questions. For one thing, I wanted to know if anyone else on the bus could corroborate his statement. I also wanted to show him the picture I took of Cantu on the stakeout and see if he could identify the car Cantu was driving. Besides Cantu's picture, I had a picture of Castillon's car in my file which I wanted to show to this particular witness. I thought showing him these two pictures might jog his memory.

Another witness I was eager to interview was Carlos De La Torre. The statement that he had talked with Sonja Johnson two days after her disappearance was of great interest to me. From the tone of the statement, Sonja had not seemed too concerned or alarmed about her situation. If he was correct about the date and time of the call, his statement provided a compelling reason to believe that at least one of the girls knew their captors and they did not realize that their lives were in peril.

The Cepeda family was from the same area in Texas as the suspects and I felt certain that the families knew each other. Long before I joined the defense for Buono, I dispatched one of my female operatives, a Spanish speaking investigator named Gessell Montiforte, to the Cepeda home to verify that the Castillon and Cepeda families knew one another from a time when they all lived in Laredo, Texas. I instructed her to pretend to be a friend of the Castillon family from Texas; that she was in California visiting friends; and that she was just stopping by to say hello on behalf of their common friends, the Castillons.

Gessell reported that neither parent was home when she got there but she spoke with one of the Cepeda children, their fourteen-year old son. The boy confirmed that the families knew each other and that he would tell his parents that Gessell had stopped by. Later, in an attempt to verify the statement with Mrs. Cepeda, she denied knowing the Castillon family and said her son didn't know what he was talking about. I didn't fully buy Cecilia Cepeda's denial. I felt that she was convinced Bianchi and Buono were guilty of murdering her daughter and that I was merely trying to get the killers off. While her attitude frustrated me, I couldn't blame her. I'd have felt the same way under similar circumstances.

Whether the boy was right or not, to support my theory that the killers knew the victims, I still needed to confirm the connection between the killers and the Cepeda family through a second source. My investigation of the Barry murder had produced the information that Tony Cepeda worked as an accountant for the USC Medical Center where Dennis Cantu was doing his internship. If I could find a connection there, I'd have another convincing notch linking Barry, Cepeda and Johnson to the same killers.

A few weeks before the Municipal Court preliminary hearing for Angelo Buono got underway, I urged Jim Brustman to issue a subpoena duces tecum for Cantu's medical school records, both at the Baylor Medical School in Houston, and at the USC Medical Center in Los Angeles. I wanted to find out what Cantu's professors and colleagues had to say about him and I wanted to know his personal references on his application for his internship at the USC Medical Center. For all I knew Tony Cepeda was instrumental in bringing this package from Hell to Los Angeles.

I knew cousins Eddie Castillon and Martin Smith were in Los Angeles at the time of the Hillside Strangler murders. Smith didn't move back to Laredo, Texas until the summer of 1978 and, while I didn't consider Smith a suspect in the Barry murder, it was my contention that he, along with his cousin Eddie, had abducted Dolly Cepeda and Sonja Johnson and held them hostage in their rented house on Crescent Drive; but I needed to see the dates and times of Cantu's pre-internship interviews at the USC Medical Center to determine if he too was in Los Angeles during the time of any of the Hillside Strangler murders.

Brustman issued the subpoenas and I got the Baylor Medical school records first. I poured over the personal references and notations by different professors. It made for interesting reading. A couple of Cantu's professors had considerably less than stellar things to say about his performance in medical school and his fitness to be a doctor. One professor gave him such a poor evaluation it was obvious that this professor wanted to wash him out of medical school.

I called the administrative offices at the USC Medical School several times, but it took more than a week before they finally got the records copied and ready to pick up. At the administration office, I met with a serious looking middle-aged secretary who gave the appearance of being fiercely loyal to her employer. She seemed nervous when I asked her if all the records were there. She said they were all there, but...and let her voice trail off. When I ask, "But what?" she clammed up and said they were all there.

I didn't believe her. Someone had told her what records to copy and give to me and which ones to hold back. Turning on the charm and smooth talking this secretary wouldn't get me anywhere so I didn't try the my-you-look-so-becoming-in-red line. I could promise her the moon and the stars and make her feel like the most beautiful woman in the world or conversely, I could hook a thousand volts of electricity to her ass and stick pins under her fingernails, and she wouldn't give it up. Her stonewalling incensed me. When I got back to my office, I opened the envelope and I was not surprised that there were no personal references, notes, or dates of the pre-acceptance interviews. They left the guts of what I was looking for out of the package. I didn't want to bother Brustman about it because he was a little leery about issuing the subpoena in the first place. Sometime later, I did tell Jim Wilcox about my reservations and he agreed with me that some vital information had been left out and wondered, as I did, what they were hiding.

Brustman wanted Chuck Boswell and me to work together, so I told Chuck to come up to my office and we could leave from there to interview some of the witnesses. Many of the families had moved away from the Eagle Rock area since the murders of Dolly Cepeda and Sonja Johnson, and we located the Landinguin family in the East San Gabriel Valley. Chuck arrived at my office and we used his car to drive out to talk to Louis Landinguin.

The Landinguin home was a typical ranch style tract house, built in the fifties, and located in what was once a solid middle class neighborhood, now in decline from too many people moving from the inner city. After the well-publicized murders of Cepeda and Johnson, the Landinquins had sought refuge in an area safer and better suited for raising their children than the barrio of Eagle Rock afforded them. I had a feeling that if the Landinguin family had moved to get away from the memories and sadness caused by the Cepeda/Johnson murders talking to them now would not be easy.

On the porch, I rang the doorbell and waited for a response. A man of about my age, or maybe a few years older, came to the door.

"Mr. Landinguin?" I asked not certain of the pronunciation of his name.

"Yes?" He answered with a question mark in his voice.

"My name is Ron Crisp and this is my partner, Chuck Boswell." I introduced us. "We're private investigators working for the defense of Angelo Buono in the Hillside Strangler case. I read the report that the police filed on their interview with your son, Louis, and we would like to talk to him just briefly about the statement he gave to the police concerning seeing a car pull up and the occupants talking with Dolly and Sonja on the day they disappeared. Is Louis around?"

"He's around," Mr. Landinguin replied without making a move to get him. "but you can't talk to him." He added firmly.

Trying to overcome this concerned father's pigheaded obstinacy would be difficult if not impossible. It was the USC Medical Center employee all over again. I could argue, plead, threaten, cajole, and throw an embarrassing tantrum and never get a response out of him if he was determined to stand in my way. I wondered if I was experiencing the thorough job the media had done in convincing the public that Angelo Buono was the Hillside Strangler, or if something more personal was going on. I didn't know what was happening, but I had the feeling that someone was a step ahead of me talking to these people before I got there. I sensed from his attitude that someone had warned Mr. Landinguin about allowing his kids to talk to me.

Louis Landinguin was mentioned in my report to Roger Kelly. It was a report that I wrote and sent to the prosecutor in good faith. Now, I was being stonewalled and I was beginning to regret ever having sent that report. Either the cops or the prosecutor, or maybe both, must have feared that because of his youth and inexperience, Louis Landinguin might identify the car Cantu was driving and it would be another major setback for their case against Angelo Buono.

My mind was burning rubber as I tried to come up with a good argument to counter Mr. Landinguin' reservations about me when Chuck Boswell piped up.

"We're going to subpoena him anyway so he might as well talk to us now." Chuck said in a rather terse tone of voice.

I was a little surprised at Chuck's aggressiveness. Until now, I had not seen the hard ass side of him, but his conduct reminded me that he had been working for Buono's defense for over a year, and maybe he had come up against this type of attitude before. Maybe his defensiveness was the result of being treated like a social pariah just because he worked for the defense of the most hated man in America at the time.

I was not one to burn bridges with witnesses. My approach and attitude was that with enough time and effort I might be able to get them to come around and talk to me. I gave Chuck a disapproving look and steered him off the porch and back to the car. This being the first time I had worked with him I figured he was just having a bad day. In the car, I made light of it and enthusiastically told him on to the next witness. I let the incident at the door drop without further comment.

Our next stop was Carlos De La Torre. Carlos lived in a small upstairs apartment in an old wood framed house that had been converted into what appeared to be an upstairs-downstairs duplex. The stairs were on the outside of the house and in need of some repair. The stairs led directly up to his apartment.

I didn't think Carlos would have much to add to his statement, but I wanted to meet the young man and verify what he had told the police. By meeting with him face to face, I could gauge his sincerity and get a feel for his personality. I thought I might detect some hesitancy or waffling on the time period of the phone call from Sonja Johnson, and his statement would come unraveled. Not that I wanted his statement to fall apart. On the contrary, De La Torre's statement, as it stood, was a positive for the defense. If true, it indicated that the victims might have known their killers and we knew they didn't know Kenneth Bianchi or Angelo Buono. I just wanted to make sure that he was rock solid in his personality and if called to the witness stand that he wouldn't change his story or fall apart on cross-examination.

From the landing at the top of the stairs, I could see that the front door was open and when I knocked on the screen door a teenage boy, dressed in shorts, a T-shirt, and no shoes got up from the sofa and came to the door. I asked him if he was Carlos De La Torre. He replied that he was and after explaining who I was and why I was standing on his porch, I asked him if Chuck and I could come in and chat for a few minutes. He opened the screen door and invited us in.

Carlos was a handsome young Latino, polite, cordial, and respectful. From all appearances, he was a bright, clean-cut kid who had avoided gangs and other bad influences. He had no tattoos on his arms or legs and he didn't have those little dots tattooed in the web of his fingers that was so popular among young druggies and gang-bangers.

I took the police report of his statement out of my briefcase and handed him a copy to read. When he finished reading it, he handed the report back to me. I asked him if that was substantially what he had told the police and if there was anything he wanted to add or corrections he wanted to make to the statement. Carlos said everything in the statement was true and correct, including the date and time of the call from Sonja Johnson, and, he said, there was nothing he could add to the report.

"Are you absolutely certain of the day of the phone call?" I asked in a disbelieving tone of voice playing the devils advocate.

"Yes, sir," he responded. "I'm positive of the day because I didn't know they were missing and it was a day or two later that I found out. That's how I know the day is accurate."

I liked the young man and he seemed certain about the date and time of the call from Sonja Johnson. From what I knew about the case against Buono, De La Torre's statement was inconsistent with Kenneth Bianchi's statement in his confession that the girls were murdered at Buono's upholstery shop in Glendale. The tenor of the phone call from Sonja Johnson indicated that the girls knew their captors and if the Task Force failed to show a close link between Kenneth Bianchi, Angelo Buono, and either Dolly Cepeda or Sonja Johnson then De La Torre's statement would work well for the defense.

Then all of sudden, out of nowhere, Chuck Boswell pounced on the kid with a verbal attack that surprised and stunned me. I didn't know if he was buckling under the pressure or what, but Chuck was coming unglued. He didn't need to act tough for my benefit. His act was vintage Joe Carroll. Chuck started yelling at him that we were going to subpoena his ass if he didn't talk straight to us and he went on and on with the threats until I finally told him to shut up. I got up from my chair and thanked the young man for his cooperation. I couldn't believe Chuck was treating a defense witness this way. I apologized profusely for the outburst and got him out of there before he could do anymore damage.

Still in shock from Boswell's outburst, as we walked down the stairs and back to the car, I told him that if he ever did anything like that again he would never interview another witness with me. Later, after getting to know Chuck better, I discovered what the real deal was. Chuck simply couldn't distinguish defense witnesses from adversarial witnesses, and when I started to question De la Torre's credibility on the date and time of the phone call, Chuck mistakenly thought the kid was being difficult and he was attempting to break him down on his statement.

The defense got together frequently and everyone seemed to have an opinion about who the Hillside Strangler was. I thought that if a jury was representative of this group, the best defense strategy for Angelo Buono would be to put all the suspects out there; George Shamshak, Richard Reynolds, Dennis Cantu, Eddie Castillon, Martin Smith, and Kenneth Bianchi and let the jury sort it out. The fact is, an investigator is worthless if he doesn't search for the truth, and I wanted to find as much truth as I could in this case. Like the press and the prosecution, I felt that someone had to pay for all these dead women. Unlike the press, the Task Force and the families of the victims, I wanted the right person to pay for it.

Jim Wilcox told me he liked Cantu, Castillon, and Smith for the Barry, Cepeda and Johnson murders, but he thought Richard Reynolds was a better suspect for the Weckler and Hudspeth murders. Wilcox was a smart lawyer and lived up to the high praise Brustman gave him. The truth notwithstanding, Jim Wilcox knew that giving the jury a dead man was risky business unless you could find strong, conclusive, evidence to link him to the murders. Juries don't care much for dead alternatives to live defendants. If Reynolds killed any of the Hillside Strangler victims, the truth went to the grave with him.

I was developing a morbid fascination with serial killers and was reading everything I could find on the subject. The unique thing about the Hillside Strangler case was the widely accepted belief that there were multiple killers working together. It was less rare in homosexual serial murders to have more than one killer involved in the same series of murders. Having multiple killers caused confusion because each murder in the Hillside Strangler series had similarities to the other murders while also containing idiosyncratic elements not found from victim to victim.

A good example of that was the needle marks in Kristina Weckler' arm. She was the only victim linked to the Hillside Strangler who had battery acid shot in her veins. The use of a syringe had to tell the Task Force something about the killer even if only that the killer had access to drug paraphernalia. When I learned about the battery acid, I had the distinct feeling that the killer knew Weckler, at least, well enough to know about her strong aversion to drugs.

Serial killer profiles are consistent in several ways, including the debasement of their victims, and I surmised that the Hillside Strangler used the syringe and battery acid as a means of debasing Weckler through her strongly held anti-drug beliefs. Some sort of relationship between the killer and Kristina Weckler might also explain the lack of a struggle or the use of force in her abduction. But the battery acid stumped me. It is not something you would find around the average household, and I wondered what the battery acid was indicated. Where would the killer get it, and why use that, rather than drugs or lighter fluid or something easier to obtain?

Wilcox liked Richard Reynolds for some of the murders including the Weckler murder. I thought with the possibility of Reynolds being involved in the slaying of the Oxnard prostitutes he was a good suspect for the prostitute murders in the Hillside Strangler case, but I didn't agree with Wilcox about the Weckler murder. In seeking to find a solid connection between my suspects and some of the victims, I had done considerable background work on Weckler. For one thing, I learned that her father, Charles Weckler, was a professional photographer. The background work I did on Smith turned up information that Martin Smith's stepfather, John Ritterrath was an industrial film producer. I couldn't help but see the similarities of being a commercial photographer and being an industrial film producer and wondered if perhaps the two men's paths had crossed at one time or another.

In addition, John Ritterrath lived on Ontario Street very close to the Art Center College of Design where Kristina Weckler attended school. I recalled seeing on their marriage certificate that Harry Carey, Jr. was a witness to John Ritterrath' marriage and I had come into some information that Charles Weckler may have known Harry Carey, Jr. as well. If they had a common friend, it would show that the paths of the families might have indeed crossed, and while it wasn't exactly a smoking gun, that fact made the odds of Martin Smith knowing Kristina Weckler a whole lot better.

I had been working on this case for a long time; much longer than anyone on the defense team. With the time and long hours of studying the case came a mental and emotional focus that made it my case. When you talk to witnesses and analyze facts, you develop a feel for what fits and what doesn't fit -- for what's true; for what's an honest mistake or the result of an over active imagination. You know in an instant an out and out lie. It's commonly called gut feelings, and most of the time the gut feelings a detective gets while investigating a case never make it to the courtroom.

The young black woman in the apartment complex where Leslie Barry lived was a good example of gut feelings. This young woman told me about a frightening experience she had on her way through the dark tunnel to the carport area one evening. I could tell by the fear in her eyes and her quivering voice that she was reliving an experience she hadn't thought about for months. From her outward appearance and body language, I knew she was being truthful and not just imagining the scenario. Her graphic description of the incident gave me goose bumps and reinforced my belief that I was on the right track. I had the same feeling about Kristina Weckler. All the details I knew about her background and gruesome murder indicated to me that she knew her killer or killers. Other than having an apartment down the street from Kenneth Bianchi, I didn't see any connection between Weckler and the men accused of being the Hillside Stranglers.

One of the things the task force leaned heavily on as evidence of a link between the victims was the three-point ligature bruising on the neck, wrists, and ankles. I had learned from my research on serial killers that binding the feet and hands of their victims before strangulation was a control thing and a common occurrence in these types of murders. The killer might do it on some of his victims and not others and the three point ligature marks on the neck, wrists, and ankles, alone, did not amount to proof of anything. If all the Task Force had were the three point ligature marks to link the victims with each other then they didn't have squat.

The Task Force had matched Bianchi's fingerprints with fingerprints lifted from a pay phone at the downtown library and the prosecutor was using those fingerprints as evidence of a connection between Bianchi and one of the victims, Kimberly Martin. Even if those fingerprints were given as evidence against Bianchi on the Martin murder, an assumption still had to be made that the one murder was related to the series of murders in order for those fingerprints to impute guilt onto Bianchi for the other victims.

It's the same with the fact that Bianchi lived on Garfield Street in Glendale, as did two of the victims, Kristina Weckler and Cindy Hudspeth. That fact alone meant nothing regarding other victims, such as Jane King or Yolanda Washington, without the assumption that they were all related and the Task Force was linking all the murders on the flimsy evidence of the three point ligature marks.

Another anomaly of the Hillside Strangler murders were the ages and backgrounds of the victims. Some of the girls were older, the oldest being twenty-eight and the youngest twelve. Judith Miller was a fifteen-year old runaway who survived on the street by being a part time prostitute. Kristina Weckler and Cindy Hudspeth were solid, ambitious young women and straight arrows. Others like Yolanda Washington and Kimberly Martin were known prostitutes. Yolanda Washington wasn't even of the same race as the others. Delores Cepeda and Sonja Johnson were the youngest victims and the only double murders on the official Hillside Strangler victim list. The two young girls were not connected to the street scene at all. In addition, Cepeda and Johnson were the only victims where evidence suggested that they were kept alive for a few days after their abduction.

The various dissimilarities made it difficult to find a methodology the Hillside Strangler used for selecting and killing his victims. The criterion for victim selection wasn't based on the normal things profilers and detectives looked for like age, body development, hair color and style, occupation, and race. The Hillside Strangler, or stranglers as the case might be, either had to be some sort of universal killer, both organized and disorganized, or the murders had to be the work of multiple killers. Forensic psychologists and profilers, working for the task force, came to the conclusion that if multiple killers were working together, they would be acting out the same psychosis but with slightly different tastes. Profilers theorized that for multiple killers to be sharing the same psychosis they would probably be blood related and raised together in the same environment.

When Kenneth Bianchi was arrested in Bellingham, Washington for the murders of Karen Mandic and Diane Wilder, and shortly thereafter came under suspicion in the Hillside Strangler case, convinced that they were looking for multiple killers, the task force began looking for a close relative to put with him for the Hillside Strangler murders. They sweated Bianchi under the interrogation lights for hours and convinced him that he would swing from the Washington State Gallows if he didn't give it up and tell them everything about the activities of him and his cousin, Angelo Buono. With a couple of big, angry cops in his face, threatening, pleading, and cajoling, Bianchi wasn't doing much arguing. He started telling them what they wanted to hear.

The Task Force liked Buono as an accomplice because they could show a relationship between him and Bianchi and he lived in Glendale, the area they considered the heart of operation of the strangler. Buono rued the day when he conceded to his aunt's pleas to let Bianchi stay with him for a short time during the period when bodies were turning up all over Los Angeles.

The Task Force had a big problem with the Bianchi/Buono relationship in terms of the significance of that relationship to the psychological part of the profile. Bianchi and Buono were not blood related. They were only related because of Bianchi being adopted by Buono's aunt. Contrary to the police profile, the two suspects did not share the same gene pool. In additiion, Buono was much older than Bianchi and they were not raised in the same generation let alone the same environment. They were cousins by name only and that didn't match the profile of the killers.

In contrast to Kenneth Bianchi and Angelo Buono, two of my suspects, Edward Martin Castillon and Martin Anthony Smith, fit the psychological profile to a tee. They were the same age, blood related on their mothers side of the family, and raised together in Laredo, Texas by Castillon's parents. Smith and Castillon fit the profile of the Hillside Strangler in other ways as well. Because of the way some victims were abducted and found, the Task Force concluded that the killer was a good student of police procedure. One victim was found on a hillside overlooking downtown Los Angeles and intentionally positioned in a spread eagle pose with her crotch facing the LAPD Headquarters. It was partly for that reason that detectives on the Task Force believed the Hillside Strangler might have a grudge against the LAPD. Maybe he was a disgruntled cop or someone who had been turned down for a job with the department. Smith had applied to the LAPD but was rejected for employment. Eddie Castillon's father, Carlos Castillon, was a former District Attorney of Laredo, Texas and with a little boost from his uncle, Smith had been able to hire on with the Laredo Police Department.

Besides fitting the psychological profile, Castillon matched the description and resembled a composite drawing released during the investigation. I don't rely on composites because as far as I'm concerned suspects never fit the composites closely enough to make a positive identification of them. Still, Castillon came as close to matching a composite as it ever gets and he sure as hell fit the age and description from the composite better than Kenneth Bianchi or Angelo Buono.

In the early stages of the investigation, the dissimilarities created complications for the task Force and they never seemed to fully recover from those problems. The evidence linking the murders was weak and tenuous at best. By having multiple killers, the crime or drop site evidence made some of the murders appear to be work of a copycat and this frustrated the Task Force. While looking at murders in the area, the Task Force would connect a new murder then go back and disconnect an earlier one. Trying to see the big picture from looking at the crimes themselves was like looking at inkblots on a Rorschach test. Links were based on what members of the Task Force saw in them and not scientific evidence.

Trying to apply general knowledge about serial killers culled from studies on previous cases didn't work either. Neither the Task Force, nor anyone else for that matter, could tell which murders were related and which were not. Taking such a flogging from the press and media didn't help the investigation. Maybe without the added pressure from the press and local politicians, the Task Force might've looked more closely at every strangulation murder in the area. They might also have expanded their area of investigation to a wider range than the arbitrary five-mile radius they were using as a basis for investigating a murder that might be connected to the Hillside Strangler series. Leslie Barry fell within the five-mile range while Margaret Madrid and Elizabeth Cevallos did not.

With the press dogging their every move, every murder they investigated was the next morning's headlines. Public panic and frustration caused them to close up shop and go home. They quit looking at other murders and following up on leads from the public. District Attorney John Van De Kamp publicly described the LAPD mindset as a "siege mentality." I wasn't aware of it at the time but that siege mentality was ever present when I called to inform the Task Force about the facts of the Leslie Barry murder.

After the fallout from Cepeda and Johnson, the press would've crucified them for their incompetence had another child turned up murdered and linked to the Hillside Strangler. So, the Task Force simply stopped following up on leads and retreated into a political damage control mode. That was their state of mind when I called them about the Leslie Barry murder.

Once I was on the defense I looked forward to having access to all the reports, crime photographs, and clues. I wanted to study everything about the case. I was interested in the methods of operation of the stranglers. I wanted to see if I could discern what the murders would look like if the killers were operating in various combinations.

I knew that Cantu had acted alone when he murdered Leslie Barry and I was certain that the Barry murder was somehow related to the Cepeda/Johnson murders. I didn't however, have any clue whether Cantu was directly involved with the Cepeda/Johnson murders, or whether Castillon and Smith had committed those abductions and murders without him. Whatever the case, Cantu knew that his two compadres from Laredo had murdered Cepeda and Johnson. One thought or idea leads to another and I considered several possibilities:

What if Cantu committed one murder by himself, as was likely in the Barry murder, and a second with Castillon, and then a third with Smith? On the other hand, what if the combination was Castillon and Smith or either one of them acting alone? The murders could look completely different even though they were, in reality, related. The rarity of multiple serial killers made it uncharted waters, but was it an absolute must that serial killers had to kill in the same combination? With so many variations and dissimilarities in the method of operation of the stranglers it would be nothing but guess work as to which of the murders were related and which could be attributed to a copycat killer, an angry pimp, or a lovers' spat. The only real commonality between the victims was that all but one died from asphyxiation by strangulation.

Shawn Hagen had provided a solid link between Leslie Barry and Dolly Cepeda. To have two girls living less than a mile apart, both twelve years old, and attending the same small private school, and murdered by strangulation. Rape appeared to be the motive in both murders. Both bodies were found on the same day a year apart, and both girls had at least one common friend. Only a total moron or a corrupt official would deny even the possibility of a connection there.

When I discovered that Dennis Cantu was a dead ringer for Kenneth Bianchi it raised a number of questions: did the Hillside Strangler have to be one or the other of these men or could both have been killing in the same area at the same time independent of each other? What were the odds that two look alike killers could be operating at the same time in the same area? If both were killing at the same time, which one was the copycat and which one the primary and more prolific killer? Which victims belonged to which killers? How did Cantu fit into the scheme of things with the cousins? Many questions needed to be answered in this case and I had to have information and cooperation to find those answers.

Considering all the possibilities in this case was giving me a major headache. Not only did I have a complicated set of facts and circumstances to work with and no money to investigate the case, but the added element of a cover-up and politics within the LAPD was killing me. I felt that at one time during their investigation, the Task Force had come dangerously close to solving this case and coming up with the killers. Now that I had suspects in my sights, I wanted to see if I could find the clues that brought the Task Force to the brink of a solution.

Words are insufficient to describe my disappointment and anger at the request-a-clue policy the LAPD setup because of the abrasive behavior of a few investigators from the defense. Not having direct access to the clues and leads made it easy for the task force to foster their cover-up. It wasn't just my investigation they felt a need to cover-up; they also had to cover their own tracks as well.

When the LAPD investigation determined that the evidence pointed to a cop as the Hillside Strangler, the Task Force began investigating other cops. Their investigation turned up dirt on a lot of police officers within the LAPD and other police departments. It wasn't dirt like cops on the take or being bribed but more personal stuff like affairs, spousal abuse, child abuse, and that sort of thing. The Task Force wasn't acting like internal affairs or anything. They weren't a rat squad to be sure.

Nevertheless, the kind of stuff they found while investigating their own would've been a personnel nightmare had it become public information. They needed to keep this information quiet; therefore just before Buono was arrested, knowing that they would be required to turn over all the facts and evidence of their investigation to the defense, the LAPD conveniently had a "computer failure" that erased most of the information about the cops they had investigated. The "computer failure" was reported in the newspaper but it was little more than a footnote to the story about the arrest and prosecution of Angelo Buono. By then the press was fired up to promote Bianchi and Buono as the Hillside Stranglers and the story was down played insofar as most of the public was unaware of the computer failure or of its significance.

The defense on a murder case can read the police reports and give the cops credit for doing, if not a thorough investigation, then at least an honest one. By reading the police reports, defense investigators can determine what witness statements are consistent with the hard evidence and which ones are not. They can then go out and talk to the witnesses the cops missed or dismissed as not being helpful to their case, and reach a conclusion about the guilt or innocence of the defendant. From the mixture of police reports and defense investigator reports, a good defense lawyer can determine what the best defense will be for his client.

When the cops destroy evidence they destroy their credibility with the defense and anyone else who believes in the sanctity of a fair trial. The Task Force's computer failure and willingness to destroy evidence said they couldn't be trusted with anything, and every witness involved in the case had to be re-interviewed by the defense. In the Hillside Strangler case, that was a daunting chore. What is more important, it created an atmosphere of mistrust where the defense felt the cops were all corrupt public officials and caused members of both sides of the aisle to begin investigating each other.

My focus was on a murder investigation, and I thought that both the Task Force and the defense were being childish and wasting too much time and money on things that were essentially irrelevant to the issues of who committed the murders.

As things turned out for this defense team, investigating the cops used time and money they didn't have and would never get.

Chapter 23

William B. Keene gained famed and fortune as the irascible old judge on TV's Divorce Court; but, a few years before his TV stardom, Keene was the Presiding Judge of the Los Angeles County Superior Court. The position of Presiding Judge rotates every year, and with the power to assign cases to other trial judges and make appointments of defense counsel for indigent defendants, the position carries enormous clout. When the Hillside Strangler case came his way, Keene was ready to take advantage. The decisions he made in the Buono case were just a prelude to the disturbing ruling he would make a short time later involving a Sheriff's deputy charged and convicted of murder.

It didn't take long for word to get back to the prosecution that I had joined the defense for Angelo Buono. Shortly after signing up with the defense team, I got a call from detective Frank Salerno of the Sheriff's Homicide Bureau. I thought the call was about six months too late, but Salerno said he and his partner, Pete Finnegan, wanted to talk to me about my report to Roger Kelley. I was delighted with this turn of events. By that time, my Merry Miss Sunshine wasn't dead, but she was on life support, and after my experience with detectives Mellecker and Holder I was leery of their motives for calling me. With what little hope I had left, the always upbeat Merry Miss Sunshine was thinking that maybe the police were finally going to investigate the Barry murder as part of the Hillside Strangler series the way it should've been investigated from the start. Still, I was skeptical of anything the Task Force did and I wasn't going to take any chances that what was said at this meeting would be denied, misinterpreted, or taken out of context.

Since Chuck Boswell was my assigned partner on the defense, I invited him to my office for the meeting. Chuck arrived a half hour early and much to my dismay, he brought along the mouth, Joe Carroll.

Not being a particularly good housekeeper, I used Mark Sutherland's office for the meeting. The furniture was more comfortable, it was cleaner than mine and he didn't have an air mattress on the floor. While we waited for Salerno and Finnegan to arrive, Joe Carroll babbled to himself, and it gave me the heebie jeebies that he was looking in my direction while he carried on this running dialogue. I wanted to escape the torture and tell him to shut the hell up, but it wouldn't have done any good. To tell Joe Carroll to calm down and be quiet would be like telling a guy with a hair lip to stop lisping. He just couldn't help himself.

When Detective Sergeants Pete Finnegan and Frank Salerno arrived at the Green Hotel, I buzzed them in and as the two cops rounded the corner from the hotel entrance to the hallway, I waved at them to indicate we were in the first office on the right.

Frank Salerno led the way, and as they came through the office door I introduced myself, Boswell, and Carroll and held out my hand in a friendly gesture. The two detectives shook hands with me and nodded an acknowledgement to Carroll and Boswell.

Salerno was about my age, maybe a little older. He appeared to be about six feet tall, big boned, muscular, and tipped the scales at a hundred and ninety to two hundred pounds. His wire-rimmed glasses gave me the impression that he might be intelligent and maybe even studious. Shorter and slighter of build, his partner, Pete Finnegan, looked like a cop sent over from central casting; an actor right off the set of Dragnet or some other cop show. From time to time during the meeting, the distractions from Joe Carroll's rambling nearly made my ears bleed and I wondered if Finnegan might turn to

Carroll, who hadn't shut up since the two cops arrived, and say something like, 'just the facts ma'am'.

I hadn't counted on Joe Carroll attending the meeting and with five people in Mark's small office things were a little cramped. Salerno went around behind Mark's desk and took a seat in the desk chair. Carroll was sitting in one of the big comfortable armchairs unaware that Pete Finnegan was looking for a place to sit. He sat there with his legs crossed and mumbling to himself about God knows what. I kept my cool but I wanted to kill him. Joe Carroll was a classless act. He was unfocused, rude and most importantly ineffectual as an investigator.

I was sitting in a big armchair under the window and in front of the desk. I forced myself to ignore Joe Carroll's rudeness and directed my attention back to Frank Salerno. I noticed that he had produced a copy of my report to Roger Kelley. His elbows on the desk and holding the report in one hand, he looked down at it, fumbling with the paperclip that attached the picture of Cantu to the report. Removing the picture, he studied it for a few seconds in silence.

"This picture is definitely a thorn in our side," he said without looking up from the photograph.

"It looks like...." he let his voice trail off. It was not a tapering off like he was stumped for an answer as to who the photograph really looked like. We both knew that the picture of Cantu showed him to be a dead ringer for Kenneth Bianchi. I had said as much in my report to Kelley. It was more like he was looking for or expecting an interjection of a different sort. If that was his intention, I didn't disappoint him.

"Yeah," I said, "it looks like Jerry Beck."

"Hmm, Jerry Beck," He echoed more to himself than to me.

It did.

Sheriff's deputy and newly anointed homicide detective, Jerry Beck, was very similar in appearance to the person the Task Force had been searching for as the Hillside Strangler. Furthermore, he was a cop and they were looking for a cop or someone with a police background. I had thought, since early in my investigation, that Beck was taking the Barry murder too personal. I attributed his overreaction in arresting Anzures without evidence to be the result of first homicide jitters. I figured he was just trying to make a good impression with his bosses on his first outing as a murder cop. Still, the Hillside Strangler case was huge and if he wanted to impress his superiors what better way to do it than to solve what had become a political albatross around the police department's neck?

Being a cop suspected in the infamous Hillside Strangler murders had to be pure agony. Nobody would want to go through that ordeal twice, and it occurred to me that Beck, not wanting to bring further attention to himself, would have a strong motive to close the books on the Barry murder as quickly and quietly as possible. Because of the "computer failure" at the LAPD, most of the information on cops collected during their marathon investigation had been deleted. My theory about Beck was not easily proven, at least not by me, but Salerno and Finnegan had been members of the Task Force from its inception and they were also Sheriff's deputies. I figured if Beck had been investigated as a suspect in the Hillside Strangler murders they would know about it. I didn't think they would confirm my suspicions, but I still wanted to give Salerno something to think about and let him know that I saw something in the physical appearance of Jerry Beck that might explain why the Barry murder had fallen through the cracks.

The rest of the meeting was something of a blur to me. Joe Carroll wanted to set his own agenda and talk about other murders not mentioned in my report. I was getting tired of his constant rambling and none of us cared about his theories concerning who murdered Lauren Wagner, nor his anger that Salerno and Finnegan were framing Buono for murder. I had my own frustrations about the case. This was my meeting and I was furious at Carroll's disruptions. To this day, I don't have a clear memory of how the meeting ended.

What I do remember about the aftermath of that meeting, is that when I came out of the Green Hotel, I looked around for my car and it was gone. The repo fairy had paid me a visit during the meeting and my Datzun 260Z was by now safely tucked away in the secure parking lot of the Datzun dealership. In my already depressed mood, I responded to my car being gone like any self-respecting private eye—I went across the street to the John Bull Pub and got blasted on beer and a couple of carafes of cheap Chablis.

Standing at the bar thinking about the meeting, I didn't have an overwhelming sense that Frank Salerno and Pete Finnegan were ready to sign up for my team. I was delighted with Salerno's statement that the photograph of Cantu was "a thorn in our side," but his use of the word "photograph" in the proclamation about Cantu being a "thorn" in their side bothered me. It bothered me because it indicated that Salerno wasn't thinking about Cantu as a suspect in the murders. As Far as I was concerned, the report was more important than the picture of Cantu. The report contained the dots they needed in order to connect Barry to the Cepeda/Johnson murders and facts about Castillon and Smith fitting the profile of the killers. To the cops, and everyone else for that matter, it was all about the picture of Cantu being a damaging piece of evidence that could discredit their star witness and demolish the prosecution's case against Angelo Buono.

I feared they were focusing too much on the downside of losing their case and not enough on the upside of taking down three dangerous serial killers. I was curious about what they intended to do with my report, and since I was still gathering evidence, what they would do about me. Judge William B. Keene, presiding Judge of the Los Angeles County Superior Court, held the answer to their dilemma.

Judge Keene had political ambitions that went way beyond the judiciary, and to use the cop's code for nuts, his personal political goals were strictly fifty-one fifty. As the presiding judge of the Superior Court at the time Angelo Buono was arrested, he saw the opportunity to make political hay while the sun was shinning. His political ambition, however, didn't have anything to do with becoming the host of his own courtroom TV show. His detour on the road to big time politics came about as a result of a stupid decision he made in the Robert Armstrong murder trial a short time after he had helped the Task Force set up Angelo Buono to take the rap as the Hillside Strangler.

Robert Armstrong was a Sheriff's Deputy who had called in a phony report of a disturbance at an apartment the deputy thought to be the center of drug activity. After calling in a false disturbance report, Armstrong was dispatched to the apartment where he busted down the door and was confronted by a frightened and pregnant black female. He shot the woman once in the stomach wounding her and killing her unborn baby. He was arrested and charged with murder. At the end of the trial, the jury convicted Armstrong of second degree murder for killing the unborn baby.

Judge Keene would do anything to gain and keep the support of the powerful police officers' unions and associations. His political ambitions made him a police officer's dream judge. However, when he threw out the jury's verdict in the Robert Armstrong case, thus reducing the second degree murder conviction to the lesser crime of killing an unborn fetus, it nearly started a riot in the black community of South Central Los Angeles. At the time, the killing of a fetus wasn't even the law in California, and the black community was outraged. What his racist decision said to blacks was that they could be victimizers in his courtroom but never the victim and especially not a victim of a white cop. He seemed to be sending the message to the police that it was perfectly okay for them skirt the necessity for a search warrant as long as they could be as creative as Armstrong.

The powers that be thought it would be safer for society to have Keene hearing divorce cases on TV. I thought giving him a TV show was a feeble punishment for flaunting the law. Instead of a TV show, he should've been busted for inciting to riot. He needed a serious attitude adjustment and some rehabilitation. Maybe 500 hours of community service in Watts and a little prison time would've straightened him out. The Armstrong case was just one more powder keg heaped on the pile of racial injustice that would explode into riots in South Central Los Angeles after the Rodney King beating.

Before his judicial credibility and political aspirations came crashing down, Keene saw his career as being on the fast track to real power and he exerted the same heavy-handed control in the Buono case as he did later in the Armstrong trial.

To further his political ambitions, Keene had put together a small group of private lawyers that he could appoint on cases where the public defender's office could not represent the defendant because of a possible conflict of interest. Most of these indigent cases were pled out and they could be extremely lucrative for sole practitioners or lawyers in small law firms, but joining Keene's group of private public defenders came at the cost of autonomy for its members. Member lawyers of his cluster were expected to share his judicial philosophy and cater to his political ambitions. In most situations that meant pleading the defendant guilty, filing an inflated bill, and going on to the next case.

If a defendant did go to trial, Keene's lawyers were expected to keep in mind that, even though he was paying their legal fees with taxpayer money, he was their ultimate client, not the defendant, and Keene didn't want his lawyers zealously discrediting police investigations. A favored member of Keene's cabal was a lawyer named Gerald Chaleff.

After my meeting with Salerno and Finnegan, I felt I was making some real headway into pressuring the police to properly investigate the Leslie Barry murder. It was more likely than not that Deputy District Attorney Roger Kelley had sent the two detectives to talk to me about my report. From his hesitation in filing murder charges against Angelo Buono at the beginning of the case, I suspected that there was more to Kelley's foot dragging than insufficient evidence. I felt that the lead prosecutor had some serious reservations about whether Angelo Buono was truly guilty of the murders. My report on the Barry murder and the photograph of Dennis Cantu acted to reinforce the grave doubts Kelley had about the truthfulness of Kenneth Bianchi's testimony and the guilt of Angelo Buono.

The Jim Brustman defense team was large, aggressive and a constant irritant to the Task Force. Most of the team was made up of volunteers who believed completely that Angelo Buono was getting screwed for political reasons. The Task Force was looking for relief from the pressure and wanted Brustman and Wilcox, and by extension me, the thorn in their side, off the case. Whatever the cops wanted, Judge Keene wanted to make it happen for them and this is how he decided to do it.

To support the motive for the murders and buck up the prosecution's case, Buono had been charged with pimping, pandering and procurement for sex. With a weak case proving that the defendant was really a serial killer, it was a part of the prosecutions trial strategy to show that Angelo Buono used and abused women and was an over-all rotten son-o-bitch and thus the Hillside Strangler. It wasn't much but it was all Kelley had to work with and he had to make do. If Kelley lost the pimping and pandering charges, he would have nothing left to shore up his star witness's ever wavering testimony that Buono was the mastermind of the murders.

Over the spirited objections of the prosecutor, Keene severed the lesser charges of pimping and pandering from the more serious murder charges. The legal term for severing charges is called bifurcation. At first glance, gutting the prosecution's case looked like a favorable ruling for the defense, but Keene had something more ominous in mind. He knew that the sex charges were a major part of the murder charges and that there would never be separate trials for the sex crimes and the ten counts of murder. By chopping the case up, he was able to appoint Gerald Chaleff, his trusted sidekick and a lawyer from his cabal, to represent Buono on the lesser sex charges while temporarily leaving Brustman to represent Buono on the murder counts.

In a way, Keene's scheme was like a shell game and the object of the game was to win favor with the police by helping them frame Buono for murder. Chaleff was the shill; the law was the pea; and Jim Brustman was the pigeon. In the end though, the public was the real chump in the game. The public was conned into believing that they were safe and their tax dollars were being used to bring a dangerous serial killer to justice. More than twenty years later the cost of Keene's game playing with human life, freedom and misery are still undetermined.

This ploy served another useful purpose in Keene's over-all plan. It gave Chaleff access to Buono so that he could undermine Buono's confidence in his lawyers. Furthermore, it put him in close contact with the defense to spy for Keene and keep him informed as to what was happening as the case wound its way through the various stages of the process.

In the short time that we had been on the Buono defense team, Wilcox and I had become fast friends. We often discussed the case over lunch and sometimes over dinner at his house. One afternoon Wilcox and I were venting our rage at a watering hole on Ventura Boulevard in the San Fernando Valley. Jim was bitter about the display of cronyism between Judge Keene and Gerald Chaleff. He related to me an incident that happened in a meeting in the Judge's chambers just a few days earlier.

To the Buono Defense team, Chaleff was an outsider, held in low esteem and looked upon with contempt. He was not trusted and never included in strategy meetings or shared information about what was going on with the defense. Everyone close to the case, including the cops, knew that Chaleff was a mole for Keene. Simply put, he served no purpose for the defense and had no good reason for being there.

During the preliminary stages of motions and appeals, Keene had continually refused Brustman's request to declare Buono indigent, claiming that the value of Buono's upholstery shop in Glendale exceeded the legal limit on personal assets to qualify him for a court appointed lawyer. Brustman argued that Buono's assets, while technically a little high, if liquidated, were still insufficient to properly defend himself against ten counts of murder. Brustman told Keene that Angelo Buono was willing to sign all of his property over to the state of California thus making him a pauper. Once the property was sold, the money could be used by the state to help defray the cost of his defense. Keene would not budge from his position and it was becoming increasingly apparent that the wily judge was trying to starve Brustman and his defense team off the case.

Wilcox and Brustman had gone to see Keene to again try to persuade him to declare Buono indigent, release state funds for his defense, and officially appoint Brustman to represent the notorious defendant. Since he had been appointed by Keene to represent Buono on what Brustman and Wilcox referred to as the "junk charges," Chaleff had a right to attend any meetings between the judge and the actual defense lawyers.

Brustman had worked the case for nearly a year without getting paid or having the money to pay investigators and experts, and he and Jim Wilcox wanted to make a last ditch plea for financial relief.

During the meeting, when Keene said something negative about appointing Brustman to represent Buono, Chaleff chimed in with a reference to another high profile case he had been appointed on.

"You mean just like the Alphabet Bomber case?"

Wilcox saw the judge flash Chaleff a look that could've stopped a freight train in its tracks. The incident confirmed Wilcox's suspicions that something devilish was up between Keene and Chaleff and he knew then that our days on the case were numbered. Judge William Keene again refused to declare Buono indigent and appoint Brustman to represent him.

From what Wilcox was telling me, I, too sensed that the Brustman defense was doomed, and I had a short time left in my effort to unearth evidence against Cantu, Castillon and Smith for the Hillside Strangler murders. I was flat ass broke, with no place to live, no car to drive, and with Keene and Chaleff doing the hokey pokey on the case, my prospects for the future were dim. While sitting in my office one day, mentally ticking off facts to myself, and putting my mind in overdrive, there was something nagging at me. It was like a piece of evidence or a clue that had caught my eye during research on the Barry murder that I really wanted to explore further; but I couldn't remember what it was. I thought my brain was going to explode trying to retrace the many steps of my investigation before I could recall what it was. Suddenly it hit me.

It was my interest in a letter written to Mayor Tom Bradley in January of 1978. The letter had fascinated me when I read about it in the newspaper and I wondered what the entire text of the letter said. Maybe something in the letter would fit with what I knew about my suspects.

I picked up the phone and dialed the number for the Task Force to request a copy of the letter and the envelope it came in.

"Robbery/Homicide Detective Thiel speaking." The voice on the other end answered.

"I don't know what the clue number is," I began after telling Thiel who I was, "but I would like to see the letter that was written and sent to Tom Bradley on January 17, 1978."

Detective Thiel was cordial and friendly.

"Yes, I'm familiar with that clue," he said.

"I'll make a copy of it for you. How would you like for me to get it to you?" he asked, "Would you like to come down to the Parker Center and pick it up?

The preliminary hearing for Angelo Buono was underway and I knew I would be spending a lot of time at the courthouse in meetings and getting investigative assignments from the defense lawyers.

"No." I said, "Why don't you send it over to the courthouse and I'll pick it up from one of the defense lawyers."

"No problem," He responded in an upbeat voice.

A few days later, I went down to the courthouse and as I approached the courtroom where the Buono prelim was being held, I spotted Jim Wilcox standing in the hallway just outside the courtroom having a cigarette.

"Hi Jim, how are you doing?" I asked.

I was eager to know if the letter had been delivered to the courthouse and the friendly amenities over I ask.

"Did the Task Force send a letter over for me?"

"Yes." He said stubbing out his cigarette and going back into the courtroom.

As the heavy doors between the courtroom and the hallway swung open, Wilcox approached me holding the letter up in front of his face and flipping the pages as if he were quickly scanning the document.

"Here you go he said," Handing me the letter.

I took the letter back to the office and if I read it once I read it fifty times. I could almost see something in the content but when I came close to understanding what the letter was about the premonition evaporated like a puff of smoke. The letter was fascinating reading, but because the writer had requested publicity, I considered it was probably a prank by one of the many loonies looking for media attention. Nevertheless, I knew that serial killers sometimes liked to toy with the police to throw them off track by sending coded messages or letters. I thought it would be wise to take the letter seriously until I could determine if it was legit or a very sick joke. Again, I dialed the phone number for the Task Force.

This time, as luck would have it, I got another detective on the phone. He was gruff and not at all friendly. Kind of reminded me of the way Ed Henderson answered the phone. He identified himself as Sergeant Bob Grogan. He didn't strike me as a chitchat sort of guy so after telling him who I was I got right to the point.

"I've been studying this letter that was sent to Mayor Bradley and I was wondering if your lab was able to lift any latent prints off the envelope." I inquired.

"Which letter?" He growled, "The first one or the second one?" Damn. Just as I was about to dismiss the letter as a sick prank by a nut, I learn that there was another letter.

"Second letter? I asked with utter, wide-eyed surprise. "I didn't know about a second letter." I quickly added. "Could you please make a copy of it along with a copy of the envelope it came in and deliver it to the courthouse for me?" I asked condescendingly as if he was nothing more than a messenger boy.

"Now, back to my original question. Were there any fingerprints lifted off this letter or the envelope it came in?" I asked, by now irritated at his lousy attitude.

"No." He snapped.

"Okay," I said, "thanks for the information." I added smugly.

Grogan grumbled something and hung up the phone.

I was at the courthouse nearly every day for the next week or two, attending strategy meetings and getting investigative assignments from Wilcox or Brustman. It became a routine with me that the first thing out of my mouth when I saw either of the defense lawyers was to inquire whether the letter had arrived. Each time, when they told me it hadn't, I was disappointed and I would go back to my office and call the Task Force to inquire why the letter hadn't been turned over to the defense. The Task Force stonewalled me with one excuse after another. "ugh, we'll look into it. Requests are taking longer than usual." Or one of my favorites,

"What was that clue number again?"

Finally, two weeks after requesting the clue from Grogan, I showed up at the courthouse and saw Wilcox in the hallway. Again, I asked him if the second Bradley letter had arrived from the Task Force.

"Yes, it just came this morning," he said, disappearing into the courtroom to get the clue. He came out of the courtroom and handed me the letter.

"Those letters are a couple of bizarre documents." Wilcox said handing me the second letter. "Do you know who wrote them?" He asked, hopeful that I might have an answer for him.

"I don't know," I answered honestly.

Wanting to play to the hope in his voice, and my own desire to find out who the author was, I added. "Maybe Castillon or Smith. If it were any of my three suspects, my guess would be Smith. I'll have to study it and see if I can get anything out of if."

We were having a strategy meeting during the noon break that day and as I followed Wilcox through the courtroom back to the conference room, I caught a glimpse of prosecutor Roger Kelley. Our eyes met briefly and he winked at me. I nodded to him and kept walking. I didn't think Kelley was flirting with me. The wink was an acknowledgement that he got my report and perhaps agreed with some of the conclusions in it.

Maybe it was because I didn't feel completely in step with the defense, but I didn't understand a lot of what went on in our strategy meetings. They talked in short hand and it made me feel like I was entering in the middle of a conversation. In the strategy meeting, Brustman started out by warning us generally about making editorial comments to the police or the press. I wasn't sure what he was referring to but I figured it had something to do with Joe Carroll and his big mouth. Brustman told us that in a couple of days we would be conducting interviews of all the witnesses he had subpoenaed. He said that the judge had made a darkened courtroom available to us and the witnesses would be showing up at the courthouse at nine o'clock for their interview. Brustman told us that there would be a hundred to a hundred and fifty witnesses and he needed the whole team present to conduct the interviews.

After the meeting, on the instructions of Jim Brustman, Chuck Boswell and I were sent to Sybil Brand, the Los Angeles County women's jail, to interview a witness who, because of her current living arrangements, would not be able to attend the mass interview. This Hollywood prostitute claimed that she saw Bianchi force one of the victims into his car. The woman had been busted for prostitution and Jim Brustman wanted me to take my picture of Cantu with me to see if she could identify Cantu as the person she saw forcing the woman into the car. It didn't really matter which way the identification went. The two men were like identical twin brothers and her credibility was damned if she did and damned if she didn't. If she couldn't identify Cantu then she couldn't identify Bianchi either. If she identified Cantu then she would have fingered a man that was inconsistent with her original identification of Kenneth Bianchi.

We signed in at Sybil Brand and waited for the witness to be brought to the visitor's window. I was sitting at the window to do the interview and Chuck was sitting in a chair next to me. When she was brought out in her jail jumpsuit she looked as if she was strung out on drugs or coming down from drugs. She took a seat on the prisoner side of the window opposite me and picked up the phone.

"Hi. My name is Ron Crisp. I'm a private investigator." I began.

She nodded at me but didn't say anything. Not even a "hi" or "do you want a date, sailor?" " Man," I thought, "this woman is hard."

I had a copy of her statement to the police in front of me and after reading it to her, I asked if that was pretty much what she could testify to. She nodded an assent without voicing an answer.

I took the photograph of Cantu out of a folder and held it up to the window for her to see. I asked her if that was the man she saw force the victim into the car.

"I'm not going to talk to you." She responded.

"Why not?" I started to argue.

She got up from her seat and left the interview without looking at the photograph or even saying goodbye.

I knew this hooker wasn't that smart. Not making an identification of the picture one way or the other was the only thing she could have done to avoid comprising the credibility of her testimony. The only way she could possibly have known the significance of the photograph of Cantu was if someone had told her. The cops were at it again telling witnesses not to talk to me. A week or so later, Jim Wilcox told me my name had come up in court. Roger Kelley had asked a witness or two if they talked to a private investigator named Ron Crisp. The hooker from Sybil Brand could almost answer without perjuring herself that she hadn't.

When Boswell dropped me off at my office in Pasadena, I asked him if he could stop by on the day of the mass interviews and give me a ride down to the courthouse. He told me he would be at my office around eight and that would give us plenty of time to get to courthouse.

Back in the comfort and solitude of my office, I was eager to study this second letter to Tom Bradley and see how it differed from the first letter and if I could glean anything of importance from it. The first thing I noticed was that the writer said he thought requesting publicity in the first letter had been a mistake and he did not want any publicity about this second letter. That explained why no one except the Task Force knew about the existence of the second letter. Yet, that statement raised questions? Why had the writer considered publicity from the first letter to be a mistake? Had the Task Force been close to capturing the suspects because of the publicity? If so, how close had they come? Were there clues among the thousands on the computer that named suspects and the author of this letter was one of them? Were any of them named Cantu, Castillon or Smith?

I considered the possibility that maybe he caught hell from his accomplice for sending the letter. The person he mentioned in the first letter that he wanted to turn into the police along with himself. Whatever he meant it was apparent that the writer was a sick puppy. The two letters, taken together as one strange piece of evidence, had a frightening air of legitimacy about them. Although anonymous, it seemed to me that these documents were real confessions to the Hillside Strangler murders.

Besides the usual expression of hating his mother, 'my mother makes my head hurt...," another part of the letter that caught my attention was a sentence that read in part:

"I don't want to go back to that place. That doctor who cut on my head..."

In analyzing that part of the letter, one logical interpretation the Task Force had for that statement was that the writer was a former mental patient and "that place" was a mental hospital. They concluded that, "That doctor" might be a psychiatrist who had tried to help him get his head screwed on straight.

Applied to my investigation the letter could be interpreted a little differently on those passages. "That Doctor" could be Dennis Cantu and "cut on my head," meant that Cantu was the leader. He was the one with the stronger personality who influenced, controlled, and persuaded him to kill. Going back to "that place" was about Laredo, Texas. Smith had to go back there to be a police officer. It's speculation but it made sense and I wanted to further investigate that possibility.

Another interpretation with Cantu as the possible writer might be "That Doctor who cut on my head" was the medical school professor who wanted to wash him out of med school.

It was obvious that the Task Force had taken these letters seriously because they had done just as the letter writer requested. In the first letter, he requested publicity and they gave him publicity. In the second letter, he said that the publicity was a mistake and he didn't want any publicity for the second letter and they kept it quiet. Even if the letters were not written by Cantu or one of my other suspects, neither Kenneth Bianchi nor Angelo Buono had written them either. That made these frightening documents a powerful piece of evidence that could help in establishing a reasonable doubt on behalf of Angelo Buono.

I was so close to dismissing the first letter as a sick prank, and of no evidentiary value at all, until Bob Grogan let it slip about the second letter. Both letters would have amounted to nothing more than dust collectors had the loose lips that sunk ships (or high profile murder cases)zipped his donut hole. They did anyway, but that omission is on Gerald Chaleff.

If it did nothing else, the letter incident reinforced my belief that the request-a-clue policy set up by the LAPD was to the benefit of no one except the police and their efforts to cover-up the case. I made a few more inquiries about the letters, but what I really wanted after discovering these bizarre, forgotten, and hidden documents, was to get into the massive data bank of clues on the Task Force computer that they collected as a result of nearly two years of intense publicity. I wondered what else besides these letters might be hidden from me in the police computer on the Hillside Strangler case, but my involvement in the case would end involuntarily before I could ever get an answer to that question.

Chapter 24

With Kenneth Bianchi changing his story every five minutes; my report and the picture of Cantu; the two Bradley letters, and Bob Grogan throwing tantrums all the time, the Hillside Strangler case had become a major headache for the Deputy DA and Chief Prosecutor Roger Kelley. It would take something stronger than an aspirin to cure it. He was ready to call it quits.

Besides his lack of evidence to support Bianchi's shaky confession, Kelley had other problems with the case. The Task Force was more than resistant to investigating the information on Cantu, Castillon, and Smith. Some Task Force members were actively trying to cover up exculpatory evidence and Kelley's knowledge of the cover-up gave him ethical fits. He was caught between the rock of doing what was morally right and the hard place of political expediency. He knew if he dismissed charges against Buono, the cops would have a fit and the ire of the LAPD could translate into big political problems for his boss. Kelley's uncertainty about the case didn't escape the watchful eye of the Task Force and it was causing them to feel the pinch. They needed to do something to relieve the pressure.

Jim Wilcox kept me informed as to what went on inside the courtroom particularly if it had anything to do with me or if it held any special interest to me. Jim told me about what happened in the courtroom shortly after Grogan had told me about the second letter to Tom Bradley.

Grogan was his own worst enemy and letting it slip about the second Bradley letter was a good example of how his oversized, out of control ego did more damage to the prosecution than good. Other than talking to him on the phone that one time and seeing him around the courthouse, I never had any other direct contact with Bob Grogan, but people who knew him filled me in.

A big, loud mouthed, red-faced, Irish bully, Grogan was an enforcer. He was the kind of enforcer you might find on a hockey team. He wasn't the fastest skater or the most coordinated athlete on the team. He might not even be able to skate backwards or stand up straight on the skates, but he was the roughest, toughest, baddest man on the ice. He was the player the coach called on when he wanted to establish physical superiority over the other team by drawing blood. He would spend more time during a game in the penalty box than on the ice, but if he could take out the hottest scorer on the other team then that was his contribution to the effort.

No one was more outspoken on the Task Force than Bob Grogan. The media loved Grogan because he was a bigger than life character. The late Bill Hazzlet, a reporter covering the courts for the Los Angeles Times, thought Bob Grogan walked on water. He was a cop philosopher who had no problem, when it served his purposes, presenting himself as the protector of the weak and downtrodden victims of crime, but it was more image than substance. The truth of the matter is that Grogan was a cop's cop and he was ferociously protective of other cops and the image of the Los Angeles Police Department.

Grogan was an end-justifies-the-means type detective and he saw his job as doing whatever it took to get a conviction against the person he arrested. To Grogan, the end didn't always have to be about putting bad guys in jail. He loved the power and authority that the badge brought him and hated anyone who questioned his authority. Roger Kelley stood as a reminder to Grogan that he was not the ultimate authority on the Hillside Strangler case and Grogan despised him for it.

Bob Grogan was one of the members of the Hillside Strangler Task Force who went to Bellingham, Washington to coerce a confession out of Kenneth Bianchi though fear and intimidation. He was one of the reasons Kenneth Bianchi's confession sounded suspiciously like it had come right out of a police report. During the interrogation, when Bianchi was stumped for an answer or didn't know a detail, Bob Grogan would thunder at him and then supply the answer as another question. He was good at asking leading questions.

An example of how that works might go something like this: During the interrogation, a cop asks the suspect an alibi question like, "Where were you on the afternoon of November 20, 1977?" If the suspect can't remember or gives the wrong answer, the interrogator yells at him, threatens him with the worse thing he can think of, then slaps him up the side of the head and asks him a leading question, "Were you driving down York Boulevard on the afternoon of November 20, 1977?" At some point, the suspect will tire of the verbal, and sometimes physical abuse, and get the idea that the right answer to the question is that he was driving down York Boulevard on the afternoon of November 20, 1977. Once the suspect starts cooperating, the interrogator can go back, and for the record, ask the question properly.

The problem with coercing a false confession from a person suspected of committing ten murders is that there's too much information for the suspect to digest and remember and too many details about all the murders to keep straight. Kenneth Bianchi couldn't remember from one day to the next what he confessed. He became so confused that he couldn't distinguish between what he really did and what he told the Task Force he had done.

Kelley felt it was time to cut his loses. Part of the plea bargain arrangement, in which Bianchi agreed to plead guilty to five counts of murder in the Hillside Strangler case and turn states evidence against his cousin, was that Bianchi would testify truthfully. If Bianchi was changing his story daily, he couldn't be telling the truth. Roger Kelley wanted to extricate himself from the case gracefully by revoking Bianchi's plea bargain and, to save a total embarrassment to the DA and the LAPD, try to make a deal with Angelo Buono. He could send Bianchi back to the state of Washington and the recalcitrant suspect would be their problem. Authorities in Washington could either try him for the murders of Karen Mandic and Diane Wilder or stick to their plea bargain with him. Whether they tried him again or stuck to their plea bargain, Kelly knew Bianchi wouldn't get out of the state pen in Walla Walla, until he was carried out feet first.

The plea bargain that Kelley was trying out on Jim Brustman had Angelo Buono pleading guilty to one count of second-degree murder and serving a substantial prison sentence. Bob Grogan hated Angelo Buono, partly because of what he thought Buono was, but mostly because Buono was cocky and defied authority. Grogan would do anything to get a conviction against Buono, and he intensely disliked anyone who might suggest that Angelo Buono was not the real Hillside Strangler. The idea of a plea bargain, especially the one Kelley was suggesting, didn't go down well with him; in fact, it stuck in his craw and he nearly choked to death on it.

He and Roger Kelley were constantly at each other's throats. Kelley, being an honest and ethical prosecutor, didn't like what he saw Grogan doing. For one thing, he didn't like Grogan telling witnesses not to talk to the defense. That kind of activity involved him in the cover-up and he didn't want any part of it. For another, Kelley didn't like the way key witness statements seemed to change after Grogan re-interviewed them. It smacked of suborning to perjury and it infuriated Kelley. Besides being suspicious of the authenticity of the new statements, it was embarrassing for Kelley to turn those modified statements over to the defense. Grogan may have thought he was helping the case, but as the saying goes, the road to Hell is paved with good intentions.

One such witness Grogan re-interviewed was an elderly woman who claimed to have seen two men force a young woman into a car at around ten o'clock on the night Lauren Wagner disappeared. At the time of the alleged incident, it was dark, the woman lived alone, and she was blind as a bat. According to her original statement, she would've been looking through thick shrubbery at an event happening at least a hundred feet away in the dark of night. She couldn't have possibly seen what she stated she saw. The defense figured her to be a lonely, frightened, old woman who just wanted some company and a little attention.

Grogan needed corroborating evidence to support Bianchi's confession to the murder of Lauren Wagner in the worst way, and this old woman was the best he had. He knew that her original statement was questionable and would fall apart on cross-examination by the defense. After Grogan "re-interviewed" the woman, her statement about her position in the house changed to a location more conducive to seeing what Grogan wanted her to see.

When I learned about the possibility of the case being pled out, I wasn't very happy. I felt Kelley was only trying to appease the police and was playing politics with the case. On the other hand, Bianchi only pled guilty to five of the ten murders, and I could see the benefit of an arrangement that would keep the murders I was interested in open and unsolved. By then the only thing that would have really made me happy would have been to have gotten into the databank compiled during the Task Force's investigation.

Everyone involved in the Buono case, as well as many courthouse observers, knew that Chaleff worked for, and was reporting everything, to Judge Keene. A few weeks after I learned about the second Bradley letter, Grogan pulled a maneuver that would never have worked on a strong, united, defense. Grogan felt bad about letting the existence of the second letter to Tom Bradley out of the bag and he needed to do something to make up for his slip of the tongue. Furthermore, he knew his case wasn't getting stronger with me working for the defense.

One day, before the preliminary hearing was to begin the afternoon session, Brustman and Wilcox had not yet returned from lunch and Chaleff had come back to court early. The bailiff brought Buono in from the holding cell to await the beginning of the afternoon session. With Chaleff and Buono sitting alone in the courtroom, the stage was set.

Bob Grogan entered the courtroom on cue. His face as red as the rising sun on a Japanese flag, his blue eyes bulging, he stood menacingly over the two men. Throwing one of the Bradley letters down on the defense table and in a loud, booming voice, dripping with anger and sarcasm, he demanded that Buono copy the letter word for word and sign the document. Somehow, Grogan managed to spit out my name, as if I were the one responsible for him being there, looming over Buono and getting in his face. It was high drama and the suddenness of the attack startled and scared the shit out of Chaleff and Buono. Buono supplied Grogan with a sample of his handwriting, but as Jim Wilcox condescended about Chaleff later, "At least Chaleff had the presence of mind not to allow Buono to copy the letter verbatim and sign it."

I didn't think getting a signed confession from Buono was the only objective of this theatrical tactic. Through Chaleff, Grogan was sending a message to Keene that they desperately needed his help in getting Jim Brustman, and by extension, me off the case.

Shortly after the courtroom theatrics, and over the objections of the defendant, Chaleff was appointed to represent Buono on the entire case. The pimping and pandering charges were rejoined to the murder charges and with the case put back together, Buono was declared indigent and state funds made available for his defense. Before the longest trial in history was over, Chaleff would be paid over a million dollars of taxpayers money to supposedly represent Angelo Buono.

Once he was installed on the case, to mollify Angelo Buono, Chaleff began looking for a woman lawyer to second chair the defense. His first choice for second banana was Leslie Abramson, the bulldog defense lawyer who later represented the Mendendez Brothers. Abramson was already a well-respected defense lawyer and she turned him down. He finally settled on an inexperienced young lawyer named Kathryn Mader.

Adding insult to injury, Chaleff, in all of his arrogance, called Jim Brustman and Jim Wilcox to the stand and questioned their integrity by inquiring in open court if they had turned over all the police reports and evidence to him. There was little doubt in my mind that this scheme was a result of me sending Chaleff a copy of a few police reports I had found stashed away in my closet. I knew he already had those reports but I wanted to remind him that I was still out there following the case.

He really rubbed salt in the open wound when he hired Joe Carroll, Jim Brustman' brother-in-law, to work on the case as one of his investigators. Chaleff was a piece of work. It was as if the

Brustman defense was his biggest adversary and not the prosecution. Sadly, there was more truth to that than anyone wanted to admit.

My frustration at being stonewalled by the Task Force, not getting paid for my work, and being unable to afford to follow up on leads, was reaching the boiling point. When Keene and Gerald Chaleff sandbagged the defense, it threw me into a blind rage. I had never experienced such intense anger, not even when Art Anzures was convicted. At one point, I felt like taking the law into my own hands, but I wasn't certain of whom I wanted to shoot. I believed in the idea of a fair trial and felt that with a little more evidence Dennis Cantu could be brought to trial. With Chaleff's, appointment to the defense, Buono's case had moved to Kangaroo Court. A fair trial wasn't in the cards for anyone. It was a good thing I didn't own a gun or I'd have put a round between Chaleff's eyes and not felt any remorse for having done it. Instead, I internalized my anger and took an extended vacation into la la land.

Frustration and depression had put me in a daze and I never had a real sense of being fired from the Buono case. In all the month's I worked for the defense, I never received a fee or income from the case. It was like one day I was struggling to find evidence to prove that the same killer, or killers, who took the lives of Dolly Cepeda, Sonja Johnson, and Kristina Weckler, also murdered Leslie Barry and then suddenly the struggle changed to one of personal survival.

I had one parting shot to take at the case.

Even before Art Anzures was ever convicted, I had approached the Los Angeles Times with the story idea that they do a Barry murder-linked-to-the-Hillside Strangler type expose. It was a great story and I was surprised at their lack of interest in it.

Over the following months, I kept the Times apprised of developments in my ongoing investigation. All the reporters I talked to told me how much they admired what I was doing, but they did nothing to help.

Admiration doesn't do much for you. It doesn't free an innocent man from prison or bring the guilty to justice. It won't buy you a cup of coffee let alone pay the rent and I thought if I heard one more person tell me how much they admired me, I'm putting them on my hit list along with Gerald Chaleff.

Finally, on Sunday, August 3, 1980, the Times published a story about me. It was a major puff piece with a picture of me on the front page of the Metro section of the Sunday edition of the Los Angeles Times. I hated the article. Not so much for what it said, although the content was mostly bullshit, but for what it didn't say. The article mentioned my report to Roger Kelley, but it didn't say anything about the content of the report. In fact, the article didn't even identify Roger Kelley as the Chief Prosecutor in the Hillside Strangler case. Either the reporter, the editor or maybe both didn't want to give the slightest hint to the public that the Leslie Barry murder was linked to the Hillside Strangler murders. The story went out over the Times Wire Service and was picked up by the Atlanta Journal and Constitution. They ran it on the third page of the front section.

As luck would have it, Ma Bell shut my phone service off for nonpayment of a two hundred dollar phone bill on the Friday before the article came out. Anyone who read the article and wanted to contact me about my investigation would have to do a major skip trace just to find me. Nevertheless, some people did reach me. Most were TV producers wanting to do a movie of the week based upon the article. I met a few of them for lunch and soon realized that we weren't on the same page. They wanted to tell the Times story and that wasn't the true story.

One producer had the idea to do a movie of the week with a story line that was similar to the "Fugitive" TV series. His premise was that I would run around like a chicken with my head cut off trying to find the one armed man who killed Leslie Barry or some such nonsense. He was a legitimate producer and we went as far as getting a contract drawn up for the purchase of an option to the story. When he phoned me one day and told me that he hoped Anzures didn't get out of prison before his movie of the week came out, I decided that our purposes were at odds and turned him down. It was too bad. I desperately needed the money, but I didn't need Hollywood sabotaging my efforts to clear an innocent man of murder.

One man who got through to me identified himself as a lawyer in Venice. He told me that he was a friend of Gerald Chaleff' and could put me in touch with the defense lawyer. I didn't know if he was playing with me or not. He certainly didn't know much about the history of the Hillside Strangler case or he would've known that the last person Chaleff wanted to hear from would be me. Anyway, he invited me to his house for dinner and I accepted his invitation.

I intended to give this lawyer my report to Roger Kelley to pass on to Chaleff. I wanted to make sure that Chaleff couldn't claim later that he was duped by the Task Force and didn't know anything about my investigation. When I got to his house I discovered that the lawyer had invited Chaleff's investigator to dine with us. While we waited for dinner to be prepared, I gave the investigator a brief run down on my investigation and handed him a copy of the Kelley report along with the exhibits attached to it. After a delicious steak dinner, the investigator left and in true California fashion, the host suggested that we all get naked and sit in the hot tub. I declined the naked invite, but I did sit on the deck and visit a bit while watching his wife's ample boobs float on top of the water until my glasses steamed up.

If the Times article wasn't bad enough, to add to my woes, in spite of getting a supervisor at the phone company to go to bat for me from the inside, I was unable to get the phone company to turn my phones back on until long after the Times article had faded from public memory. By then the frustrations of the case, my righteous indignation at Chaleff, stress caused by my dismal financial situation, and alcohol had turned my life into shit. I was headed for a total emotional collapse that would take me years to recover from and no matter how hard I tried, I couldn't seem to put the brakes on this skid into hell. I saw everyone's life moving forward except mine, and mine was spiraling into a dark abyss like a gunnysack full of sand through the trap doors of a gallows.

June Elliott leased a one-room office at the Green Hotel to use as her studio and art gallery. June was an animator for Hanna Barberra at Disney Studios and an outstanding portrait artist on her own. A friend of Mark Sutherland's, she moved into the hotel a short time after I was evicted from my office and we became good friends. She painted a beautiful portrait of my son, sitting in a tree, dressed in bibbed overalls without a shirt, and holding a puppy he found during his visit that summer. I could never afford to buy the painting so

June gave it a generic name like "A Boy and His Dog" and used it in her art shows.

She didn't keep the office for long, and by the time she moved out, I was in dire straights and in desperate need of a place to sleep. June had signed a one-year lease with the Hotel and she still had a month left on her paid up lease. Knowing my need for living quarters, she gave me the key to her studio and told me to use it any time I needed a place to stay.

Shortly after June's lease expired, the Green hotel converted the room into a TV room for their senior citizen residents. It was comfortably furnished with a couple of armchairs, two sofas, and blinds over the windows to keep out the light. The seniors all had TV's in their own apartments so they rarely used the room.

I kept a key to the outside security door after I was evicted from my office and knowing the TV room was never in use by the residents, I would sneak into the hotel at night after the managers office closed and crash on one of the sofas. The door had a lock on it so I didn't worry about being discovered by a resident wanting to watch television. I got up early every morning and hit the streets before the hotel office opened. When the office closed at night, I would sneak back in to watch TV and sleep. I kept this routine up for nearly six months and during that period only once did anyone ever try to come in. When he realized the door was locked he gave up and went on his way.

For some reason, the public bathrooms on the ground floor of the hotel had showers installed in them and while the toilets and lavatories were available for anyone to use, the hotel kept the doors to the showers secured under lock and key. After a few days without bathing, my body was beginning to smell like a decaying corpse. I hated to be dirty and it was driving me nuts. One night I went into the men's bathroom and tried to break down the shower door. Even though my considerable beer consumption had ballooned me into a two hundred and forty pound fat ass drunk, there wasn't enough room between the wall and the door to get a running start at it and when I slammed my shoulder against it, I just bounced off. It was pathetic that a big man like me couldn't knock down a hollow core door. I tried kicking it in and the sound echoed off the tile floor like a shotgun blast. I was frantic to get clean, but I was making so much racket I was afraid someone might hear me.

I went next door to the women's bathroom and discovered that it had a slightly different floor plan than the men's room. The shower was in the front of the bathroom and the shower door was only three of four feet across from the wall. I was able to leverage my back against the wall and with my foot on the door, push hard enough to break the doorjamb without making much noise. In all the time I was sneaking in and out the hotel, maintenance never fixed the door and I was able to take my daily shower without causing any more damage.

New to this homeless business, my daylight hours were spent walking the streets aimlessly or sitting at the outside counter at Gill's Grill on the corner of Fair Oaks and Colorado Boulevard. I would sit there drinking coffee and reading the newspaper for most of the morning. Occasionally, I would just sit there and stare off into space like I was in a catatonic state. Wendy, visiting from New York, drove by and she said she honked and waved at me and I looked at her without the slightest hint of recognition. She said I looked haunted. It wasn't so much that I was haunted as much as feeling empty after finding out that everything I'd been raised to believe in and been taught in government and civics classes about patriotism and liberty and justice for all, were in reality, a crock of shit.

Before I became homeless myself, I had befriended another homeless man I met at one of my regular watering holes in Old Town, the Loch Ness Monster Pub. This guy knew the ins and outs of being homeless better than anyone. When I wasn't sitting at Gill's Grill, we would spend a lot of time walking the streets together and he introduced me to the invisible world of the homeless.

One chilly day, as I walked alone down Colorado Boulevard, I pulled my jacket collar up to my ears to keep the cool air off my neck. I was headed east on Colorado and I ran into my friend walking west toward Old Town. I was happy to see him, and after catching up on the latest street news, he told me he knew a place where we could get a warm meal and maybe a pitcher of beer. I was all for it and together we started walking toward the Pasadena Mall with high expectations of warm food, cold beer, and a camaraderie that gave us the feeling that we weren't alone in the world.

Since we still had a few friends willing to put us up for a night or two and we stayed reasonably clean, my friend and I considered ourselves to be borderline homeless. Staying clean and well groomed, we managed to hide our situation from most of our family and friends. Being clean also enabled us to occasionally come up with enough money to buy our own food and booze for a night. Most of my old Crisp and Marley clients were not aware that I had fallen on such hard times and every now and then I would pick up a job serving legal papers on someone.

While drinking in one of our regular watering holes, it wasn't out of the question that one or the other of us could get lucky and pick up a woman. This was usually a major turn of events, for we knew we could count on room and board, sometimes for a week or more, if she could remember who we were the next morning and how we came to be in her bed. The relationship would seldom last longer than a week, because at some point the woman would expect us to spring for dinner, and when we couldn't produce she would know we were bums, and it would be the end of that gig.

One day as we walked toward the promise and expectations of a warm meal and a pitcher of beer, my friend and I met another homeless man. He was filthy from head to toe and shabbily dressed in jeans that were a size to big for him and showed his butt crack. He wore an old army field jacket, and boots without shoelaces. He seemed to be well acquainted with my friend and they started chatting like they hadn't seen each other in years. The man asked if we had scored any money and while I was flat broke, my friend reached into his coat pocket and took out a five-dollar bill. It was the all the money he had in the world and he handed it to the man. The man thanked him and as we walked on toward the Pasadena mall, I asked him why he gave that guy all of his money. My friend didn't say anything. He just looked at me and gave me a knowing smile that seemed to say; 'you'll learn buddy.'

My friend had seven drunk-driving arrests and his California Drivers license was permanently suspended. The last I heard he had met a schoolteacher, married her, and persuaded her to cash in her retirement benefits so the two of them could move to Ireland. Word got back to me that after he moved to Ireland, he picked up his eighth drunk-driving arrest and a short time later returned to the

United States. Whatever he did or has done with his life since then, I'll never forget him giving that homeless man his last five dollars. It was the finest act of compassion I've ever witnessed.

Months of hard drinking and living on the streets took a toll on me both physically and mentally. I contacted my brother and he flew me back to Oklahoma on his private plane for a little rest and recuperation at my parent's home in the Tulsa area. Off and on over the next few years I tried to jump start my private investigator careerl, but after being royally screwed on the Anzures and Buono cases, I didn't have much motivation to investigate anything for lawyers.

By the time the preliminary hearing on the Buono case ended, I was living in Oklahoma. When the case moved to the Los Angeles Superior Court of Judge Ronald George, Roger Kelley surprised everyone by making a motion to dismiss the murder charges against Angelo Buono. The preliminary hearing had given Kelley a pretty good idea of what his case would look like at trial and without any strong corroborating evidence to support Kenneth Bianchi's ever changing story, the prosecutor's case looked like a loser. I'm sure Kelly couldn't help but notice my absence from the case since Chaleff had taken over the defense.

As the presiding Judge of the Superior Court for Los Angeles County, it was Judge Keene's duty to assign the Buono case to a trial judge. It was not surprising that he chose another politically ambitious judge to preside over the trial. Ronald George made no bones about his political ambition. He wanted to someday sit on the California Supreme Court and the Hillside Strangler case was the kind of high profile trial that could bring recognition his way. He wasn't going to allow a little thing like a bad witness or perjured testimony take away a golden opportunity for him to shine in the spotlight. Ruling that it was up to a jury to decide if Kenneth Bianchi was credible or not, Judge George denied the motion to dismiss charges against Buono.

If Kelley's motion to dismiss the case came as a surprise to everyone, what he did next shocked the legal and political establishment. It's one thing to bail on a case because your evidence is weak and your primary witness is perjuring himself and everyone knows it. When the Judge hearing the case denies the motion and wants to let a jury hear the case, the judge takes the responsibility for what happens at the end of the trial. The prudent thing for a prosecutor to do, if they really believe in the guilt of the defendant, is to continue with the trial knowing that if the case is lost they have a big "I told you so' to toss at the judge.

When the judge denied the motion, Kelley refused to prosecute saying that he no longer believed in the case. He had made a statement about belief and not about law. Saying he didn't want to take a weak case to trial was one thing, but saying he no longer believed in the case was the same as saying he didn't believe the right man was being tried for the murders. Kelley told the court that they could ask the Attorney General to take up the prosecution and it gave me a few days of hope while the Attorney General's Office decided whether to get involved with the case.

Ronald George, a life-long Republican, felt that his time had come to begin campaigning for the highest court in California. The International media could make his name a household word. If he could show wisdom and courage in his decisions and judicial restraint in his demeanor, it would go a long way toward getting recognition from the Republican Party. Since Jerry Brown had already served his two terms in office, the governorship was up for grabs and the favored candidate to be the next Governor of California was the Republican Attorney General, George Deukmejian.

Crime is always a hot button political issue in California, and year after year, law and order is the main plank in the Republican platform. For Ronald George, continuing the prosecution of Angelo Buono was an opportunity to help George Deukmejian win the law and order vote. If everything went according to plan, it could put George on the short list for a nomination to a higher court.

The last thing a political candidate needs is to be portrayed in the media as soft on crime. For a District Attorney looking to move up the political ladder, a high profile case can make him or break him. The media always equates the conviction of defendants with the execution of justice and the acquittal of a defendant, particularly in high profile murder cases, as a blatant injustice. If the DA takes a case to trial and loses, he's a DA who can't win the big one. It's media driven, but the lynch mob-gas-the-bastards mentality of the public will not tolerate letting someone charged with a heinous crime go free without some serious political ramifications. After dismissing the charges against Angelo Buono, the only way for Roger Kelley and his boss John Van De Kamp to come out of this with their political heads intact was for the Buono trial to end with an acquittal.

Like Judge Keene and Ronald George, George Deukmejian knew he could harvest some political hay out of the Hillside Strangler case but his campaign for Governor didn't need a big controversy over the trial of Angelo Buono. If Roger Kelley was right and the case against Buono was that weak, an acquittal during his campaign for Governor could be a momentum wrecker. It would make him look like he was trying to exploit the publicity from the case purely for political gain. However, if the trial didn't end until the campaign was over, politically it wouldn't matter which way it went. An acquittal would be forgotten by the time he was up for reelection in four years and a conviction against Buono could be used to make John Van De Kamp look soft on crime, when and if, Van De Kamp, ever ran for Governor.

By holding a hearing on every motion brought before him; and by allowing the prosecutor to call every witness who knew the victims, the defendants, or had anything remotely relevant to say about the case, (excluding me of course), Judge George could stall a verdict until after the gubernatorial campaign was over. This stalling tactic would work to make the Judge appear to be prudent, judicious, and fair. The election was nearly two years away and by the time the trial ended, it was the longest and most expensive in the history of US Jurisprudence.

Going against a daring decision by the District Attorney's Office not to prosecute the case could be politically risky. The judge believed in insurance and one thing he needed to protect himself, if the trial went south on him, was a friend he could count on to put a favorable spin on what went wrong. He didn't want to fall victim to bad publicity and he was delighted when he got a call from Darcy O'Brien.

O'Brien was a professor of English Literature and an old friend and college roommate of Ronald George when they attended Princeton University. O'Brien told the judge that he wanted to do a book on the Hillside Strangler case. George knew he could count on his old friend not to give too objective an account of the case. The book, <u>Two of a Kind, The Hillside Stranglers</u>, featured Bob Grogan as the star detective and touted the courage of Ronald George in denying the motion by the District Attorney to dismiss the charges and see the case through to the end. The book canonized Bob Grogan, and it might make you want to stand up and applaud this detective's dedication to the case. Hell, I almost wanted to kiss him myself after reading the book.

Roger Kelley's boss, District Attorney John Van De Kamp, was running for Attorney General that year and the stalling tactic in the Buono trial inadvertently helped him win election. Without a guilty verdict in the case, he wouldn't face embarrassing questions from the media about his approval of Kelley's decision to dismiss charges against Angelo Buono.

During the long trial, I bounded from here to there, living in Oklahoma for a while then moving to San Francisco for a few months just trying to find myself. By the time the Buono trial ended, I was back in Los Angeles and following the closing arguments of the trial in the newspaper. When Chaleff told the jury that Kenneth Bianchi acted alone in killing all the victims, it felt like a slap at me. The Taxpayers had spent millions of dollars for the investigation and millions more for the trial of Angelo Buono. Now the defense lawyer, who was supposed to be challenging the state's case, was instead agreeing with them. The Task Force believed Bianchi was the Hillside Strangler, or at least pretended they did, and now the defense was saying they believe it too. Where's the advocacy? Where's the conflict?

While Investigating the Leslie Barry murder on a shoestring budget of five thousand dollars, I had come up with a better, and more logical, solution to the crimes. I had turned that information over to the Task Force, and they still couldn't solve the case. The reward I got for the great job I did on the Leslie Barry murder was poverty and homelessness. Now this squirrelly son-of-a-bitch was taking a pot shot at me by announcing to the world that Kenneth Bianchi was the one and only Hillside Strangler. What an arrogant bastard to think that just because he says it people will believe it!

Not long after deliberations began, the jury notified the judge that they had reached a verdict in one of the murders. The judge decided to allow the jury to announce the verdicts as they were reached rather than wait until deliberations were completed on all the charges. The jury's first verdict was a not guilty on the charge of murdering Yolanda Washington.

Lawyers are fond of saying you can never predict what a jury will do. In this case, I could predict exactly what they would do and I did. The day after the verdict was announced on the Yolanda Washington murder, I was having lunch and drinks with Jim and Susan Wilcox at the Pineapple Hill Saloon in Van Nuys. We were discussing the verdict and Jim asked me what I thought the outcome on the rest of the charges would be. I said, Chaleff telling the jury that Bianchi acted alone in killing all the victims reestablished the credibility of his confession, and the jury will return a verdict of guilty on most, if not all, the remaining charges.

When the jury delivered the last verdict in the Hillside Strangler trial, Angelo Buono had been convicted of nine murders.

Bob Grogan was elated with the outcome of the trial, and according to the ending of Darcy O'Brien's book, he felt comfortable enough to share his elation with Judge George by taking a bottle of champagne into the judge's chambers for a victory celebration. Judge George, always concerned about the appearance of judicial impropriety, told him it was improper for him to be there and asked him to leave. Bob Grogan had screwed up again. His display of solidarity with the judge was more proof of how the deck had been stacked against Angelo Buono.

A fair trial comes about when all the known, relevant facts of a crime are argued before a jury so that the jury can make an informed decision about the guilt or innocence of a defendant. That didn't happen in the trials of Arthur Anzures and Angelo Buono. No one knows whether I'm right or wrong about Dennis David Cantu, Edward Martin Castillon, and Martin Anthony Smith being the Hillside Stranglers. It's been more than two decades since I first brought these suspects to the attention of the police and the District Attorney and this approach to the case has yet to be investigated thoroughly. However, if I'm right about who the real killers are, the system took a terrible gamble with the lives of innocent and unsuspecting women who have since become victims of the so-called Hillside Stranglers.

I could never understand why the Los Angeles Times didn't run the story on my investigation. Several reporters at the Times knew that Chaleff was assisting the prosecution in the cover-up of my investigation. Media conglomerates like the Los Angeles Times are always looking for scoops on the big case. They often cite the intense competition from other media sources as an excuse for getting their facts mixed up and the story completely wrong.

I got my answer a few years after the Buono trial ended. I was discussing the case with a friend and he told me that the Times Mirror Company, the parent company of the Los Angeles Times, owned a book publishing company named New American Library. While the case was still in progress, New American Library signed book deals with several authors to write books that assumed Angelo Buono was the Hillside Strangler. Not surprisingly, one of those books was Darcy O'Brien's, Two of Kind, The Hillside Stranglers. The Los Angeles Times wasn't interested in a Buono-didn't-do-it story because it would've hit them in the pocket book.

I wish I could report a positive, upbeat ending where the system works, the good guys win, and the sun sets on a safer more secure world; but this is a true story and real life doesn't always work that way. Perhaps the success of the cover-up in the Hillside Strangler case can be measured by how few people have ever heard about this aspect of the case. There was just too much power working against my efforts to see justice done in the case twenty years ago. Maybe with the passage of time people will be able to see things more clearly than they did during the heat of the case and the cover-up will end here.

If not, God only knows how many more young girls and women will become victims of the Hillside Stranglers.

The End

Any questions, comments, complaints, offers and hate mail about this book can be sent to oldflamepi@aol.com Attn Ron Crisp. If you want me to reply, please put your name (preferably your real name) and phone number in the subject box of the email.